RDA
ESSENTIALS

RDA
ESSENTIALS

THOMAS BRENNDORFER

AMERICAN LIBRARY ASSOCIATION, *Chicago*

CANADIAN LIBRARY ASSOCIATION, *Ottawa*

CILIP: CHARTERED INSTITUTE OF LIBRARY AND INFORMATION PROFESSIONALS, *London*

Chicago | *2016*

THOMAS BRENNDORFER began his career in cataloging at the National Library of Canada in 1990. While working at the Guelph Public Library in 1997 he learned about FRBR, which had been presented at a conference on the future of AACR2 in nearby Toronto. He followed the development of FRBR to its full incorporation into a draft of RDA ten years later in 2007. Having seen the importance of FRBR for the future of catalogs he began giving presentations introducing FRBR and RDA concepts to catalogers (and others eager to learn) at conferences hosted by the Ontario Library Association and Canadian Library Association.

© 2016 by the American Library Association, the Canadian Library Association, and CILIP: Chartered Institute of Library and Information Professionals

ISBNs
U.S.: 978-0-8389-1328-4
U.K.: 978-1-78330-056-3
Canada: 978-0-88802-347-6

Library of Congress Cataloging-in-Publication Data

Names: Brenndorfer, Thomas, author.
Title: RDA essentials / Thomas Brenndorfer.
Description: Chicago : ALA Editions, an imprint of the American Library
    Association, 2016. | Includes bibliographical references and index.
Identifiers: LCCN 2015033083 | ISBN 9780838913284 (print : alk. paper)
Subjects: LCSH: Resource description & access—Handbooks, manuals, etc. |
    Descriptive cataloging—Standards—Handbooks, manuals, etc.
Classification: LCC Z694.15.R47 B74 2016 | DDC 025.3/2—dc23 LC record
available at http://lccn.loc.gov/2015033083

Cover design by Alejandra Diaz. Cover image © natrot/Shutterstock.
Composition in the Minion Pro and Gotham typefaces.

⊗ This paper meets the requirements of ANSI/NISO Z39.48-1992 (Permanence of Paper).

Printed in the United States of America
20 19 18 17 16   5 4 3 2 1

CONTENTS

INTRODUCTION

Whom is *RDA Essentials* written for?

RDA Essentials is for catalogers who provide comprehensive descriptions and access for a variety of simple library resources. *RDA Essentials* provides basic instructions for recording values for each RDA element. However, some resources require more specialized vocabulary or more complex instructions for constructing access points than is provided here. For these resources catalogers should consult appropriate specialized vocabulary lists, the full text of RDA, and applicable specialized cataloging community guidelines or agency policies.

For all catalogers and cataloging students, *RDA Essentials* is a quick reference source for the RDA element set. Each element is accompanied by the RDA definition, scope note, core element information, and basic instructions. While *RDA Essentials* does not provide encoding instructions, such as those for MARC, catalogers are encouraged to use the element set approach in *RDA Essentials* as a template to map-related encoding conventions.

Background

With the introduction of RDA, cataloging in libraries has undergone a major transformation. The last major change occurred in the early 1980s as the Anglo-American Cataloguing Rules, 2nd edition (AACR2), entered widespread use as the main tool for the creation of descriptions of library resources. The International Conference on the Principles and Future Development of AACR held in 1997 in Toronto, Canada, was a turning point. The papers delivered at the conference[1] addressed concerns that had been raised in the library community about the viability of traditional cataloging in light of technological innovations such as the World Wide Web. Among the new concepts were the Functional Requirements for Bibliographic Records (FRBR), which entailed a major rethinking of bibliographic data supported by a database modeling technique called an entity-relationship analysis.

How does one make sense of the mass of bibliographic data in library catalogs? In rethinking bibliographic data, two categories of data are useful in understanding the different decisions that go into the cataloging process: *content* and *carrier*.

The *carrier* category includes data about the inventory control of physical things—the world of publishers, distributors, prices, titles, page counts, and ISBNs. FRBR refines the carrier category into two entities: the *manifestation* and the *item*. Previously, the manifestation information had typically formed the basis of a catalogue record—a description of a publication, with identifying data transcribed from the publication such as title, statement of responsibility, edition statement, and publication statement. The item entity represents each copy a library holds of a publication.

The *content* category includes data about the intellectual or creative content that exists in the carrier. FRBR refines this category into two entities: the *work* and the *expresssion*. Catalogers gather data about the intellectual or creative content, identifying works and recording their attributes. Shakespeare's *Hamlet* is a work, and when this work is identified, a library catalog user is able to find it in the mass of physical carriers that have appeared over time. The expression entity covers the transformations a work can undergo while still being recognizably the same work. A text can be translated from English into a French expression. The work in a printed book may reappear as a spoken word expression in an audiobook. A work may undergo revisions in different editions, but these expressions will still be recognized as the same work.

Described in FRBR terms, a cataloger records data defined by the four bibliographic entities of work, expression, manifestation, and item. This orderly approach to recording data leads to another activity defined by FRBR, which is the recording of relationships between particular works (e.g., adaptations or sequels), expressions, manifestations, and items, as well as relationships for the agents associated with those particular entities. The relationships for agents include authors of works, editors of expressions, publishers of manifestations, and owners of items. Agents fall into three entity categories—Person, Family, and Corporate Body. Relationships can also exist between particular persons, families, and corporate bodies. Recording all of these types of relationships supports users in discovering related resources.

Resource Description and Access (RDA)

What began as AACR3, a FRBR-inspired revision of the AACR2 cataloging rules, eventually became Resource Description and Access (RDA). RDA was published in 2010, the culmination of years of effort in fully recasting AACR2 in FRBR terms. The FRBR conceptual model is reflected in RDA's structure. RDA first covers elements used to record attributes of entities of interest to users of bibliographic data. RDA then covers elements used to record relationships between those entities. As RDA was developed, the text was influenced further by FRAD (Functional Requirements for Authority Data) and FRSAD (Functional Requirements for Subject Authority Data).

Another layer of organization also exists in RDA—that of organizing elements for each entity by *user task*. The FRBR user tasks are *identify*, *select*, *find*, and *obtain*. For example some manifestation elements are used primarily in *identifying* the manifestation (e.g., title, date of publication, ISBN), while others are used mostly in *selecting* a particular manifestation based upon some characteristic, such as extent (e.g., number of pages). Many elements can be indexed and are used in *finding* library resources. A few elements are used for information supporting a user in *obtaining* or acquiring a resource. FRAD and FRSAD introduced additional user tasks, but the primary focus of *RDA Essentials* is on the FRBR user tasks.

Description of a resource

When following the RDA instructions in order, a cataloger first prepares a description of a resource, such as a simple book, by following this sequence of steps.

First, the cataloger looks at the book and transcribes identifying information such as the title proper and other titles that appear on the book as variants (e.g., a different spine title), the statement of responsibility (a statement of who the book is by), any edition statement, and publication details such as the place of publication, the publisher's name, and the date of publication. All of these elements support the *identify* user task. Then the cataloger proceeds to look at the physical characteristics of the book and records elements such as the extent and the book's dimensions. If the book is in large print, the Font Size element can be recorded to support a user in *selecting* the book. Some additional elements for details such as price relate to how a user can *obtain* the book.

Then the cataloger considers the content of the book. The title of the work needs to be determined to assist in the *identify* user task, especially if the work has been published under different titles. Several other elements may be used in identifying the work, such as Form of Work and Date of Work.

Many of these elements for the work are used to construct an *authorized access point representing a work*. In the RDA Toolkit (rdatoolkit.org), the elements used to identify a work are followed by instructions for constructing authorized access points. An authorized access point identifies an entity, and catalogers make an effort to construct unique access points. The construction of the authorized access point for a work begins with determining the Preferred Title for the Work. Some additional identifying elements for the work (e.g., Date of Work) may be added to distinguish the access point. To complete the construction of the authorized access point for a work, the Preferred Title for the Work is often preceded by the access point for the creator of the work (e.g., author, artist, or composer). This step in identifying a creator is comparable to what catalogers have known as choosing a "main entry." The resulting authorized access point representing a work is an orderly means of identifying the work entity.

Access Point	Example
Authorized access point representing a work	Hemingway, Ernest, 1899–1961. For whom the bell tolls

With the work identified, the cataloger continues to consider the content, and records other RDA elements that support users in *selecting* works and expressions, such as Intended Audience, Summarization of the Content, Illustrative Content, Colour Content, and Award.

Throughout RDA several elements are identified as *core*. These are the elements that should be recorded at a minimum if applicable and readily ascertainable. Other elements can become core if needed to distinguish entities. Agencies responsible for producing bibliographic descriptions may opt to designate additional RDA elements as core.

Access to a resource

Using the next set of instructions in RDA, the cataloger switches focus from the resource being described to the persons, families, and corporate bodies that have a relationship to the resource. The cataloger records a separate set of identifying elements for each person, family, and corporate body. For a person, these identifying elements include Preferred Name for the Person, Date of Birth, Place of Birth, Profession or Occupation, and Biographical Information.

With these identifying elements, the cataloger then follows the RDA instructions for constructing authorized access points to represent persons, families, and corporate bodies. The cataloger constructs an authorized access point using the preferred name of the entity, and adds additional elements (e.g., adding Date of Birth for a person) as required or as needed to create a unique access point. The cataloger then follows RDA instructions for constructing variant access points, which historically have formed the basis of *see* references pointing from variant forms to authorized headings in catalogs.

Access Point	Example
Authorized Access Point Representing a Person	Orwell, George, 1903–1950
Variant Access Point Representing a Person	Blair, Eric Arthur, 1903–1950
Real name for George Orwell treated as a variant name.	

Once the attributes of each entity are recorded in RDA elements and access points created, the cataloger proceeds to record the relationships between all the entities identified. One important relationship was already encountered in constructing the authorized access point representing a work. The work-creator relationship can be applied to all authors of a book if there are multiple authors, but only one creator is chosen to construct the authorized access point representing a work (following the main instruction in RDA 6.27.1.3). RDA also defines this single work-creator relationship as a *core* element.

The cataloger proceeds to record other RDA relationship elements based upon cataloger judgment or agency policy to support users in finding resources. The cataloger considers expression-contributor relationships (e.g., editors, illustrators, performers, and translators), as well as several possible relationships of persons, families, and corporate body to manifestations and items, such as Publisher and Owner.

RDA provides basic instructions for relating a work to its subjects. It instructs the cataloger to include as a core element at least one subject relationship that is applicable or readily ascertainable. Instead of providing specific instructions for subject relationships, RDA relies on guidance provided in external identifiable subject systems.

Continuing with the order of instructions in RDA, the cataloger then sees instructions for recording the many possible types of relationships between works, expressions, manifestations, and items. The cataloger can choose from several techniques to record the relationships. Authorized access points representing works is a technique that is often used, but some relationships are written out as structured or free-text descriptions of the entity or entities involved in the relationship. Relationships between works, expressions, manifestations, and items can be derivative (e.g., adaption of, remake of), whole-part (e.g., in series), accompanying (e.g., index to, issued with), sequential (e.g., continuation of, sequel to), and equivalent (e.g., reproduced as).

The last set of instructions in RDA covers the relationships between persons, families, and corporate bodies. Catalogers have known these as *see also* relationships. These relationships assist in resource discovery, because users can employ these relationships to find further resources associated with persons, families, and/or corporate bodies that are related to those associated with the resource being described.

Mode of Issuance, presentation format, and the preferred source of information

When considering the manifestation, the cataloger needs to determine the Mode of Issuance. This element affects the choices for data in several other elements. Mode of Issuance is defined as a categorization reflecting whether a resource is issued in one or more parts, the way it is updated, and its intended termination. Choices are: *single unit* (a single physical unit such as a single-volume monograph, or a logical unit like a PDF file), *multipart monograph* (resource issued in finite number of parts either simultaneously or successively), *serial* (resource issued in parts with no predetermined conclusion), and *integrating resource* (resource with integrated updates, such as loose-leaf publications and websites that are continuously updated).

While Mode of Issuance affects the choices for data in several elements, another category the cataloger needs to determine before recording information is *presentation format*. This category affects the choice for the preferred source of information that identifies a resource. Determining a preferred source of information for a resource is required for determining the title proper of the manifestation (the title normally used when citing the resource).

RDA Essentials lists the sources of information used to record elements at the beginning of each chapter rather than with each element. In many cases, the elements in each chapter of *RDA Essentials* have the same source of information. For many manifestation elements, listing all sources of information for each element at the beginning of the chapter shows that several manifestation elements are dependent on the source for other manifestation elements.

To determine the preferred source for the title proper to be recorded, the cataloger first determines the presentation format (for example, a book format usually has a title page, which becomes the preferred source). The cataloger considers other possible sources if the book lacks a title page. For each element after Title Proper, the cataloger reviews the preferences for sources of information, and refers back to the presentation format. The element Mode of Issuance can also affect the choice for a source of information. The cataloger also makes notes on decisions made about sources. In many cases, the cataloger indicates that information came from outside the resource if the data was not found on a source in the resource.

Conventions in *RDA Essentials*

In *RDA Essentials* elements are capitalized (e.g., Copyright Date, Place of Birth, Creator).

Some elements have element sub-types, and in many cases only the sub-types are used to record data. The element sub-types are generally presented with the parent element to provide clarity and context (e.g., Title » Title Proper, Extent » Extent of Text, Video Characteristic » Video Format).

Several elements are organized into sub-elements, and these sub-elements are intended to be recorded together to form the value for the parent element. For example, Publication Statement is generally formed by its sub-elements Place of Publication, Publisher's Name, and Date of Publication. In *RDA Essentials* the sub-elements are presented with the parent element (e.g., Edition Statement » Designation of Edition, Series Statement » Title Proper of Series).

RDA Essentials presents the basic instructions used to record each RDA element. Common guidelines often apply to groups of elements, and the chapters for these guidelines are found together in *RDA Essentials*. For example, many elements are used to transcribe data found on the resource, and the guidelines chapter 14, *Transcription* (p. 263), applies to these elements. There are common instructions for recording names of persons, families, and corporate bodies, and *RDA Essentials* directs the reader to consult the guidelines chapter 23, *Names of Persons, Families, and Corporate Bodies* (p. 297) in these cases.

Examples in *RDA Essentials* consist of the name of the element followed by a recorded value.

Element	Example
Extent of Text	327 pages

Side bars in *RDA Essentials* alert the reader to related elements, alternatives, optional additions, optional omissions, and exceptions.

Related elements. For instructions on recording the color characteristics of a digital file, see *Colour Content.*

For alternatives and options, the agency responsible for creating the data establishes policies and guidelines, or the decisions can be left to individual cataloger judgment.

Alternative. Omit an initial article when recording a characterizing word or phrase.

Optional addition. Add a term even if there is no need to distinguish one access point from another.

An exception is an instruction that is not an alternative or an option, but takes precedence over the immediately preceding instruction.

Exception. Record *Online* for a conference that was held online.

What is not in *RDA Essentials*

RDA Essentials provides instructions for creating a comprehensive description of the resource as a whole. Instructions for analytical and hierarchical descriptions are omitted. See RDA 1.5.3 for cases where an analytical description is used to describe a part of a larger resource.

RDA Essentials does not cover exceptions for early printed resources. Instructions for transliteration of names are omitted, nor does it cover instructions for recording titles and constructing access points for musical works, religious works, and legal works.

RDA Essentials covers all RDA elements, but catalogers will need to consult the full RDA text for instructions on constructing access points from several elements for musical works, religious works, and legal works. For example, Medium of Performance is listed in *RDA Essentials*, but see RDA 6.28.1.9.1 for instructions on using the element in access points for musical works.

RDA Essentials generally omits instructions for changing descriptions because of the Mode of Issuance. For descriptions of multipart monographs, serials, and integrating resources, previously recorded elements can be updated to reflect new information. Similarly, notes and access points can also be added to a description to reflect new information from new parts, new issues, or updates to the resource. See the full RDA text for instructions at elements affected by changes arising from the resource's Mode of Issuance.

RDA vocabulary terms are not listed except for some common cases such as Content Type and Carrier Type. Check the RDA Registry (www.rdaregistry.info) for updates that cover RDA vocabulary.

Detailed instructions for capitalization, abbreviations, initial articles, and names in other languages are omitted. In many cases, *RDA Essentials* flags elements where these additional instructions are important and provides a basic instruction. References are provided to more detailed instructions in the RDA appendixes. The examples in *RDA Essentials* follow the RDA guidelines, such as those on capitalization (RDA appendix A). There is an alternative at RDA 1.7.1 for using in-house guidelines for capitalization, punctuation, abbreviations, etc.

RDA Essentials omits instructions for displaying elements. For these, see RDA appendix D for International Standard Bibliographic Description (ISBD) presentation and RDA appendix E for punctuation rules for access points. If the following is encountered in *RDA Essentials,* a cataloger would record the data in accordance with the display conventions chosen. For example, applying ISBD punctuation for the two titles (RDA D.1.2.2) results in *Clock symphony ; Surprise symphony*.

Element	Example
Title Proper	Clock symphony
	Surprise symphony

Similarly, *RDA Essentials* omits instructions for encoding elements in MARC, or in any other particular encoding standard. RDA was written in anticipation of being implemented in different encoding standards. Three different scenarios for RDA were envisioned in the document *RDA Database Implementation Scenarios*.[2] RDA supports all these scenarios, which cover the range from card catalogs to MARC-based systems to relational and object-oriented databases.

For catalogers, an important lesson is that RDA is about recording well-formed *data* and recording *relationships*, and that specific record structures and displays are a secondary issue. For the last several decades, catalogers have thought of catalogs as separated into bibliographic records and authority records, but data for FRBR entities may be scattered across both these record types. Catalogers have been creating bibliographic records that are composite descriptions of different FRBR entities. Because RDA is based on FRBR's entity-relationship model, catalogers are now required to focus first on recording data about entities (e.g., manifestations, works, persons), and then recording the relationships between them. The data and relationships recorded should support many implementation scenarios. The transformation in cataloging represented by RDA is about using the rigor of the entity-relationship model from FRBR to record robust and reliable data in order to maximize support for users engaged in resource discovery.

NOTES

1. International Conference on the Development and Principles and Future Development of AACR, Toronto, Ontario, Canada, on October 23–25, 1997, www.rda-jsc.org/intlconf1.html.

2. RDA Database Implementation Scenarios, July 1, 2009, www.rda-jsc.org/docs/5editor2rev.pdf.

Elements

1

Identifying Manifestations and Items

Manifestation refers to the physical embodiment of an expression of a work.

Item refers to a single exemplar or instance of a manifestation.

Resource, in the context of this chapter, refers to a manifestation or an item.

SUPPORTING THE USER

When following the instructions in this chapter, a cataloger looks at the resource and considers how it is identified in terms of the attributes of manifestations and items. These attributes include information typically used by the producers of resources to identify their products (e.g., title, statement of responsibility, edition statement).

By recording these attributes in separate elements, a cataloger supports a user in *identifying* the resource described (i.e., confirming that the resource described corresponds to the resource sought, or distinguishing between two or more resources with the same or similar characteristics). The data recorded can also be used in *finding* resources that correspond to the user's stated search criteria.

Elements

Core designates a core element—see element instructions for more details.
Transcribed designates an element covered by the guidelines: *Transcription* (p. 263).

Elements for Manifestations			
Elements	*Sub-types or Sub-elements*	*Core*	*Transcribed*
Mode of Issuance			X
Title			
	Title Proper	X	X
	Parallel Title Proper		X
	Other Title Information		X
	Parallel Other Title Information		X
	Variant Title		X
	Earlier Title Proper		X
	Later Title Proper		X
	Key Title		
	Abbreviated Title		
Statement of Responsibility			
	Statement of Responsibility Relating to Title Proper	X	X
	Parallel Statement of Responsibility Relating to Title Proper		X
Edition Statement	*Sub-elements:*		
	Designation of Edition	X	X
	Parallel Designation of Edition		X
	Statement of Responsibility Relating to the Edition		X
	Parallel Statement of Responsibility Relating to the Edition		X
	Designation of a Named Revision of an Edition	X	X
	Parallel Designation of a Named Revision of an Edition		X
	Statement of Responsibility Relating to a Named Revision of an Edition		X
	Parallel Statement of Responsibility Relating to a Named Revision of an Edition		X
Numbering of Serials			
	Numeric and/or Alphabetic Designation of First Issue or Part of Sequence	X	X
	Chronological Designation of First Issue or Part of Sequence	X	X
	Numeric and/or Alphabetic Designation of Last Issue or Part of Sequence	X	X
	Chronological Designation of Last Issue or Part of Sequence	X	X
	Alternative Numeric and/or Alphabetic Designation of First Issue or Part of Sequence		X
	Alternative Chronological Designation of First Issue or Part of Sequence		X

Elements for Manifestations			
Elements	**Sub-types or Sub-elements**	**Core**	**Transcribed**
	Alternative Numeric and/or Alphabetic Designation of Last Issue or Part of Sequence		X
	Alternative Chronological Designation of Last Issue or Part of Sequence		X
Production Statement	*Sub-elements:*		
	Place of Production		X
	Parallel Place of Production		X
	Producer's Name		X
	Parallel Producer's Name		X
	Date of Production	X	
Publication Statement	*Sub-elements:*		
	Place of Publication	X	X
	Parallel Place of Production		X
	Publisher's Name	X	X
	Parallel Publisher's Name		X
	Date of Publication	X	
Distribution Statement	*Sub-elements:*		
	Place of Distribution		X
	Parallel Place of Distribution		X
	Distributor's Name		X
	Parallel Distributor's Name		X
	Date of Distribution		
Manufacture Statement	*Sub-elements:*		
	Place of Manufacture		X
	Parallel Place of Manufacture		X
	Manufacturer's Name		X
	Parallel Manufacturer's Name		X
	Date of Manufacture		
Copyright Date			
Series Statement	*Sub-elements:*		
	Title Proper of Series	X	X
	Parallel Title Proper of Series		X
	Other Title Information of Series		X
	Parallel Other Title Information of Series		X
	Statement of Responsibility Relating to Series		X
	Parallel Statement of Responsibility Relating to Series		X
	ISSN of Series		X

Elements for Manifestations			
Elements	*Sub-types or Sub-elements*	*Core*	*Transcribed*
	Numbering within Series	X	X
	Title Proper of Subseries	X	X
	Parallel Title Proper of Subseries		X
	Other Title Information of Subseries		X
	Parallel Other Title Information of Subseries		X
	Statement of Responsibility Relating to Subseries		X
	Parallel Statement of Responsibility Relating to Subseries		X
	ISSN of Subseries		X
	Numbering within Subseries	X	X
Frequency			
Identifier for the Manifestation		X	
	Publisher's Number for Music		
	Plate Number for Music		
Preferred Citation			
Note on Manifestation			
	Note on Title		
	Note on Statement of Responsibility		
	Note on Edition Statement		
	Note on Numbering of Serials		
	Note on Production Statement		
	Note on Publication Statement		
	Note on Distribution Statement		
	Note on Manufacture Statement		
	Note Copyright Date		
	Note on Series Statement		
	Note on Frequency		
	Note on Issue, Part, or Iteration Used as the Basis for the Identification of the Resource		

Elements for Items			
Elements	*Sub-types or Sub-elements*	*Core*	*Transcribed*
Custodial History of the Item			
Immediate Source of Acquisition of Item			
Identifier for the Item			
Note on Item			

Choosing sources of information

Choose the preferred source of information for a resource in order to record the Title Proper, which is used to identify the resource. The source with the Title Proper then becomes the preferred source of information for several other identifying elements.

Determine the presentation format and the mode of issuance in order to choose the preferred source of information. See *Mode of Issuance* for instructions for choosing the preferred source of information for single units, multipart monographs, serials, and integrating resources. Make notes about sources of information, as applicable (see *Note on Manifestation* elements).

The following instructions apply when describing the resource using a comprehensive description. See RDA 2.2 for instructions for analytical descriptions.

Choosing the preferred source of information based on presentation format (RDA 2.2.2)

Resources consisting of one or more pages, leaves, sheets, or cards, or images of them

A printed book may have a title page, but a microfilm resource or an online PDF may have an image of a title page. The first preference for a source is the title page, title sheet, or title card, or an image of them, if available.

> **Alternative.** If the resource consists of microform or computer images of one or more pages, leaves, sheets, or cards, use an eye-readable label with the title instead of the image of the title page, title sheet, or title card. The label must be permanently printed on or affixed to the resource.

Subsequent preferences for the source with a title are, in descending order: cover or jacket (or an image), caption (or an image), masthead (or an image), colophon (or an image), or another source within the resource that has a title (preference is given to a source in which the information is formally presented).

Resources consisting of moving images, which can be tangible resources (e.g., film reels, DVDs) or online resources (e.g., MP4 files, streaming videos)

The first preference for a source is the title frame or frames, or title screen or screens, if available and if the source lists a formally presented collective title.

> **Alternative.** Use a label with a title that is permanently printed on or affixed to the resource in preference to the title frame or frames, or title screen or screens. This alternative does not apply to labels on accompanying textual material or a container.

For tangible moving image resources, subsequent preferences for a source with a title are, in descending order: a label that is permanently printed on or affixed to the resource, a container or accompanying material issued with the resource, or an internal source forming part of the resource (e.g., a disc menu).

Other resources that are tangible, such as objects or audio resources (e.g., compact discs)

The first preference for a source is a textual source on the resource, or a label that is permanently printed on or affixed to the resource. Subsequent preferences for a source with a title are, in order: an internal source with textual content, a container, or accompanying material issued with the resource.

Other resources that are online, such as websites or online audio resources

The first preference is the first of the following sources with a title: a) textual content or b) embedded metadata. Subsequent preferences are sources forming part of the resource itself in which the information is formally presented.

More than one preferred source of information (RDA 2.2.3)

If there is more than one preferred source of information in a resource, generally choose the first occurring source. For resources with multiple preferred sources of information in different languages or scripts, the first preference is a source in the language or script of the content. See RDA 2.2.3 for additional exceptions for resources with multiple preferred sources of information.

Parts of the resource considered as sources (RDA 2.2.2.1)
and other sources of information outside the resource (RDA 2.2.4)

Treat as part of the resource itself any of the following for a comprehensive description:

- storage medium (e.g., paper, tape, film)
- any housing that is an integral part of the resource (e.g., a cassette, a cartridge)
- accompanying material (e.g., a leaflet, an "about" file)
- container issued with the resource.

If information required to identify the resource does not appear on a source forming part of the resource itself, take it from one of the following sources (in order of preference for a comprehensive description):

a) other published descriptions of the resource
b) a container that is not issued with the resource itself (e.g., a box or case made by the owner)
c) any other available source (e.g., a reference source)

Sources for elements identifying Manifestations and Items

Determining Mode of Issuance

Use evidence presented by the resource itself (or on any accompanying material or container). Take additional evidence taken from any source.

See *Mode of Issuance* for additional instructions on choosing a source of information identifying the resource.

Supplied information

RDA identifies specific elements that require an indication that information is supplied from a source outside the resource itself. For those elements, indicate that information is supplied by means of a note (*see Note on Manifestation*) *or* by some other means (e.g., through coding or the use of square brackets).

Element	Example
Date of Publication	[1988–1991]

Element	Example
Place of Publication	Dublin [Ohio]

Element	Example
Designation of Edition	F major edition
Note on Edition Statement	Edition statement from publisher's catalog

Exception. Do not indicate that the information was taken from a source outside the resource itself if the resource is of a type that does not normally carry identifying information (e.g., a photograph, a naturally occurring object, a collection).

RDA ESSENTIALS TIP

In the following list, the elements marked with an asterisk (*) require an indication, such as square brackets, for information supplied from outside the resource itself.

Sources for Title and Statement of Responsibility element sub-types

* Title Proper

> a) preferred source of information established from presentation format (e.g., title page for a book) and Mode of Issuance
>
> b) if there is no title provided on the resource itself, then source outside the resource

* Other Title Information

> same source as Title Proper

* Statement of Responsibility Relating to Title Proper—in order of preference:

> a) same source as Title Proper
>
> b) another source within the resource
>
> c) source outside the resource

Earlier Title Proper

> source specified for Title Proper in earlier iterations of the integrating resource

Later Title Proper

> source specified for Title Proper in later issues or parts of a multipart monograph or serial

* Parallel Title Proper
 a) any source within the resource
 b) if Title Proper is taken from outside the resource, then same source as Title Proper

* Parallel Other Title Information
 a) same source as corresponding Parallel Title Proper
 b) if there is no corresponding Parallel Title Proper, then same source as Title Proper

* Parallel Statement of Responsibility
 a) same source as corresponding Parallel Title Proper
 b) if there is no corresponding Parallel Title Proper, then same source as Title Proper

Variant Title—any source

Abbreviated Title—any source

Key Title—in order of preference:
 a) ISSN register
 b) source within the resource
 c) any other source

Sources for Edition Statement sub-elements

* Designation of Edition—in order of preference:
 a) same source as Title Proper
 b) another source within the resource
 c) source outside the resource

* Statement of Responsibility Relating to the Edition—same source as Designation of Edition

* Parallel designation of edition—in order of preference:
 a) same source as Designation of Edition
 b) another source within the resource
 c) source outside the resource

* Parallel Statement of Responsibility Relating to the Edition
 a) same source as corresponding Parallel Designation of Edition
 b) if there is no corresponding Parallel Designation of Edition, then same source as designation of edition

* Designation of a Named Revision of an Edition—in order of preference:
 a) same source as Designation of Edition
 b) another source within the resource
 c) source outside the resource

* Statement of Responsibility Relating to a Named Revision of an Edition—same source as Designation of a Named Revision of an Edition

* Parallel Designation of a Named Revision of an Edition—in order of preference:
    a) same source as Designation of a Named Revision of an Edition
    b) another source within the resource
    c) source outside the resource

* Parallel Statement of Responsibility Relating to a Named Revision of an Edition
    a) same source as corresponding Parallel Designation of a Named Revision of an Edition
    b) if there is no corresponding Parallel Designation of a Named Revision of an Edition,
       then same source as Designation of a Named Revision of an Edition

Sources for Numbering of Serials element sub-types

* All designations of first issue or part of sequence—in order of preference:
    a) source on first issue or part of that sequence that has Title Proper
    b) another source within the first issue or part of that sequence
    c) source outside the resource

* All designations of last issue or part of sequence—in order of preference:
    a) source on last issue or part of that sequence that has Title Proper
    b) another source within the last issue or part of that sequence
    c) source outside the resource

Sources for Production Statement sub-elements

* Producer's Name—in order of preference:
    a) same source as Title Proper
    b) another source within the resource
    c) source outside the resource

* Place of Production—in order of preference:
    a) same source as Producer's Name
    b) another source within the resource
    c) source outside the resource

* Parallel Place of Production—in order of preference:
    a) same source as Place of Production
    b) another source within the resource
    c) source outside the resource

* Parallel Producer's Name—in order of preference:
    a) same source as Producer's Name
    b) another source within the resource
    c) source outside the resource

* Date of Production—any source

Sources for Publication Statement sub-elements

* Publisher's Name—in order of preference:

a) same source as Title Proper

b) another source within the resource

c) source outside the resource

* Place of Publication—in order of preference:

a) same source as Publisher's Name

b) another source within the resource

c) source outside the resource

* Parallel Place of Publication—in order of preference:

a) same source as Place of Publication

b) another source within the resource

c) source outside the resource

* Parallel Publisher's Name—in order of preference:

a) same source as Publisher's Name

b) another source within the resource

c) source outside the resource

* Date of Publication—in order of preference:

a) same source as Title Proper

b) another source within the resource

c) source outside the resource

For multipart monographs and serials, take the beginning and/or ending date of publication from the first and/or last released issue or part, or from another source.

For integrating resources, take the beginning and/or ending date of publication from the first and/or last iteration, or from another source.

Sources for Distribution Statement sub-elements

* Distributor's Name—in order of preference:

a) same source as Title Proper

b) another source within the resource

c) source outside the resource

* Place of Distribution—in order of preference:

a) same source as Distributor's Name

b) another source within the resource

c) source outside the resource

* Parallel Place of Distribution—in order of preference:

a) same source as Place of Distribution

b) another source within the resource

c) source outside the resource

* Parallel Distributor's Name—in order of preference:
  a) same source as Distributor's Name
  b) another source within the resource
  c) source outside the resource

* Date of Distribution—in order of preference:
  a) same source as Title Proper
  b) another source within the resource
  c) source outside the resource

For multipart monographs and serials, take the beginning and/or ending date of distribution from the first and/or last released issue or part, or from another source.

For integrating resources, take the beginning and/or ending date of distribution from the first and/or last iteration, or from another source.

Sources for Manufacture Statement sub-elements

* Manufacturer's Name—in order of preference:
  a) same source as Title Proper
  b) another source within the resource
  c) source outside the resource

* Place of Manufacture—in order of preference:
  a) same source as Manufacturer's Name
  b) another source within the resource
  c) source outside the resource

* Parallel Place of Manufacture—in order of preference:
  a) same source as Place of Manufacture
  b) another source within the resource
  c) source outside the resource

* Parallel Manufacturer's Name—in order of preference:
  a) same source as Manufacturer's Name
  b) another source within the resource
  c) source outside the resource

* Date of Manufacture
  a) same source as Title Proper
  b) another source within the resource
  c) source outside the resource

For multipart monographs and serials, take the beginning and/or ending date of manufacture from the first and/or last released issue or part, or from another source.

For integrating resources, take the beginning and/or ending date of manufacture from the first and/or last iteration, or from another source.

Sources for Series Statement sub-elements

* Title Proper of Series—in order of preference:

    a) series title page

    b) another source within the resource

    c) source outside the resource

* Other Title Information of Series—same source as Title Proper of Series

* Statement of Responsibility Relating to Series—same source as Title Proper of Series

* ISSN of Series—in order of preference:

    a) series title page

    b) another source within the resource

    c) source outside the resource

* Title Proper of Subseries—in order of preference:

    a) series title page

    b) another source within the resource

    c) source outside the resource

* Other Title Information of Subseries—same source as Title Proper of Series

* Statement of Responsibility Relating to Subseries—same source as Title Proper of Sub-series

* ISSN of Subseries—in order of preference:

    a) series title page

    b) another source within the resource

    c) source outside the resource

* Parallel Title Proper of Subseries—any source within the resource

* Parallel Other Title Information of Series

    a) same source as corresponding Parallel Title Proper of Subseries

    b) if there is no corresponding Parallel Title Proper of Subseries, then same source as Title Proper of Series

* Parallel Statement of Responsibility Relating to Series

    a) same source as corresponding Parallel Title Proper of Subseries

    b) if there is no corresponding Parallel Title Proper of Subseries, then same source as Title Proper of Series

* Parallel Title Proper of Subseries—any source within the resource

* Parallel Other Title Information of Subseries

    a) same source as corresponding Parallel Title Proper of Subseries

    b) if there is no corresponding Parallel Title Proper of Subseries, then same source as Title Proper of Subseries

* Parallel Statement of Responsibility Relating to Subseries
    a) same source as corresponding Parallel Title Proper of Subseries
    b) if there is no corresponding Parallel Title Proper of Subseries, then same source as
       Title Proper of Subseries

* Numbering within Series
    a) series title page
    b) another source within the resource
    c) source outside the resource

* Numbering within Subseries
    a) series title page
    b) another source within the resource
    c) source outside the resource

Use any source of information for these elements
Copyright Date
Frequency
Identifier for the Manifestation and element sub-types
Preferred Citation
Note on Manifestation and element sub-types
Custodial History of Item
Immediate Source of Acquisition
Identifier for the Item
Note on Item

Mode of Issuance

Mode of Issuance (RDA 2.13)

A categorization reflecting whether a resource is issued in one or more parts, the way it is updated, and whether its termination is predetermined or not.

> **Related elements.** For notes, see *Note on Manifestation » Note on Issue, Part, or Iteration Used as the Basis for the Identification of the Resource.*

Recording

Record one or more RDA terms. Record as many terms as are applicable to the resource being described.

RDA terms for Mode of Issuance

Single Unit	A *single unit* is a resource that is issued either as a single physical unit (e.g., as a single-volume monograph) or, in the case of an intangible resource, as a single logical unit (e.g., as a PDF file posted on the web).
Multipart Monograph	A *multipart monograph* is a resource issued in two or more parts (either simultaneously or successively) that is complete or intended to be completed within a finite number of parts (e.g., a dictionary in two volumes, three audiocassettes issued as a set).
Serial	A *serial* is a resource issued in successive parts, usually having numbering that has no predetermined conclusion (e.g., a periodical, a monographic series, a newspaper). Includes resources that exhibit characteristics of serials, such as successive issues, numbering, and frequency, but whose duration is limited (e.g., newsletters of events) and reproductions of serials.
Integrating Resource	An *integrating resource* is a resource that is added to or changed by means of updates that do not remain discrete but are integrated into the whole (e.g., a loose-leaf manual that is updated by means of replacement pages, a website that is updated continuously).

RDA ESSENTIALS TIP

The following instructions for choosing a source of information based on Mode of Issuance apply when describing the resource using a comprehensive description.

See RDA 2.1.3 for instructions for analytical descriptions.

Choosing a source of information for a single unit (e.g., a textbook in one volume, an audio recording on one audio disc) (RDA 2.1.2.2)

Resource embodies one work
Choose a source identifying the resource as a whole.

Resource embodies multiple works
Prefer a source that has a collective title.

No source identifying resource as a whole, but one source has a title identifying a main or predominant work or content
Consider that source to identify the resource as a whole.

No source identifying resource as a whole, and no source has a title identifying a main or predominant work or content
Treat the sources identifying its individual contents as a collective source of information for the resource as a whole.

Choosing a source of information for a multipart monograph or a serial (e.g., a compact disc set, a periodical) (RDA 2.1.2.3)

Issued as a set that is unnumbered, or numbering does not help establish an order

Choose a source identifying the resource as a whole, preferring a source that has a collective title.

Sequentially numbered issues or parts

Choose a source identifying the lowest numbered issue or part available.

Unnumbered issues or parts, or numbering does not help establish an order

Choose a source identifying the issue or part with the earliest date of issue.

No source identifying resource as a whole, but one source has a title identifying a main or predominant work or content

Consider that source to identify the resource as a whole.

No source identifying resource as a whole, and no source has a title identifying a main or predominant work or content

Treat the sources identifying the individual parts as a collective source of information for the resource as a whole.

Making notes identifying part or issue used for the preferred source for multipart monographs and serials (RDA 2.17.13)

In some cases, the identification of a multipart monograph or serial is not based on the first released part or issue.

For a multipart monograph

Make a note identifying the part of a multipart monograph on which the identification of the resource is based and/or its number or publication date, as appropriate. If more than one part has been consulted, make a separate note identifying the latest part consulted in making the description.

Element	Example
Note on Issue, Part, or Iteration Used as the Basis for Identification of the Resource	Identification of the resource based on: part 2, published 1998

For a numbered serial

Make a note identifying the issue or part used as the basis for the identification. If more than one issue or part has been consulted, make a separate note identifying the latest issue or part consulted in preparing the description. Do not make a note of earliest and/or latest issues or parts consulted if they are the same as those recorded in the numbering of serials element (see *Numbering of Serials*).

Element	Example
Note on Issue, Part, or Iteration Used as the Basis for Identification of the Resource	Identification of the resource based on: no. 8 (Jan./June 1997)

Element	Example
Note on Issue, Part, or Iteration Used as the Basis for Identification of the Resource	Latest issue consulted: no. 12 (Jan./June 1999)

For an unnumbered serial

Make a note identifying the earliest issue or part consulted and its date of publication. If other issues or parts have also been consulted, make a separate note identifying the latest issue or part consulted and its date.

Element	Example
Note on Issue, Part, or Iteration Used as the Basis for Identification of the Resource	Identification of the resource based on: Labor and economic reforms in Latin America and the Caribbean, 1995

Choosing a source of information for an integrating resource (e.g., a loose-leaf volume, an updating website) (RDA 2.1.2.4)

Choose a source of information identifying the current iteration of the resource as a whole.

No source of information identifying the current iteration of the integrating resource as a whole

Treat the sources of information identifying its individual contents as a collective source of information for the whole.

More than one source of information

Use the first occurring of these sources. However, if an integrating resource contains preferred sources of information with different dates, then use as the preferred source of information the source with the later or latest date.

Making notes identifying iteration used for the preferred source for integrating resources (RDA 2.17.13)

Make a note identifying the latest iteration of an integrating resource consulted in preparing the description.

Element	Example
Note on Issue, Part, or Iteration Used as the Basis for Identification of the Resource	Identification of the resource based on version consulted: Oct. 26, 2000

For online resources, make a note identifying the date on which the resource was viewed for description.

Element	Example
Note on Issue, Part, or Iteration Used as the Basis for Identification of the Resource	Former title (as viewed October 6, 1999): Washington newspapers database

Titles

Title (RDA 2.3)

A word, character, or group of words and/or characters that names a resource or a work contained in it.

It is possible for more than one title to appear in sources of information (e.g., on a title page, title frame; as a caption title, running title; on a cover, spine; on a title bar) *or* on a jacket, sleeve, container, etc. *or* in material accompanying the resource.

It is also possible for a resource to have one or more titles associated with it through reference sources *or* through assignment by a registration agency (e.g., a key title) *or* by an agency preparing a description of the resource (e.g., a cataloger's translation of the title).

Core element

Title Proper is a core element. Other titles are optional.

> **Related elements.** For notes, see *Note on Manifestation » Note on Title.*

Title » Title Proper (RDA 2.3.2)

The chief name of a resource (i.e., the title normally used when citing the resource). An alternative title is treated as part of the title proper.

Element	Example
Title Proper	The hobbit, or, There and back again

> **Related elements.** The title proper does not include: parallel titles proper (see *Parallel Title Proper*), other title information (see *Other Title Information*), and parallel other title information (see *Parallel Other Title Information*).

Core element

Choosing the title proper

In more than one language or script on source

If the content is written, spoken, or sung, *then* choose as the title proper the title in the language or script of the main content of the resource. If the content is not written, spoken, or sung *or* there is no main content in a single language *then* choose the title proper on the basis of the sequence, layout, or typography of the titles.

In more than one form on source; same language and script

Choose title based on sequence, layout, or typography of the titles on source.

> **Exception.** *Serials and integrating resources.* If the title of a serial or integrating resource appears on the source of information for the title proper in full as well as in the form of an acronym or initialism, choose the full form as the title proper.

Transcribe other title or titles in Other Title Information or Variant Title if considered important for identification or access.

Collective title with titles of individual contents on source

Choose the collective title.

> **Related elements.** Record the titles of the individual contents as the titles of related manifestations (see Related Manifestation), if considered important for identification or access.
>
> See *Related Work* for instructions on recording the relationship to the related works.

Transcribing

Apply guidelines: *Transcription* (p. 263) and *Titles Associated with a Manifestation* (p. 271).

Element	Example
Title Proper	Revised Washington State flood damage reduction plan

Resource lacking a collective title (RDA 2.3.2.9)

Transcribe the titles proper of the parts as they appear on the source of information for the resource as a whole.

Element	Example
Title Proper	Lord Macaulay's essays ; and, Lays of ancient Rome

If the sources of information identifying the individual parts are being treated as a collective source of information for the resource as a whole, transcribe the titles proper of the parts in the order in which they appear in the resource.

Element	Example
Title Proper	Clock symphony
	Surprise symphony

> **Alternative.** Devise a collective title. If considered important for identification or access, transcribe the titles of individual parts as the titles proper of related manifestations (see Related Manifestation).

Resource with no title (RDA 2.3.2.10)

If there is no title in the resource itself, transcribe as the title proper *either* a) a title taken from another source *or* b) a devised title.

Transcribing devised titles (RDA 2.3.2.11)

If the resource itself has no title *and* a title cannot be found in any of the other sources of information *then* devise a brief descriptive title that indicates *either* a) the nature of the resource (e.g., map, literary manuscript, diary, advertisement) *or* b) its subject (e.g., names of persons, corporate bodies, objects, activities, events, geographical area and dates), *or* c) a combination of the two, as appropriate.

Title » Parallel Title Proper (RDA 2.3.3)

The title proper in another language and/or script.

An alternative title in another language and/or script is treated as part of the parallel title proper.

Transcribing

Apply guidelines: *Transcription* (p. 263) and *Titles Associated with a Manifestation* (p. 271).

More than one Parallel Title Proper element

Transcribe the titles in the order indicated by the sequence, layout, or typography of the titles on the source or sources of information.

Element	Example
Title Proper	Strassenkarte der Schweiz
Parallel Title Proper	Carte routière de la Suisse
Parallel Title Proper	Road map of Switzerland

Title » Other Title Information (RDA 2.3.4)

Information that appears in conjunction with, and is subordinate to, the title proper of a resource.

Other title information can include any phrase appearing with a title proper that is indicative of the character, contents, etc., of the resource, or the motives for, or occasion of, its production, publication, etc.

Other title information includes subtitles, etc. It does not include variations on the title proper such as spine titles, sleeve titles, etc., or designations and/or names of parts, sections, or supplements.

In more than one language or script on source

Choose the other title information that is in the language or script of the title proper. If this criterion does not apply, choose the other title information that appears first.

Transcribing

Apply guidelines: *Transcription* (p. 263) and *Titles Associated with a Manifestation* (p. 271).

Element	Example
Title Proper	Kerouac
Other Title Information	the definitive biography

More than one Other Title Information element

Transcribe the elements in the order indicated by the sequence, layout, or typography of the elements on the source of information.

Element	Example
Title Proper	ACoRN
Other Title Information	acute care of at-risk newborns
Other Title Information	a resource and learning tool for health care professionals

---

Title » Parallel Other Title Information (RDA 2.3.5)

Other title information in a language and/or script that differs from that transcribed in the other title information element.

Transcribing

Apply guidelines: *Transcription* (p. 263) and *Titles Associated with a Manifestation* (p. 271).

More than one Parallel Other Title Information element

Transcribe in the same order as the parallel titles proper to which the information corresponds.

Element	Example
Parallel Other Title Information	masterpieces of botanical illustration
Parallel Other Title Information	chefs-d'œuvre de l'illustration botanique
Title Proper in German. Parallel titles proper in English and in French. Parallel Other Title Information elements transcribed separately in the same order as the corresponding Parallel Title Proper.	

***RDA ESSENTIALS* TIP**

RDA appendix E provides instructions for ISBD (International Standard Bibliographic Description) presentation of elements. For example, each parallel title is preceded by an equals sign and each unit of other title information is preceded by a colon.

> Ein Garten Eden : Meisterwerke der botanischen Illustration = Garden of Eden : masterpieces of botanical illustration = Un jardin d'Eden : chefs-d'œuvre de l'illustration botanique

Title » Variant Title (RDA 2.3.6)

A title associated with a resource that differs from a title transcribed as the title proper, a parallel title proper, other title information, parallel other title information, earlier title proper, later title proper, key title, or abbreviated title.

> **Related elements.** Variations in the title proper appearing on an earlier iteration of an integrating resource are treated as earlier titles proper (see *Earlier Title Proper*).
>
> Variations in the title proper appearing on a later issue or part of a multipart monograph or serial are treated as later titles proper (see *Later Title Proper*).

Transcribing

Apply guidelines: *Transcription* (p. 263) and *Titles Associated with a Manifestation* (p. 271).

Variant titles include the following

- those that appear in the resource itself (e.g., on a title page, title frame, title screen; as a caption title, running title; on a cover, spine), on a jacket, sleeve, container, etc., or in accompanying material
- those associated with a resource through reference sources
- those assigned by an agency registering or preparing a description of the resource (e.g., a title assigned by a repository, a cataloger's translation or transliteration of the title)
- those assigned by the creator or by previous owners or custodians of the resource, etc.
- corrections to titles that appear in the resource in an incorrect form
- part of a title (e.g., an alternative title or a section title transcribed as part of the title proper)
- variations in parallel titles proper, other title information, or parallel other title information appearing on an earlier iteration of an integrating resource or on a later issue or part of a multipart monograph or serial

Element	Example
Title Proper	Aging in the Americas into the XXI century
Variant Title	Aging in the Americas into the twenty-first century

Element	Example
Title Proper	SSP, a civil defense manual for cultural survival
Variant Title	Strategic sustainable planning
Note on Title	Title on cover: Strategic sustainable planning

Title » Earlier Title Proper (RDA 2.3.7)

A title proper appearing on an earlier iteration of an integrating resource that differs from that on the current iteration.

Transcribing

Apply guidelines: *Transcription* (p. 263) and *Titles Associated with a Manifestation* (p. 271).

Title » Later Title Proper (RDA 2.3.8)

A title proper appearing on a later issue or part of a multipart monograph or serial that differs from that on the first or earliest issue or part.

Transcribing

Apply guidelines: *Transcription* (p. 263) and *Titles Associated with a Manifestation* (p. 271).

Title » Key Title (RDA 2.3.9)

The unique name assigned to a resource by an ISSN registration agency.

Recording

Record the key title as it appears on the source.

Element	Example
Key Title	Image (Niagara ed.)

Title » Abbreviated Title (RDA 2.3.10)

A title that has been abbreviated for purposes of indexing or identification.

An abbreviated title is created either by the agency preparing the description or by another agency (e.g., an ISSN registration agency, an abstracting or indexing service).

Recording

Record the abbreviated title as it appears on the source.

Element	Example
Abbreviated Title	Can. j. infect. dis. med. microbial.

Statements of Responsibility

Statement of Responsibility (RDA 2.4)

A statement relating to the identification and/or function of any persons, families, or corporate bodies responsible for the creation of, or contributing to the realization of, the intellectual or artistic content of a resource.

A statement of responsibility sometimes includes words or phrases that are neither names nor linking words.

> **Related elements.** See guidelines: *Statements of Responsibility* (p. 25) for statement of responsibility sub-elements in Edition Statement and Series Statement.
>
> See guidelines: *Name of Producer, Publisher, Distributor, and Manufacturer* (p. 285) for statements identifying persons, families, or corporate bodies in Production Statement, Publication Statement, Distribution Statement, and Manufacture Statement.

Core element

Statement of Responsibility Relating to Title Proper is a core element (if more than one, only the first transcribed is required). Other statements of responsibility are optional.

> **Related elements.** For notes, see *Note on Manifestation » Note on Statement of Responsibility*.

Statement of Responsibility » Statement of Responsibility Relating to Title Proper (RDA 2.4.2)

A statement associated with the title proper of a resource that relates to the identification and/or function of any persons, families, or corporate bodies responsible for the creation of, or contributing to the realization of, the intellectual or artistic content of the resource.

Core element

If more than one statement of responsibility relating to title proper appears on the source of information, only the first transcribed is required.

In more than one language or script on source

Choose the statement in the language or script of the Title Proper. If this criterion does not apply, choose the statement that appears first.

Transcribing

Apply guidelines: *Transcription* (p. 263) and *Statements of Responsibility* (p. 25).

Element	Example
Statement of Responsibility Relating to Title Proper	by James Clavell

Element	Example
Statement of Responsibility Relating to Title Proper	L.H. Booth, P. Fisher, V. Heppelthwaite, and C.T. Eason

Element	Example
Statement of Responsibility Relating to Title Proper	University of London Audio Visual Centre
Statement of Responsibility Relating to Title Proper	produced, directed, and edited by N.C. Collins
Only the first statement of responsibility is a core element.	

Element	Example
Statement of Responsibility Relating to Title Proper	starring, in alphabetical order: Josie Bissett, Thomas Calabro, Doug Savant, Grant Show, Andrew Shue, Courtney Thorne-Smith, Daphne Zuniga
Statement of Responsibility Relating to Title Proper	special guest star: Heather Locklear, as Amanda
Statement of Responsibility Relating to Title Proper	created by Darren Star

If not all statements of responsibility appearing on the source or sources of information are being transcribed, give preference to those identifying creators of the intellectual or artistic content. In case of doubt, transcribe the first statement.

Make a note on persons, families, or corporate bodies not transcribed in the statement of responsibility if considered important for identification, access, or selection (see *Note on Manifestation » Note on Statement of Responsibility*).

Statement of Responsibility » Parallel Statement of Responsibility Relating to Title Proper (RDA 2.4.3)

A statement of responsibility relating to title proper in a language and/or script that differs from that transcribed in the Statement of Responsibility Relating to Title Proper element.

Transcribing

Apply guidelines: *Transcription* (p. 263) and *Statements of Responsibility* (p. 25).

More than one Parallel Statement of Responsibility Relating to Title Proper element

Transcribe the statements in the same order as the parallel titles proper to which they correspond. If that is not applicable, transcribe them in the order found on the resource.

Element	Example
Statement of Responsibility Relating to Title Proper	Mary E. Bond, compiler and editor
Parallel Statement of Responsibility Relating to Title Proper	Mary E. Bond, rédactrice et réviseure

Edition Statements

Edition Statement (RDA 2.5)

A statement identifying the edition to which a resource belongs.

> An edition statement sometimes includes a designation of a named revision of an edition.
>
> An edition statement sometimes includes a statement or statements of responsibility relating to the edition and/or to a named revision of an edition.

For resources in an unpublished form, statements indicating the version of the work contained in the resource are treated as edition statements. Some examples of a resource in an unpublished form are manuscript drafts or video recordings that have not been commercially released or broadcast.

Core element

Designation of Edition and Designation of a Named Revision of an Edition are core elements. Other sub-elements of edition statements are optional.

❚ **Related elements.** For notes, see *Note on Manifestation » Note on Edition Statement.*

> **Optional addition.** If a resource lacks an edition statement but is known to contain significant changes from other editions, supply an edition statement, if considered important for identification or access. Indicate that the information was taken from a source outside the resource itself (e.g., by using square brackets).

Edition Statement » Designation of Edition (RDA 2.5.2)

A word, character, or group of words and/or characters, identifying the edition to which a resource belongs.

Note that in some languages the same term or terms can be used to indicate both edition and printing. A statement detailing the number of copies printed is not a designation of edition.

In case of doubt about whether a statement is a designation of edition, consider the presence of these words or statements as evidence that it is a designation of edition:

(a) a word such as *edition, issue, release, level, state,* or *update* (or its equivalent in another language)

or

(b) a statement indicating: a difference in content, a difference in geographic coverage, a difference in language, a difference in audience, a particular format or physical presentation, a different date associated with the content, or a particular voice range or format for notated music

Core element

In more than one language or script on source

Choose the statement in the language and/or script of the Title Proper. If this criterion does not apply, choose the statement that appears first.

Capitalization

Capitalize the first word or abbreviation of the first word (RDA A.5).

Transcribing

Apply guidelines: *Transcription* (p. 263).

Element	Example
Designation of Edition	World Cup ed.

Element	Example
Designation of Edition	Abridged

Element	Example
Designation of Edition	Northern ed.

Element	Example
Designation of Edition	Canadian edition

Element	Example
Designation of Edition	Widescreen version

Element	Example
Designation of Edition	Draft, May 2000

More than one Designation of Edition element

Transcribe the statements in the order indicated by the sequence, layout, or typography of the statements on the source of information.

If a designation of edition consists of a letter or letters and/or a number or numbers (expressed either as numerals or as words) without accompanying words, add an appropriate word. Indicate that the information was taken from a source outside the resource itself (e.g., by using square brackets).

Element	Example
Designation of Edition	[Version] 1.1

Element	Example
Designation of Edition	First [edition]

Related elements. Other elements for statements indicating regular revision or numbering (RDA 2.5.2.5).

For serials and integrating resources, transcribe statements indicating regular revision as a note on frequency (see *Note on Manifestation* » *Note on Frequency*).

Element	Example
Note on Frequency	Revised edition issued every 6 months

Element	Example
Note on Frquency	Frequently updated

For serials, transcribe statements indicating numbering as numbering (see *Numbering of Serials elements*).

Element	Example
Numeric and/or Alphabetic Designation of First Issue or Part of Sequence	First edition

Related elements. Other elements that integrate a designation of edition (RDA 2.5.2.6).

If a designation of edition is an integral part of the title proper, other title information, or statement of responsibility or the designation is grammatically linked to any of these elements then transcribe the designation of edition as part of the element to which it is integrated or linked. Do not transcribe it again as a designation of edition.

Element	Example
Title Proper	The compact edition of the Oxford English dictionary

Edition Statement » Parallel Designation of Edition
(RDA 2.5.3)

A designation of edition in a language and/or script that differs from that transcribed in the designation of edition element.

Transcribing

Apply guidelines: *Transcription* (p. 263).

Element	Example
Designation of Edition	Canadian ed.
Parallel Designation of Edition	Éd. canadienne

More than one Parallel Designation of Edition element

Transcribe the statements in the order indicated by the sequence, layout, or typography of the statements on the source or sources of information.

Edition Statement » Statement of Responsibility Relating to the Edition (RDA 2.5.4)

A statement relating to the identification of any persons, families, or corporate bodies responsible for the edition being described but not to all editions.

In more than one language or script on source

Choose the statement in the language or script of the Title Proper. If this criterion does not apply, choose the statement that appears first.

Transcribing

Apply guidelines: *Transcription* (p. 263) and *Statements of Responsibility* (p. 25).

Element	Example
Designation of Edition	New edition
Statement of Responsibility Relating to the Edition	revised and updated by Alan Powers

Element	Example
Designation of Edition	New Wessex ed.
Statement of Responsibility Relating to the Edition	introduction by J. Hillis Miller
Statement of Responsibility Relating to the Edition	notes by Edward Mendelson

Related elements. If there is doubt about whether a statement of responsibility applies to all editions or only to some or there is no designation of edition then transcribe the statement of responsibility as a statement of responsibility relating to title proper (see Statement of Responsibility » Statement of Responsibility Relating to Title Proper).

When describing the first edition, transcribe all statements of responsibility as statements of responsibility relating to title proper (see *Statement of Responsibility » Statement of Responsibility Relating to Title Proper*).

Element	Example
Title Proper	Everyman's dictionary of abbreviations
Statement of Responsibility Relating to Title Proper	[edited by] John Paxton

Edition Statement » Parallel Statement of Responsibility Relating to the Edition (RDA 2.5.5)

A statement of responsibility relating to the edition in a language and/or script that differs from that transcribed in the statement of responsibility relating to the edition element.

Transcribing

Apply guidelines: *Transcription* (p. 263) and *Statements of Responsibility* (p. 25).

More than one Parallel Statement of Responsibility Relating to the Edition element

Transcribe the statements in the same order as the parallel designations of edition to which they correspond. If that is not applicable, transcribe them in the order found on the resource.

Edition Statement » Designation of a Named Revision of an Edition (RDA 2.5.6)

A word, character, or group of words and/or characters, identifying a particular revision of a named edition.

Core element

In more than one language or script on source

Choose the statement in the language or script of the Title Proper. If this criterion does not apply, choose the statement that appears first.

Transcribing

Apply guidelines: *Transcription* (p. 263). Apply also instructions for *Designation of Edition*.

If the source of information has a statement indicating a revision of an edition (e.g., a named reissue of a particular edition containing changes from that edition), transcribe that statement.

Element	Example
Designation of Edition	World's classics edition
Designation of a Named Revision of an Edition	new edition, revised, reset, and illustrated

Do not transcribe statements relating to a reissue of an edition that contains no changes unless the resource is considered to be of particular importance to the agency preparing the description.

More than one Designation of a Named Revision of an Edition element

Transcribe the statements in the order indicated by the sequence, layout, or typography of the statements on the source of information.

Edition Statement » Parallel Designation of a Named Revision of an Edition (RDA 2.5.7)

A designation of a named revision of an edition in a language and/or script that differs from that transcribed in the designation of a named revision of an edition element.

Transcribing

Apply guidelines: *Transcription* (p. 263).

More than one Parallel Designation of a Named Revision of an Edition element

Transcribe the parallel statements in the order indicated by the sequence, layout, or typography of the statements on the source or sources of information.

Edition Statement » Statement of Responsibility Relating to a Named Revision of an Edition (RDA 2.5.8)

A statement relating to the identification of any persons, families, or corporate bodies responsible for a named revision of an edition.

In more than one language or script on source

Choose the statement in the language or script of the Title Proper. If this criterion does not apply, choose the statement that appears first.

Transcribing

Apply guidelines: *Transcription* (p. 263) and *Statements of Responsibility* (p. 25).

Element	Example
Designation of Edition	Rev. ed.
Statement of Responsibility Relating to the Edition	with revisions, an introduction, and a chapter on writing by E.B. White
Designation of a Named Revision of an Edition	2nd ed.
Statement of Responsibility Relating to a Named Revision of an Edition	with the assistance of Eleanor Gould Packard

Edition Statement » Parallel Statement of Responsibility Relating to a Named Revision of an Edition (RDA 2.5.9)

A statement of responsibility relating to a named revision of an edition in a language and/ or script that differs from that transcribed in the statement of responsibility relating to a named revision of an edition element.

Transcribing

Apply guidelines: *Transcription* (p. 263) and *Statements of Responsibility* (p. 25).

More than one Parallel Statement of Responsibility Relating to a Named Revision of an Edition element

Transcribe the statements in the same order as the parallel designations of a named revision of an edition to which they correspond.

Numbering of Serials

Numbering of Serials (RDA 2.6)

The identification of each of the issues or parts of a serial

Numbering of serials may include a numeral, a letter, any other character, or the combination of these with or without an accompanying caption (e.g., volume, number) and/or a chronological designation.

A serial sometimes has more than one sequence of numbering. A new sequence generally begins when a new system of numeric and/or alphabetic designations begins.

A serial sometimes has more than one concurrent system of numeric and/or alphabetic designations.

> **Related elements.** For numbering within series, see Series Statement » Numbering within Series.
>
> For numbering within subseries, see *Series Statement » Numbering within Subseries.*

Core element

Core elements are *Numeric and/or Alphabetic Designation of First Issue or Part of Sequence; Chronological Designation of First Issue or Part of Sequence; Numeric and/or Alphabetic Designation of Last Issue or Part of Sequence;* and *Chronological Designation of Last Issue or Part of Sequence.* Transcribing and recording other designations are optional.

> **Related elements.** For notes, see *Note on Manifestation » Note on Numbering of Serials.*

In more than one language or script

For each Numbering of Serials element sub-type choose the designation that is in the language or script of the Title Proper. If this criterion does not apply, choose the designation that appears first.

Recording and transcribing—Common instructions for Numbering of Serials element sub-types

Record numbers by applying guidelines: *Numbers Expressed as Numerals or as Words* (p. 267). Transcribe other words, characters, or groups of words and/or characters as they appear on the source of information by applying guidelines: *Transcription* (p. 263).

Element	Example
Chronological Designation of First Issue or Part of Sequence	July/August 2005

Element	Example
Numeric and/or Alphabetic Designation of First Issue or Part of Sequence	Vol. 1, no. 1

Element	Example
Alternative Numeric and/or Alphabetic Designation of First Issue or Part of Sequence	4th issue

> **Exception.** If necessary for clarity, replace a slash with a hyphen.
>
> | Element | Example |
> |---|---|
> | Chronological Designation of First Issue or Part of Sequence | 1961/1962 |
> | *Designation appears on issue as 1961-2. Note also that inclusive dates are recorded in full according to guidelines: Numbers Expressed as Numerals or as Words.* | |

If the numeric and/or alphabetic designation consists of a year and a number that is a division of the year, record the year before the number. (RDA 2.6.2.3)

Element	Example
Numeric and/or Alphabetic Designation of First Issue or Part of Sequence	97-1
Instead of 1-97. Do not record as a chronological designation.	

Recording numbering for first and last issue or part

Record the numbering for the first issue or part (see *Numeric and/or Alphabetic Designation of First Issue or Part of Sequence* and *Chronological Designation of First Issue or Part of Sequence*).

When describing a serial that has ceased publication, record the numbering for the last issue or part (see *Numeric and/or Alphabetic Designation of Last Issue or Part of Sequence* and *Chronological Designation of Last Issue or Part of Sequence*).

Element	Example
Numeric and/or Alphabetic Designation of First Issue or Part of Sequence	Vol. 3, no. 6
Chronological Designation of First Issue or Part of Sequence	Aug./Sept. 1970
Numeric and/or Alphabetic Designation of Last Issue or Part of Sequence	volume 5, number 3
Chronological Designation of Last Issue or Part of Sequence	Mar. 1972
Designations for first and last issue of a serial.	

Numbering that starts a new sequence with a different system

If the numbering starts a new sequence with a different system, record the numbering of the first issue or part of each sequence *and* the numbering of the last issue or part of each sequence.

Record each sequence of numbering in the order in which they occur.

Element	Example
Numeric and/or Alphabetic Designation of First Issue or Part of Sequence	Vol. 1, no. 1
Chronological Designation of First Issue or Part of Sequence	November 1943
Numeric and/or Alphabetic Designation of Last Issue or Part of Sequence	volume 10, number 12
Chronological Designation of Last Issue or Part of Sequence	June 1973
Numeric and/or Alphabetic Designation of First Issue or Part of Sequence	number 1
Chronological Designation of First Issue or Part of Sequence	July 1974
Designations for first and last issues of first sequence; designations for first issue of new sequence starting with number 1 (July 1974).	

Variations in designations

Make notes on variations in designations (see *Note on Manifestation » Note on Numbering of Serials*) if there are variations in designations that do not constitute a new sequence *and* the variations are considered important for identification.

Element	Example
Note on Numbering of Serials	Issues for Aug. 1973–Dec. 1974 also called v. 1, no. 7–v. 2, no. 12

Supplying a designation for . . .

Numeric and/or Alphabetic Designation of First Issue or Part of Sequence

Chronological Designation of First Issue or Part of Sequence

Numeric and/or Alphabetic Designation of Last Issue or Part of Sequence

Chronological Designation of Last Issue or Part of Sequence

If the issue or part has no designation *and* subsequent or previous issues or parts as applicable define a designation pattern, *then* supply a designation based on the pattern.

If the identification of the resource is based on another issue or part *and* a designation can be readily ascertained, *then* supply a designation.

For supplied designations, indicate that the information was taken from a source outside the resource itself (e.g., by using square brackets). (RDA 2.6.2.3, 2.6.3.3, 2.6.4.3, 2.6.5.3)

Element	Example
Numeric and/or Alphabetic Designation of First Issue or Part of Sequence	[Part 1]

Subsequent issues numbered: Part 2, Part 3, *etc.*

Element	Example
Numeric and/or Alphabetic Designation of Last Issue or Part of Sequence	[issue 12]

No numeric and/or alphabetic designation on last issue of sequence. Designation on previous issue: issue 11.

Element	Example
Numeric and/or Alphabetic Designation of First Issue or Part of Sequence	[Vol. 1, no. 1]
Chronological Designation of First Issue or Part of Sequence	[Jan. 1978]
Note on Issue, Part or Iteration Used as the Basis for the Identification of the Resource	Identification of the resource based on: Vol. 1, no. 3 (Mar. 1978)

Identification of resource not based on first issue; designations for first issue can be readily ascertained.

Numbering of Serials » Numeric and/or Alphabetic Designation of First Issue or Part of Sequence (RDA 2.6.2)

Numbering presented in numeric and/or alphabetic form on the first issue or part of a sequence of numbering for a serial.

Core element

Numeric and/or alphabetic designation of first issue or part of sequence for the first or only sequence is a core element.

Capitalization

Capitalize the first word or abbreviation of the first word. (RDA A.6)

Transcribing and recording

Apply guidelines: *Transcription* (p. 263) and *Numbers Expressed as Numerals or as Words* (p. 267).

Element	Example
Numeric and/or Alphabetic Designation of First Issue or Part of Sequence	Volume 1, no. 1

Alternative. Make a note on the numbering of the first issue or part of the sequence (see *Note on Manifestation » Note on Numbering of Serials*).

Element	Example
Note on Numbering of Serials	Began with volume 1, no. 1 in 2006
Note on numbering of serials as alternative to designation.	

Designation continued from a previous serial

In some cases, the sequence of numeric and/or alphabetic designation is continued from a previous serial. When this occurs, record the numeric and/or alphabetic designation of the first issue or part of the serial represented by the new description, continuing the numbering from the previous serial.

Element	Example
Numeric and/or Alphabetic Designation of First Issue or Part of Sequence	Vol. 1, no. 6
Designation appears on last issue of previous serial as: vol. 1, no. 5.	

Second or subsequent sequence of numbering

If a second or subsequent sequence of numbering is accompanied by wording to differentiate the sequence, such as *new series*, include this wording.

Element	Example
Numeric and/or Alphabetic Designation of First Issue or Part of Sequence	V. 1, no. 1
Numeric and/or Alphabetic Designation of Last Issue or Part of Sequence	v. 5, no. 12
Numeric and/or Alphabetic Designation of First Issue or Part of Sequence	new series, v. 1, no. 1
First sequence completed; second sequence has wording: new series.	

If a new sequence with the same system as before is not accompanied by wording such as *new series*, supply *new series* or another appropriate term. Indicate that the information was taken from a source outside the resource itself.

Element	Example
Numeric and/or Alphabetic Designation of First Issue or Part of Sequence	[2nd series], number 1
Previous sequence completed: number 1-number 6. Subsequent sequences have: 3rd series, 4th series.	

Numbering of Serials » Chronological Designation of First Issue or Part of Sequence (RDA 2.6.3)

Numbering presented in the form of a date (e.g., a year; year and month; month, day, and year) on the first issue or part of a sequence of numbering for a serial.

Core element

Chronological designation of first issue or part of sequence for the first or only sequence is a core element.

Capitalization

If Numeric and/or Alphabetic Designation of First Issue or Part of Sequence element is lacking, capitalize the first word or abbreviation of the first word (RDA A.6).

Transcribing and recording

Apply guidelines: *Transcription* (p. 263) and *Numbers Expressed as Numerals or as Words* (p. 267).

> **Alternative.** Make a note on the numbering of the first issue or part of the sequence (see *Note on Manifestation » Note on Numbering of Serials*).

Numbering of Serials » Numeric and/or Alphabetic Designation of Last Issue or Part of Sequence (RDA 2.6.4)

Numbering presented in numeric and/or alphabetic form on the last issue or part of a sequence of numbering for a serial.

Core element

Numeric and/or alphabetic designation of last issue or part of sequence for the last or only sequence is a core element.

Transcribing and recording

Apply guidelines: *Transcription* (p. 263) and *Numbers Expressed as Numerals or as Words* (p. 267).

> **Alternative.** Make a note on the numbering of the last issue or part of the sequence (see *Note on Manifestation » Note on Numbering of Serials*).

Numbering of Serials » Chronological Designation of Last Issue or Part of Sequence (RDA 2.6.5)

Numbering presented in the form of a date (e.g., a year; year and month; month, day, and year) on the last issue or part of a sequence of numbering for a serial.

Core element

Chronological designation of last issue or part of sequence for the last or only sequence is a core element.

Transcribing and recording

Apply guidelines: *Transcription* (p. 263) and *Numbers Expressed as Numerals or as Words* (p. 267).

> **Alternative.** Make a note on the numbering of the last issue or part of the sequence (see *Note on Manifestation » Note on Numbering of Serials*).

ALTERNATIVE DESIGNATIONS

If a serial has more than one concurrent system of numbering, record the second or subsequent systems as alternative numbering. Record them in the order in which they are presented.

Element	Example
Numeric and/or Alphabetic Designation of First Issue or Part of Sequence	Vol. 3, no. 7
Alternative Numeric and/or Alphabetic Designation of First Issue or Part of Sequence	No. 31
Two concurrent systems of numbering.	

> ***RDA ESSENTIALS* TIP**
>
> For each of the alternative designations, apply the same guidelines used to transcribe and to record the main designations: *Transcription* (p. 263) and *Numbers Expressed as Numerals or as Words* (p. 267).

Numbering of Serials » Alternative Numeric and/or Alphabetic Designation of First Issue or Part of Sequence (RDA 2.6.6)

A second or subsequent system of numbering presented in numeric and/or alphabetic form on the first issue or part of a sequence of numbering for a serial.

Capitalization

Capitalize the first word or abbreviation of the first word (RDA A.6).

Numbering of Serials » Alternative Chronological Designation of First Issue or Part of Sequence (RDA 2.6.7)

A second or subsequent system of numbering presented in the form of a date (e.g., a year; year and month; month, day, and year) on the first issue or part of a sequence of numbering for a serial.

An alternative chronological designation may include a date in a different calendar.

Capitalization

If Alternative Numeric and/or Alphabetic Designation of First Issue or Part of Sequence element is lacking, capitalize the first word or abbreviation of the first word (RDA A.6).

Numbering of Serials » Alternative Numeric and/or Alphabetic Designation of Last Issue or Part of Sequence (RDA 2.6.8)

A second or subsequent system of numbering presented in numeric and/or alphabetic form on the last issue or part of a sequence of numbering for a serial.

Numbering of Serials » Alternative Chronological Designation of Last Issue or Part of Sequence (RDA 2.6.9)

A second or subsequent system of numbering presented in the form of a date (e.g., a year; year and month; month, day, and year) on the last issue or part of a sequence of numbering for a serial.

An alternative chronological designation may include a date in a different calendar.

Production, Publication, Distribution, and Manufacture Statements, and Copyright Date

Production Statement (RDA 2.7)

A statement identifying the place or places of production, producer or producers, and date or dates of production of a resource in an unpublished form.

Production statements include statements relating to the inscription, fabrication, construction, etc., of a resource in an unpublished form.

Record a production statement or statements for a resource that is in an unpublished form (e.g., a manuscript, a painting, a sculpture, a locally made recording).

Core element

Date of Production is a core element for resources issued in an unpublished form. Other sub-elements of production statements are optional.

❙ **Related elements.** For notes, see *Note on Manifestation* » *Note on Production Statement.*

> ### *RDA ESSENTIALS* TIP
>
> For each Production Statement sub-element, apply the same techniques used for transcribing or recording the corresponding Publication Statement sub-element.

Production Statement » Place of Production (RDA 2.7.2)

A place associated with the inscription, fabrication, construction, etc., of a resource in an unpublished form.

Production Statement » Parallel Place of Production (RDA 2.7.3)

A place of production in a language and/or script that differs from that transcribed in the place of production element.

Production Statement » Producer's Name (RDA 2.7.4)

The name of a person, family, or corporate body responsible for inscribing, fabricating, constructing, etc., a resource in an unpublished form.

Production Statement » Parallel Producer's Name (RDA 2.7.5)

A producer's name in a language and/or script that differs from that transcribed in the producer's name element.

Production Statement » Date of Production (RDA 2.7.6)

A date associated with the inscription, fabrication, construction, etc., of a resource in an unpublished form.

Core element

Date of Production is a core element for resources issued in an unpublished form. If the date of production appears on the source of information in more than one calendar, only the date in the calendar preferred by the agency preparing the description is required.

RDA ESSENTIALS **TIP**

For Production Statement, only Date of Production is a core element.

Use *Date of Production* for unpublished resources, such as for the date a document was produced for in-house use, or for the date an object like a sculpture was made.

Element	Example
Date of Production	2014

Publication Statement (RDA 2.8)

A statement identifying the place or places of publication, publisher or publishers, and date or dates of publication of a resource.

Publication statements include statements relating to the publication, release, or issuing of a resource.

Consider all online resources to be published.

> **Related elements.** Record a publication statement or statements for a published resource. For statements relating to the production of resources in an unpublished form, see *Production Statement.*

Core element

Place of Publication, Publisher's Name, and Date of Publication are core elements for published resources. Other sub-elements of publication statements are optional.

> **Related elements.** For notes, see Note on Manifestation » Note on Publication Statement.

RDA ESSENTIALS **TIP**

A Publication Statement has three core sub-elements, which must be recorded if they are applicable and readily ascertainable.

Element	Example
Place of Publication	New York
Publisher's Name	McGraw-Hill
Date of Publication	2009

Publication Statement » Place of Publication (RDA 2.8.2)

A place associated with the publication, release, or issuing of a resource.

Core element

If more than one place of publication appears on the source of information, only the first transcribed is required.

In more than one language or script on source

Choose the form that is in the language or script of the Title Proper. If this criterion does not apply, choose the place name in the language or script that appears first.

Transcribing

Apply guidelines: *Transcription* (p. 263) and *Place of Production, Publication, Distribution, and Manufacture* (p. 281).

More than one Place of Publication element

Transcribe the place names in the order indicated by the sequence, layout, or typography of the names on the source of information.

If there are two or more publishers *and* there are two or more places associated with one or more of the publishers, *then* transcribe the place names associated with each publisher in the order indicated by the sequence, layout, or typography of the place names on the source of information.

Publication Statement » Parallel Place of Publication (RDA 2.8.3)

A place of publication in a language and/or script that differs from that transcribed in the place of publication element.

Transcribing

Apply guidelines: *Transcription* (p. 263).

More than one Parallel Place of Publication element

Transcribe the names in the order indicated by the sequence, layout, or typography of the names on the source or sources of information.

Element	Example
Place of Publication	Genf
Parallel Place of Publication	Genève

Publication Statement » Publisher's Name (RDA 2.8.4)

The name of a person, family, or corporate body responsible for publishing, releasing, or issuing a resource. For early printed resources, printers and booksellers are treated as publishers.

Core element

If more than one publisher's name appears on the source of information, only the first transcribed is required.

In more than one language or script on source

Choose the form that is in the language or script of the Title Proper. If this criterion does not apply, choose the name in the language or script that appears first.

Transcribing

Apply guidelines: *Transcription* (p. 263) and *Name of Producer, Publisher, Distributor, and Manufacturer* (p. 285).

More than one Publisher's Name element

Transcribe the publishers' names in the order indicated by the sequence, layout, or typography of the names on the source of information.

Publication Statement » Parallel Publisher's Name
(RDA 2.8.5)

A publisher's name in a language and/or script that differs from that transcribed in the publisher's name element.

Transcribing

Apply guidelines: *Transcription* (p. 263).

More than one Parallel Publisher's Name element

Transcribe the names in the order indicated by the sequence, layout, or typography of the names on the source or sources of information.

Element	Example
Publisher's Name	Health Canada, Pest Management Regulatory Agency
Parallel Publisher's Name	Santé Canada, Agence de réglementation de la lutte antiparasitaire

Publication Statement » Date of Publication (RDA 2.8.6)

A date associated with the publication, release, or issuing of a resource.

Core element

If the date of publication appears on the source of information in more than one calendar, only the date in the calendar preferred by the agency preparing the description is required.

Recording

Apply guidelines: *Date of Production, Publication, Distribution, and Manufacture* (p. 289).

Date of Publication in different calendars

Record the dates in the order indicated by the sequence, layout, or typography of the dates on the source of information.

Distribution Statement (RDA 2.9)

A statement identifying the place or places of distribution, distributor or distributors, and date or dates of distribution of a resource in a published form.

Related elements. For notes, see *Note on Manifestation » Note on Distribution Statement*.

***RDA ESSENTIALS* TIP**

For each Distribution Statement sub-element, apply the same techniques used for transcribing or recording the corresponding Publication Statement sub-element.

Distribution Statement » Place of Distribution (RDA 2.9.2)

A place associated with the distribution of a resource in a published form.

Distribution Statement » Parallel Place of Distribution (RDA 2.9.3)

A place of distribution in a language and/or script that differs from that transcribed in the place of distribution element.

Distribution Statement » Distributor's Name (RDA 2.9.4)

The name of a person, family, or corporate body responsible for distributing a resource in a published form.

Distribution Statement » Parallel Distributor's Name
(RDA 2.9.5)

A distributor's name in a language and/or script that differs from that transcribed in the distributor's name element.

Distribution Statement » Date of Distribution (RDA 2.9.6)

A date associated with the distribution of a resource in a published form. Record if the date of distribution differs from the date of publication *and* the date of distribution is considered important for identification.

Manufacture Statement (RDA 2.10)

A statement identifying the place or places of distribution, distributor or distributors, and date or dates of distribution of a resource in a published form.

> **Related elements.** For notes, see *Note on Manifestation » Note on Manufacture Statement.*

> ### *RDA ESSENTIALS* TIP
> For each Manufacture Statement sub-element, apply the same techniques used for transcribing or recording the corresponding Publication Statement sub-element.

Manufacture Statement » Place of Manufacture
(RDA 2.10.2)

A place associated with the printing, duplicating, casting, etc., of a resource in a published form.

Manufacture Statement » Parallel Place of Manufacture
(RDA 2.10.3)

A place of manufacture in a language and/or script that differs from that transcribed in the place of manufacture element.

Manufacture Statement » Manufacturer's Name (RDA 2.10.4)

The name of a person, family, or corporate body responsible for printing, duplicating, casting, etc., a resource in a published form.

Manufacture Statement » Parallel Manufacturer's Name
(RDA 2.10.5)

A manufacturer's name in a language and/or script that differs from that transcribed in the manufacturer's name element.

Manufacture Statement » Date of Manufacture (RDA 2.10.6)

A date associated with the printing, duplicating, casting, etc., of a resource in a published form.

Copyright Date (RDA 2.11)

A date associated with a claim of protection under copyright or a similar regime.

Copyright dates include phonogram dates (i.e., dates associated with claims of protection for audio recordings).

> **Related elements.** For notes, see *Note on Manifestation » Note on Copyright Date.*

Recording

Apply guidelines: *Numbers Expressed as Numerals or as Words* (p. 267).

Precede the date by the copyright symbol (©) or the phonogram copyright symbol (℗). If the appropriate symbol cannot be reproduced, precede the date by *copyright* or *phonogram copyright*.

Element	Example
Copyright Date	©2002

> **Optional addition.** If the date as it appears in the resource is not of the Gregorian or Julian calendar, add the corresponding date or dates of the Gregorian or Julian calendar. Indicate that the information was taken from a source outside the resource itself (e.g., by using square brackets).
>
> | Element | Example |
> |---|---|
> | Copyright Date | ©2556 [2013] |
>
> *Copyright date appears in Buddhist calendar on the source of information.*

Copyright date in different calendars

Record the dates in the order indicated by the sequence, layout, or typography of the dates on the source of information.

Multiple copyright dates applying to various aspects (e.g., text, sound, graphics)

Record any that are considered important for identification or selection.

Element	Example
Copyright Date	℗2009
Copyright Date	©2010

Multiple copyright dates applying to a single aspect (e.g., text, sound, graphics)

Record only the latest copyright date.

Series Statements

Series Statement (RDA 2.12)

A statement identifying a series to which a resource belongs and the numbering of the resource within the series.

A series statement sometimes includes additional sub-elements such as those for one or more subseries, statements of responsibility relating to a series or subseries, and ISSNs of series and subseries.

Related elements. For instructions on recording a series or subseries as a related work, see *Related Work*.

RDA ESSENTIALS TIP

While a Series Statement is used to transcribe the series information as found on a particular manifestation, the series may also be considered a work in a whole-part relationship to the resource being described. As one of the identifying elements for a work, the title of the series may also be recorded in Preferred Title for the Work, which is used in constructing an authorized access point representing the series as a work. Variant titles of the series may be recorded in Variant Title for the Work. The authorized access point representing the series may be used in a Related Work element with the relationship designator *in series* to support users in finding all resources related to the series.

Core element

Core elements are Title Proper of Series, Numbering within Series, Title Proper of Subseries, and Numbering within Subseries. Other sub-elements of series statements are optional.

Related elements. For notes, see *Note on Manifestation* » *Note on Series Statement*.

Series Statement » Title Proper of Series (RDA 2.12.2)

The chief name of a series (i.e., the title normally used when citing the series).
   An alternative series title is treated as part of the title proper of series.

Core element

Choosing the Title Proper of Series

In more than one language or script on source

If the content is written, spoken, or sung, *then* choose as the title proper of series the title in the language or script of the main content of the resource.

   If the content is not written, spoken, or sung *or* there is no main content in a single language, *then* choose the title proper of series on the basis of the sequence, layout, or typography of the titles.

In more than one form on source; same language or script

Choose the title based on sequence, layout, or typography.

Transcribing

Apply guidelines: *Transcription* (p. 263) and *Titles Associated with a Manifestation* (p. 271).

Element	Example
Title Proper of Series	The Oxford history of England

   If the title proper of the series includes numbering as an integral part of the title, transcribe the numbering as part of the title proper of the series (do not apply to a multipart monograph or serial if the numbering of the series varies among the parts or issues).

Element	Example
Title Proper of Series	The twenty-sixth L. Ray Buckendale lecture

Series Statement » Parallel Title Proper of Series (RDA 2.12.3)

The title proper of a series in another language and/or script.

Transcribing

Apply guidelines: *Transcription* (p. 263) and *Titles Associated with a Manifestation* (p. 271).

More than one Parallel Title Proper of Series element

Transcribe the titles in the order indicated by the sequence, layout, or typography of the titles on the source or sources of information.

Series Statement » Other Title Information of Series
(RDA 2.12.4)

Information that appears in conjunction with, and is subordinate to, the title proper of a series. Transcribe only if considered necessary for the identification of the series.

In more than one language or script on source

Choose the information that is in the language or script of the Title Proper of the Series. If this criterion does not apply, choose the other title information that appears first.

Transcribing

Apply guidelines: *Transcription* (p. 263) and *Titles Associated with a Manifestation* (p. 271).

Element	Example
Title Proper of Series	English linguistics, 1500–1750
Other Title Information of Series	a collection of facsimile reprints

More than one Other Title Information of Series element

Transcribe the elements in the order indicated by the sequence, layout, or typography of the elements on the source of information.

Series Statement » Parallel Other Title Information of Series (RDA 2.12.5)

Other title information of a series in a language and/or script that differs from that transcribed in the other title information of series element.

Transcribing

Apply guidelines: *Transcription* (p. 263) and *Titles Associated with a Manifestation* (p. 271).

More than one Parallel Other Title Information of Series element

Transcribe in the same order as the parallel titles proper of series to which the information corresponds.

Series Statement » Statement of Responsibility Relating to Series (RDA 2.12.6)

A statement relating to the identification of any persons, families, or corporate bodies responsible for a series.

Transcribe statements of responsibility associated with the series title only if considered necessary for identification of the series.

In more than one language or script on source

Choose the statement in the language or script of the Title Proper of the Series. If this criterion does not apply, choose the statement that appears first.

Transcribing

Apply guidelines: *Transcription* (p. 263) and *Statements of Responsibility* (p. 277).

Series Statement » Parallel Statement of Responsibility Relating to Series (RDA 2.12.7)

A statement of responsibility relating to series in a language and/or script that differs from that transcribed in the statement of responsibility relating to series element.

Transcribing

Apply guidelines: *Transcription* (p. 263) and *Statements of Responsibility* (p. 277).

More than one Parallel Statement of Responsibility Relating to Series element

Transcribe the statements in the same order as the parallel titles proper of series to which they correspond.

Series Statement » ISSN of Series (RDA 2.12.8)

The identifier assigned to a series by an ISSN registration agency.

Transcribing

Apply guidelines: *Transcription* (p. 263).

> **Optional omission.** If the ISSN of a subseries appears on the source of information (see *ISSN of subseries)*, omit the ISSN of the main series.

Element	Example
ISSN of Series	ISSN 0317-3127

Series Statement » Numbering within Series (RDA 2.12.9)

A designation of the sequencing of a part or parts within a series.

Numbering within series can include a numeral, a letter, any other character, or the combination of these. Numbering is often accompanied by a caption (e.g., *volume, number*) and/or a chronological designation.

Core element

In more than one language or script on source

Choose the numbering that is in the language or script of the Title Proper of the Series. If this criterion does not apply, choose the numbering that appears first.

Transcribing and recording

Apply guidelines: *Transcription* (p. 263) and *Numbers Expressed as Numerals or as Words* (p. 267).

| **Exception.** If necessary for clarity, replace a slash with a hyphen.

If the numbering consists of a year and a number that is a division of the year, record the year before the number (e.g., *2000, no. 3* instead of *no. 3, 2000*).

When the numbering is grammatically integrated with the series title, record the numbering as part of Title Proper of Series.

If the numbering that appears on the source of information is known to be incorrect, record it as it appears. Make a note giving the correct numbering (see *Note on Manifestation » Note on Series Statement*).

Capitalization

Do not capitalize a term that is part of the numbering unless capitalization is required as applicable to the language involved (RDA A.10–A.55). Capitalize other words and alphabetic devices according to the usage on the resource (RDA A.7).

Element	Example
Numbering within Series	volume 12
Source has Volume 12. *Transcribe, but do not capitalize.*	

Chronological designation

If the resource has both a numeric and/or alphabetic designation and a chronological designation, record both. Do not treat a date of production, publication, distribution, or manufacture as a chronological designation.

Element	Example
Numbering within Series	v. 3, no. 2
	Sept. 1981

New sequence of numbering

Include wording intended to differentiate a new sequence of numbering (such as *new series*).

Supply *new series* or another appropriate term if a new sequence of numbering has the same numbering as an earlier sequence *and* the new sequence of numbering is not accompanied by wording such as *new series*. Indicate that the information was taken from a source outside the resource itself (e.g., by using square brackets).

Element	Example
Numbering within Series	[new series], no. 1

Alternative numbering system

If the series has more than one separate system of numbering, record the systems in the order in which they are presented.

Series Statement » Title Proper of Subseries (RDA 2.12.10)

The chief name of a subseries (i.e., the title normally used when citing the subseries).

Core element

Choosing the title proper of subseries

In more than one language or script on source

If the content is written, spoken, or sung *then* choose as the title proper of subseries the title in the language or script of the main content of the resource. If the content is not written, spoken, or sung *or* there is no main content in a single language, *then* choose the title proper of subseries on the basis of the sequence, layout, or typography of the titles.

In more than one form on source; same language or script

Choose the title based on sequence, layout, or typography.

Transcribing

Apply guidelines: *Transcription* (p. 263) and *Titles Associated with a Manifestation* (p. 271).

Subseries or separate series

In case of doubt about whether a series title is a subseries or a separate series, treat it as a separate series.

Numeric and/or alphabetic designation of subseries

If the subseries has a numeric and/or alphabetic designation and no title, transcribe the designation as the subseries title.

Element	Example
Title Proper of Series	Music for today
Title Proper of Subseries	Series 2

If the subseries has a title as well as a designation, transcribe the title following the designation.

Element	Example
Title Proper of Series	Viewmaster science series
Title Proper of Subseries	4, Physics

> **RDA ESSENTIALS TIP**
>
> For the other Series Statement sub-elements for a subseries, apply the same techniques used for transcribing or recording the corresponding sub-element for the main series.

Series Statement » Parallel Title Proper of Subseries
(RDA 2.12.11)

The title proper of a subseries in another language and/or script.

Series Statement » Other Title Information of Subseries
(RDA 2.12.12)

Information that appears in conjunction with, and is subordinate to, the title proper of a subseries. Transcribe other title information of a subseries only if considered necessary for the identification of the series.

Series Statement » Parallel Other Title Information of Subseries (RDA 2.12.13)

Other title information of a subseries in a language and/or script that differs from that transcribed in the Other Title Information of Subseries element.

Series Statement » Statement of Responsibility Relating to Subseries (RDA 2.12.14)

A statement relating to the identification of any persons, families, or corporate bodies responsible for a subseries. Transcribe statements of responsibility associated with the title of a subseries only if considered necessary for identification of the subseries.

Series Statement » Parallel Statement of Responsibility Relating to Subseries (RDA 2.12.15)

A statement of responsibility relating to a subseries in a language and/or script that differs from that transcribed in the Statement of Responsibility Relating to Subseries element.

Series Statement » ISSN of Subseries (RDA 2.12.16)

The identifier assigned to a subseries by an ISSN registration agency.

Series Statement » Numbering within Subseries (RDA 2.12.17)

A designation of the sequencing of a part or parts within a subseries.

Numbering within subseries can include a numeral, a letter, any other character, or the combination of these. Numbering is often accompanied by a caption (e.g., *volume*, *number*) and/or a chronological designation.

Core element

Frequency, Identifiers, and Notes

Frequency (RDA 2.14)

A categorization reflecting whether a resource is issued in one or more parts, the way it is updated, and its intended termination.

❘ Related elements. For notes, see *Note on Manifestation » Note on Frequency.*

Recording

Record an RDA term.

RDA terms for Frequency

daily	semiweekly	semimonthly	annual
three times a week	three times a month	quarterly	biennial
biweekly	bimonthly	three times a year	triennial
weekly	monthly	semiannual	irregular

If none of these terms in the list is appropriate or sufficiently specific, make a note giving details of the frequency (see *Note on Manifestation » Note on Frequency*).

Identifier for the Manifestation (RDA 2.15.1)

A character string associated with a manifestation that serves to differentiate that manifestation from other manifestations.

Identifiers for manifestations include:

- registered identifiers from internationally recognized schemes (e.g., ISBN, ISSN, URN)
- other identifiers assigned by publishers, distributors, government publications agencies, document clearinghouses, archives, etc., following their internally devised schemes
- "fingerprints" (i.e., identifiers constructed by combining groups of characters from specified pages of an early printed resource)
- music publishers' numbers and plate numbers.

Related elements. For identifiers intended to provide online access to a resource using a standard Internet browser, see *Uniform Resource Locator.*

Core element

If there is more than one identifier for the manifestation, prefer an internationally recognized identifier, if applicable. Additional identifiers for the manifestation are optional.

Recording

If there is a specified display format for the identifier for the manifestation (e.g., ISBN, ISSN, URN), record it using that format.

If there is no specified display format for the identifier, record it as it appears on the source. Precede the identifier with a trade name or the name of the agency, etc., responsible for assigning the identifier, if readily ascertainable.

Qualification

If the resource has only one identifier, record the type of binding or format, if considered important for identification.

Element	Example
Identifier for the Manifestation	ISBN 978-1-107-66485-2 (paperback)

For updating loose-leafs, add the qualification *(loose-leaf)* to the identifier.

Incorrect identifiers

If an identifier is known to be incorrectly represented in the resource, record the number as it appears. Indicate that the number is incorrect, cancelled, or invalid, as appropriate.

Element	Example
Identifier for the Manifestation	ISBN 0-87068-430-2 (invalid)

More than one identifier of the same type

Record a brief qualification after the identifier.

Element	Example
Identifier for the Manifestation	ISBN 0-435-91660-2 (cased)
Identifier for the Manifestation	ISBN 0-435-91661-0 (pbk.)

Identifiers for the whole and for parts

If describing a resource consisting of two or more parts *and* there is an identifier for the resource as a whole as well as identifiers for the individual parts, *then* record the identifier for the resource as a whole.

When describing only a single part, record the identifier for that part. Follow the identifier with the designation of the part to which it applies.

Optional addition. Record both the identifier for the resource as a whole and any identifiers for individual parts. Follow each identifier with the designation of the part to which it applies.

Element	Example
Identifier for the Manifestation	ISBN 0-379-00550-6 (set)
Identifier for the Manifestation	ISBN 0-379-00551-4 (v. 1)

Alternative. If there are more than three identifiers for individual parts, record only the first identifier and the last identifier. If the identifiers are consecutive, separate them by a hyphen. If the identifiers are not consecutive, separate them with a diagonal slash.

Identifier for the Manifestation » Publisher's Number for Music (RDA 2.15.2)

A numbering designation assigned to a resource by a music publisher, appearing normally only on the title page, the cover, and/or the first page of music.

A publisher's number sometimes includes initials, abbreviations, or words identifying the publisher.

Recording

Record publishers' numbers for music. If a publisher's number is preceded by an abbreviation, word, or phrase identifying a publisher, include that abbreviation, word, or phrase as part of the number.

Identifier for the Manifestation »
Plate Number for Music (RDA 2.15.3)

A numbering designation assigned to a resource by a music publisher. The number is usually printed at the bottom of each page, and sometimes also appears on the title page.

A plate number sometimes includes initials, abbreviations, or words identifying a publisher. It is sometimes followed by a number corresponding to the number of pages or plates.

Recording

Record plate numbers for music. If a plate number is preceded by an abbreviation, word, or phrase identifying a publisher, include that abbreviation, word, or phrase as part of the number.

Preferred Citation (RDA 2.16)

A citation for a resource in the form preferred by a creator, publisher, custodian, indexing or abstracting service, etc.

Recording

Record a preferred citation in the form as it appears on the source.

Element	Example
Preferred Citation	Fletcher, P.R., (2004) PhD Thesis - How Tertiary Level Physics Students Learn and Conceptualise Quantum Mechanics (School of Physics, University of Sydney)

Note on Manifestation (RDA 2.17)

A note providing information on attributes of the manifestation.

❙ **Related elements.** For notes on describing carriers, see *Note on Carrier.*

Recording

For all Note on Manifestation elements, apply guidelines: *Notes* (p. 119).

Note on Manifestation » Note on Title (RDA 2.17.2)

A note providing information on the source from which a title was taken, the date the title was viewed, variations in titles, inaccuracies, deletions, etc., or other information relating to a title.

| **Related elements.** *Title* element sub-types.

Source of Title Proper

Make a note on the source from which the title proper is taken if it is not one of these sources:

(a) the title page, title sheet, or title card (or image of it) of a resource consisting of multiple pages, leaves, sheets, or cards (or images of them)
(b) the title frame or title screen of a resource consisting of moving images

Element	Example
Note on Title	Title from container

| **Optional omission.** If the resource has only a single title and the title appears on the resource itself, do not record the source from which the title proper is taken.

Source of Parallel Title Proper, Variant Title, Earlier Title Proper, Later Title Proper

If a parallel title proper is taken from a different source than the title proper, make a note on the source of the parallel title proper if considered important for identification or access.

Element	Example
Note on Title	French title from cover

If considered important for identification or access, make a note on the source or basis for a variant title, an earlier title proper, and a later title proper.

Element	Example
Variant Title	Rocque's map of Shropshire
Note on Title	Spine title: Rocque's map of Shropshire

Element	Example
Earlier Title Proper	Taxation of intangible assets, 1997–1998
Note on Title	Earlier title proper: Taxation of intangible assets, 1997–1998

| **Related elements.** For online resources, make a separate note indicating the date the resource was viewed (see *Note on Issue, Part, or Iteration Used as the Basis for Identification of the Resource*).

Title variations, inaccuracies, and deletions

In some cases, scattered issues or parts, or occasional iterations of a resource have different titles proper, parallel titles proper, other title information, or parallel other title information. If the differences are not considered important for identification or access, make a general note indicating that the title, etc., varies.

Element	Example
Note on Title	Title varies slightly

If an inaccuracy in a title has been transcribed as it appears on the source of information, make a note giving the corrected form of the title, if considered important for identification or access.

Element	Example
Title Proper	Heirarchy in organizations
Note on Title	Title should read: Hierarchy in organizations

If an obvious typographic error has been corrected when transcribing the title proper of a serial or integrating resource, make a note giving the title as it appears on the source of information.

Element	Example
Title Proper	Housing starts
Note on Title	Title appears on v. 1, no. 1 as: Housing sarts

Other information relating to a title

Make notes on other details relating to a title if considered important for identification or access.

Element	Example
Note on Title	The word "Brain" in the title appears with an X through it

Note on Manifestation » Note on Statement of Responsibility (RDA 2.17.3)

A note providing information on a person, family, or corporate body not named in a statement of responsibility to whom responsibility for the intellectual or artistic content of the resource has been attributed, on variant forms of names appearing in the resource, on changes in statements of responsibility, or on other information relating to a statement of responsibility.

▌ **Related elements.** *Statement of Responsibility* element sub-types.

Element	Example
Note on Statement of Responsibility	Formerly attributed to J.S. Bach

Element	Example
Note on Statement of Responsibility	Author's initials represented by musical notes

Make notes on other information relating to a statement of responsibility, including information not recorded in the Statement of Responsibility element, if considered important for identification, access, or selection. Include a word or short phrase if necessary to clarify the role of a person, family, or corporate body named in the note.

Element	Example
Note on Statement of Responsibility	At head of title: Arctic Biological Station

Element	Example
Note on Statement of Responsibility	Cast: Gilles Behat (Charles IV), Jean Deschamps (Charles de Valois), Hélène Duc (Mahaut d'Artois)

Element	Example
Note on Statement of Responsibility	Producers, Gary Usher, Curt Boettcher, Terry Melcher, Bruce Johnston, and Brian Wilson; engineer, Bill Fletcher; container notes, Joe Foster; archiving credit, Gary Usher, Jr.

Note on Manifestation » Note on Edition Statement
(RDA 2.17.4)

A note providing information on the source of an edition statement, on edition statements relating to issues, parts, etc., on changes in edition statements, or other information relating to an edition statement.

▌ **Related elements.** *Edition Statement* sub-elements.

Note on Manifestation » Note on Numbering of Serials
(RDA 2.17.5)

A note providing information on the numbering of the first and/or last issue or part, on complex or irregular numbering (including numbering errors), or on the period covered by a volume, issue, part, etc.

❚ **Related elements.** *Numbering of Serials* element sub-types.

Element	Example
Note on Numbering of Serials	Began with volume 1, no. 1 in 2006
Note made for information not recorded as part of the Numbering of Serials element.	

Element	Example
Note on Numbering of Serials	Numbering irregular; some numbers repeated or omitted

Element	Example
Note on Numbering of Serials	Report year ends June 30

Note on Manifestation » Note on Production Statement
(RDA 2.17.6)

A note providing details on place of production, producer, or date of production, or information on changes in the place of production, producer, or producer's name.

❚ **Related elements.** *Production Statement* sub-elements.

Note on Manifestation » Note on Publication Statement
(RDA 2.17.7)

A note providing details on place of publication, publisher, or date of publication, information on changes in the place of publication, publisher, or publisher's name, or on suspension of publication.

❚ **Related elements.** *Publication Statement* sub-elements.

Element	Example
Place of Publication	Belfast
Note on Publication Statement	Actually published in Dublin

Element	Example
Date of Publication	[1969?]
Note on Publication Statement	Probable year of publication based on date range in which the publisher was active

Make notes on the beginning and ending date of publication if the identification of the resource is based on an issue or part other than the first and/or last.

Element	Example
Note on Publication Statement	Began in 1988; ceased in 1991
First and last published issues not available but information about beginning and ending dates known.	

Note on Manifestation » Note on Distribution Statement
(RDA 2.17.8)

A note providing details on place of distribution, distributor, or date of distribution, or information on changes in the place of distribution, distributor, or distributor's name.

| **Related elements.** *Distribution Statement* sub-elements.

Element	Example
Note on Distribution Statement	Distributed in the U.K. by: EAV Ltd

Note on Manifestation » Note on Manufacture Statement (RDA 2.17.9)

A note providing details on place of manufacture, manufacturer, or date of manufacture, or information on changes in the place of manufacture, manufacturer, or manufacturer's name.

| **Related elements.** *Manufacture Statement* sub-elements.

Note on Manifestation » Note on Copyright Date
(RDA 2.17.10)

A note providing information on copyright dates not recorded as part of the copyright date element.

| **Related elements.** *Copyright Date.*

Element	Example
Copyright Date	©2002
Note on Copyright Date	CD-ROM is copyright 2001

Note on Manifestation » Note on Series Statement
(RDA 2.17.11)

A note providing information on complex series statements, incorrect numbering within series, or changes in series statements.

▌ **Related elements.** *Series Statement* sub-elements.

Element	Example
Note on Series Statement	Pts. 1 and 2 in series: African perspective. Pts. 3 and 4 in series: Third World series. Pt. 5 in both series

Note on Manifestation » Note on Frequency (RDA 2.17.12)

A note providing details on the currency of the contents, on the frequency of release of issues or parts of a serial or the frequency of updates to an integrating resource, or on changes in frequency.

▌ **Related elements.** *Frequency.*

Element	Example
Note on Frequency	Monthly (except Aug.)

Element	Example
Note on Frequency	Continually updated

Element	Example
Note on Frequency	Includes amendments through order of December 5, 1983, effective April 1, 1984

Element	Example
Note on Frequency	Bimonthly, Nov./Dec. 1980–Mar./Apr. 1992; monthly, May 1992–

Note on Manifestation » Note on Issue, Part, or Iteration Used as the Basis for Identification of the Resource
(RDA 2.17.13)

A note identifying the issue or part of a multipart monograph or serial, or the iteration of an integrating resource that has been used as the basis for the identification of a resource.

For an online resource, the note on issue, part, or iteration used as the basis for identification can also include the date on which the resource was viewed for description.

▎Related elements. See *Mode of Issuance* for examples and additional instructions.

Item Elements

Custodial History of the Item (RDA 2.18)

A record of previous ownership or custodianship of an item.

Recording

Record transfers of ownership, responsibility, or custody or control of the resource. Record the name of a previous owner or owners. Add the years of ownership after the name.

Element	Example
Custodial History of the Item	Previously owned by L. McGarry, 1951–1963

Immediate Source of Acquisition of Item (RDA 2.19)

The source from which the agency directly acquired an item and the circumstances under which it was received.

Recording

Record the source from which the item was acquired, the date of acquisition, and the method of acquisition, if this information is not confidential.

Element	Example
Immediate Source of Acquisition of Item	Purchased from Sotheby's, London, May 26, 2000

Identifier for the Item (RDA 2.20)

A character string associated with an item that serves to differentiate that item from other items.

Recording

If there is a specified display format for the identifier for the item, record it using that format. If there is no specified display format for the identifier, record it as it appears on the source. Precede the identifier with the name of the agency, etc., responsible for assigning the identifier, if readily ascertainable.

Incorrect identifiers

If an identifier is known to be incorrectly represented in the resource, record the number as it appears. Indicate that the number is incorrect, cancelled, or invalid, as appropriate.

Note on Item (RDA 2.21)

A note providing information on attributes of the item.

Related elements. For notes on describing item-specific carrier characteristics, see *Note on Item-Specific Carrier Characteristic.*

Recording

Apply guidelines: *Notes* (p. 269).

2

Describing Carriers

MANIFESTATIONS AND ITEMS

Manifestation refers to the physical embodiment of an expression of a work.

Item refers to a single exemplar or instance of a manifestation.

Resource, in the context of this chapter, refers to a manifestation or an item.

Carrier refers to a physical medium in which data, sound, images, etc., are stored. For certain types of resources, the carrier may consist of storage medium (e.g., tape, film) sometimes encased in a plastic, metal, etc., housing (e.g., cassette, cartridge) that is an integral part of the resource.

SUPPORTING THE USER

When following the instructions in this chapter, a cataloger continues to look at the resource, but this time considers the physical characteristics of the carrier and the formatting and encoding of the information stored on the carrier.

By recording these attributes of the carrier as separate elements, a cataloger supports a user in *selecting* a resource that is appropriate to the user's requirements. The data recorded can also support users in *finding* resources that correspond to the user's stated search criteria, and in *identifying* a resource (i.e., differentiating the resource from others with similar identifying information).

Elements

Core designates a core element—see element instructions for more details.

Elements for Manifestations		
Elements	*Sub-types*	*Core*
Media Type		
Carrier Type		X
Extent		X
	Extent of Cartographic Resource	X
	Extent of Notated Music	X
	Extent of Still Image	X
	Extent of Three-Dimensional Form	X
	Extent of Text	X
Dimensions		
	Dimensions of Map, Etc.	
	Dimensions of Still Image	
Base Material		
Details of Base Material		
Applied Material		
	Emulsion on Microfilm and Microfiche	
Details of Applied Material		
Details of Emulsion on Microfilm and Microfiche		
Mount		
Details of Mount		
Production Method		
	Production Method for Manuscript	
	Production Method for Tactile Resource	
Details of Production Method		
Details of Production Method for Manuscript		
Details of Production Method for Tactile Resource		
Generation		
	Generation of Audio Recording	
	Generation of Digital Resource	
	Generation of Microform	
	Generation of Motion Picture Film	
	Generation of Videotape	
Details of Generation		
Details of Generation of Audio Recording		
Details of Generation of Digital Resource		

Elements for Manifestations		
Elements	*Sub-types*	*Core*
Details of Generation of Microform		
Details of Generation of Motion Picture Film		
Details of Generation of Videotape		
Layout		
Details of Layout		
Book Format		
Details of Book Format		
Font Size		
Details of Font Size		
Polarity		
Details of Polarity		
Reduction Ratio		
Details of Reduction Ratio		
Sound Characteristic		
	Type of Recording	
	Recording Medium	
	Playing Speed	
	Groove Characteristic	
	Track Configuration	
	Tape Configuration	
	Configuration of Playback Channels	
	Special Playback Characteristic	
Details of Sound Characteristic		
Details of Type of Recording		
Details of Recording Medium		
Details of Playing Speed		
Details of Groove Characteristics		
Details of Track Configuration		
Details of Tape Configuration		
Details of Configuration of Playback Channels		
Details of Special Playback Characteristic		
Projection Characteristic of Motion Picture Film		
	Presentation Format	
	Projection Speed	
Details of Projection Characteristic of Motion Picture Film		
Details of Presentation Format		
Details of Projection Speed		
Video Characteristic		

Elements for Manifestations		
Elements	**Sub-types**	**Core**
	Video Format	
	Broadcast Standard	
Details of Video Characteristic		
Details of Video Format		
Details of Broadcast Standard		
Digital File Characteristic		
	File Type	
	Encoding Format	
	File Size	
	Resolution	
	Regional Encoding	
	Encoded Bitrate	
	Digital Representation of Cartographic Content	
Details of Digital File Characteristic		
Details of File Type		
Details of Encoding Format		
Details of Representation of Cartographic Content		
Equipment or System Requirement		
Note on Carrier		
	Note on Extent of Manifestation	
	Note on Dimensions of Manifestation	
	Note on Changes in Carrier Characteristic	

Elements for Items		
Elements	**Sub-types**	**Core**
Note on Item-Specific Carrier Characteristic		
	Note on Extent of Item	
	Note on Dimensions of Item	

Sources of information

Base all elements of the description of the carrier or carriers on evidence presented by the resource itself, or on any accompanying material or container. If additional information is considered important for identification or selection, take additional evidence from any source.

Media Type and Carrier Type

Media Type (RDA 3.2)

A categorization reflecting the general type of intermediation device required to view, play, run, etc., the content of a resource.

Recording

Record one or more RDA terms.

RDA terms for Media Type

audio	projected	other
computer	stereographic	unspecified
microform	unmediated	
microscopic	video	

> **Alternative.** If the resource being described consists of more than one media type, record only: a) the media type that applies to the predominant part of the resource (if there is a predominant part) or b) the media types that apply to the most substantial parts of the resource (including the predominant part, if there is one). Use one or more of the terms for Media Type, as appropriate.

RDA ESSENTIALS TIP

Media Type is a category for the device to playback or access the content. For *video* and *audio* media types, the media can have content stored in digital or analog form. For the *computer* media type, the media can be direct access (e.g., computer tapes or discs) or accessed remotely through file servers.

Unmediated means the content is perceived directly through one or more human senses without the need of an intermediary device.

Carrier Type (RDA 3.3)

A categorization reflecting the format of the storage medium and housing of a carrier in combination with the type of intermediation device required to view, play, run, etc., the content of a resource.

Core element

Recording

Record one or more RDA terms.

RDA terms for Carrier Type

Audio carriers Media Type = audio	Computer carriers Media Type = computer	Microform carriers Media Type = microform
audio belt	computer card	aperture card
audio cartridge	computer chip cartridge	microfiche
audio cylinder	computer disc	microfiche cartridge
audio disc	computer disc cartridge	microfilm cassette
audio roll	computer tape cartridge	microfilm reel
audio wire reel	computer tape reel	microfilm roll
audiocassette	online resource	microfilm slip
audiotape reel	other	microopaque
sound track reel		other
other		

Projected image carriers Media Type = projected	Unmediated carriers Media Type = unmediated	Video carriers Media Type = video
film cartridge	card	video cartridge
film cassette	flipchart	videocassette
film reel	object	videodisc
film roll	roll	videotape reel
filmslip	sheet	other
filmstrip cartridge	volume	
overhead transparency	other	
slide		
other		

Microscopic carriers Media Type = microscopic	Stereographic carriers Media Type = stereographic
microscope slide	stereograph card
other	stereograph disc
	other

If the carrier type or types applicable to the resource being described cannot be readily ascertained, record *unspecified*.

Element	Example
Media Type	unmediated
Media Type	video
Carrier Type	volume
Carrier Type	videodisc
A book published with a DVD.	

Element	Example
Media Type	unmediated
Carrier Type	volume
Carrier Type	card
Carrier Type	object
A game with a printed manual, some cards, and objects.	

Alternative. If the resource being described consists of more than one carrier type, record only: a) the carrier type that applies to the predominant part of the resource (if there is a predominant part) or b) the carrier types that apply to the most substantial parts of the resource (including the predominant part, if there is one). Use one or more of the terms for Carrier Type, as appropriate.

Extent

Extent (RDA 3.4)

The number and type of units and/or subunits making up a resource.

A *unit* is a physical or logical constituent of a resource (e.g., a volume, audiocassette, film reel, a map, a digital file).

A *subunit* is a physical or logical subdivision of a unit (e.g., a page of a volume, a frame of a microfiche, a record in a digital file).

Related elements. For instructions for specific types of resources, see *Extent of Cartographic Resource, Extent of Notated Music, Extent of Still Image, Extent of Three-Dimensional Form, and Extent of Text* (separate instructions for single volume and more than volume).

For instructions on recording duration (e.g., playing time, running time, performance time), see *Duration*.

Core element

Extent is a core element only if the resource is complete or if the total extent is known.

Record subunits only if readily ascertainable and considered important for identification or selection.

> **Related elements.** For notes, see *Note on Carrier* » *Note on Extent of Manifestation, Note on Item-Specific Carrier Characteristic* » *Note on Extent of Item*.

Recording

Record by giving the number of units and the type of unit. For the type of unit, use an appropriate Carrier Type term. Record the term in the singular or plural, as applicable. Specify the number of subunits, if applicable.

Element	Example
Carrier Type	audio disc
Extent	3 audio discs

> **Alternative.** Use a term in common usage (including a trade name, if applicable) to indicate the type of unit a) if the carrier is not in the carrier type list, *or* b) as an alternative to a carrier type term, if preferred by the agency preparing the description.

Element	Example
Media Type	computer
Carrier Type	other
Extent	1 USB flash drive

Element	Example
Carrier Type	computer disc
Extent	1 DVD-ROM

> **Related elements.** If an applicable trade name or other similar specification is not used as the term for the type of unit, record that information as instructed at *Equipment or System Requirement*.

Exact number of units not readily ascertainable (RDA 3.4.1.4)

If the exact number of units cannot be readily ascertained, record an approximate number preceded by *approximately*.

Element	Example
Extent	approximately 600 slides

| **Optional omission.** If the number of units cannot be readily approximated, omit the number.

Units cannot be named concisely (RDA 3.4.1.5)

If the units cannot be named concisely, record the number of physical units and describe them as *various pieces*.

Element	Example
Extent	48 various pieces

| **Optional omission.** If the number of units cannot be readily ascertained or approximated, omit the number.

Subunits (RDA 3.4.1.7)

Specify the number of subunits, if applicable.

COMPUTER DISCS, CARTRIDGES, ETC., AND ONLINE RESOURCES

If the resource consists of one or more files in a format that parallels a print, manuscript, or graphic counterpart (e.g., PDF), specify the number of subunits by applying the instructions for these Extent element sub-types: Extent of Cartographic Resource, Extent of Notated Music, Extent of Still Image, and/or Extent of Text.

Element	Example
Extent	1 computer disc (184 remote sensing images)

Element	Example
Extent	1 online resource (68 pages)

For other types of files (e.g., audio files, video files, data files), specify the number of files. Use one or more terms listed for Digital File Characteristic » File Type.

Element	Example
Extent	1 computer disc (1 audio file, 3 video files)

Element	Example
Extent	1 online resource (1 program file)

| **Optional addition.** For a resource consisting of one or more program files and/or data files, add the number of statements and/or records, as appropriate.

If the number of subunits cannot be stated succinctly, record the details in a note if considered important for identification or selection (see *Note on Carrier » Note on Extent of Manifestation*).

MICROFICHES AND MICROFILM

If the resource is in a format that parallels a print, manuscript, or graphic counterpart specify the number of subunits by applying the instructions for these Extent element subtypes: Extent of Cartographic Resource, Extent of Notated Music, Extent of Still Image, and/or Extent of Text.

Element	Example
Extent	3 microfiches (1 score (118 pages))

Element	Example
Extent	1 microfilm reel (255 pages)

For other microfiche and microfilm resources, specify the number of frames.

Element	Example
Extent	1 microfiche (120 frames)

FILMSTRIPS AND FILMSLIPS

Specify the number of frames or double frames.

Element	Example
Extent	1 filmstrip (10 double frames)

OVERHEAD TRANSPARENCIES

Specify the number of overlays or attached overlays.

Element	Example
Extent	1 overhead transparency (5 attached overlays)

FLIPCHARTS

Specify the number of sheets.

Element	Example
Extent	1 flipchart (8 sheets)

STEREOGRAPHS

Specify the number of pairs of frames.

Element	Example
Extent	1 stereograph disc (7 pairs of frames)

VIDEODISCS

For a videodisc that contains only still images, record the number of frames.

Element	Example
Extent	1 videodisc (45,876 frames)

Exact number of subunits not readily ascertainable (RDA 3.4.1.8)

If the subunits are unnumbered and their number cannot be readily ascertained, record an approximate number preceded by *approximately*.

Element	Example
Extent	1 filmstrip (approximately 100 frames)

Subunits in resources consisting of more than one unit (RDA 3.4.1.9)

If the resource consists of more than one unit *and* each unit contains the same number of subunits *then* specify the number of subunits in each unit, followed by *each*.

Element	Example
Extent	4 filmstrips (50 double frames each)

If the number of subunits in each unit is approximately the same, specify the approximate number of subunits in each unit, followed by *each*.

Element	Example
Extent	3 overhead transparencies (approximately 10 overlays each)

If the number of subunits in each unit is not the same (or approximately the same), apply one of these instructions, as applicable: a) specify the total number of subunits, *or* b) record an approximate total number of subunits.

Element	Example
Extent	2 overhead transparencies (20 overlays)

Element	Example
Extent	3 microfiches (approximately 300 frames)

❚ Optional omission. Omit the total number of subunits and record only the number of units.

Additional Common Instructions for Recording Extent

Apply the following instructions, as applicable, to the Extent element or its element sub-types. See RDA 3.4.1.11 for recording extent of a collection and RDA 3.4.1.12 for recording extent of a part of a larger resource.

Units and sets of units with identical content (RDA 3.4.1.6)

If the units of the resource have identical content, add *identical* before the term indicating the type of unit.

Element	Example
Extent	30 identical microscope slides

Element	Example
Extent of Text	3 identical volumes

If the resource consists of multiple sets of units *and* each set has identical content, *then* record the number of sets and the number of units in each set in the form *20 identical sets of 12 microscope slides*, etc.

Incomplete resource (RDA 3.4.1.10)

For a resource that is not yet complete, record the term indicating the type of unit without the number. Apply also for a resource when the total number of units issued is unknown.

Element	Example
Extent	microscope slides

Element	Example
Extent of Text	volumes (loose-leaf)

Element	Example
Extent of Still Image	postcards

Alternative. Do not record extent for a resource that is not yet complete (or if the total number of units issued is unknown).

Extent » Extent of Cartographic Resource (RDA 3.4.2)

The number and type of units and/or subunits making up a cartographic resource.

Application

For a printed, manuscript, graphic, or three-dimensional resource consisting of cartographic content (with or without accompanying text and/or illustrations).

> **Related elements.** For resources consisting of cartographic content in other media (e.g., microforms), see *Extent.*

Core element

Extent is a core element for cartographic resources only if the resource is complete or if the total extent is known.

> **Related elements.** For notes, see *Note on Carrier » Note on Extent of Manifestation, Note on Item-Specific Carrier Characteristic » Note on Extent of Item.*

Recording

Record the extent of the resource by giving the number of units and an appropriate term for Extent of Cartographic Resource.

RDA terms for Extent of Cartographic Resource (singular or plural)

atlas	remote-sensing image
diagram	section
globe	view
map	*another concise term or terms (use terms from* Extent of Still Image *or* Extent of Three-Dimensional Form, *if applicable)*
model	
profile	

Element	Example
Extent of Cartographic Resource	3 maps

Element	Example
Extent of Cartographic Resource	1 globe

Element	Example
Extent of Cartographic Resource	52 playing cards
Term for Extent of Still Image used.	

If the exact number of units is not readily ascertainable, record an estimated number preceded by *approximately*.

Element	Example
Extent of Cartographic Resource	approximately 800 maps

More than one cartographic unit on one or more sheets (RDA 3.4.2.3)

If the resource consists of more than one cartographic unit on one or more sheets *and* the number of cartographic units differs from the number of sheets, *then* record the number of cartographic units and specify the number of sheets.

Element	Example
Extent of Cartographic Resource	6 maps on 1 sheet

Cartographic unit presented in more than one segment (RDA 3.4.2.4)

If the cartographic unit is presented in more than one segment designed to fit together to form one or more cartographic units *and* all the segments are on a single sheet, *then* record the number of complete cartographic units followed by in and the number of segments.

Element	Example
Extent of Cartographic Resource	1 section in 4 segments

If the segments are not all on one sheet, record the number of complete cartographic units followed by *on* and the number of sheets.

Element	Example
Extent of Cartographic Resource	1 map on 4 sheets

Atlases (RDA 3.4.2.5)

Specify the number of volumes and/or pages, etc., in an atlas (see *Extent of Text*). Record this information in parentheses following the term *atlas*.

Element	Example
Extent of Cartographic Resource	1 atlas (3 volumes)

Element	Example
Extent of Cartographic Resource	1 atlas (xvii, 37 pages, 74 leaves of plates)

Extent » Extent of Notated Music (RDA 3.4.3)

The number and type of units and/or subunits making up a resource consisting of notated music, with or without accompanying text and/or illustrations.

Application

For a printed or manuscript resource consisting of notated music (with or without accompanying text and/or illustrations).

> **Related elements.** For resources consisting of notated music in other media (e.g., microforms), see *Extent.*

Core element

Extent is a core element for notated music resources only if the resource is complete or if the total extent is known.

> **Related elements.** For notes, see *Note on Carrier » Note on Extent of Manifestation, Note on Item-Specific Carrier Characteristic » Note on Extent of Item.*

Recording

Record the extent of the resource by giving the number of units and an appropriate RDA term for Extent of Notated Music. If the resource consists of more than one type of unit, record the number of each applicable type in the order specified from Format of Notated Music.

RDA terms for Extent of Notated Music (singular or plural terms from *Format of Notated Music*)

score	piano score
condensed score	chorus score
study score	part
piano conductor part	choir book
violin conductor part	table book
vocal score	*another concise term or terms*

Specify the number of volumes and/or pages, leaves, or columns as instructed for Extent of Text. Record this information in parentheses, following the term for the format of notated music.

Element	Example
Extent of Notated Music	1 score (38 leaves)

Element	Example
Extent of Notated Music	1 condensed score (2 volumes)

Exception. *Resource containing a set of parts.* If the resource contains a set of parts, record the number of parts but omit the number of volumes and/or pages, leaves, or columns applicable to the parts.

Element	Example
Extent of Notated Music	1 score (viii, 278 pages)
Extent of Notated Music	24 parts

Exception. *Resource consisting of a score and one or more parts, or of multiple parts in a single physical unit.* If the resource consists of both a score and one or more parts, or of multiple parts in a single physical unit, record the extent in the form: 1 score and 4 parts, etc., followed by the number of pages, leaves, or columns, in parentheses.

Element	Example
Extent of Notated Music	1 score and 1 part (5 pages)

Extent » Extent of Still Image (RDA 3.4.4)

The number and type of units and/or subunits making up a resource consisting of one or more still images.

Application

For a resource consisting of one or more still images in the form of drawings, paintings, prints, photographs, etc.

> **Related elements.** For resource consisting primarily of still images in a volume, see *Extent of Text.*
>
> For resources consisting of still images in other media (e.g., slides, transparencies), apply the basic instructions at *Extent.*
>
> For cartographic content in the form of still images, see *Extent of Cartographic Resource.*

Core element

Extent is a core element for still image resources only if the resource is complete or if the total extent is known.

> **Related elements.** For notes, see *Note on Carrier » Note on Extent of Manifestation, Note on Item-Specific Carrier Characteristic » Note on Extent of Item.*

Recording

Record by giving the number of units and an appropriate RDA term for Extent of Still Image. If the resource consists of more than one type of unit, record the number of each applicable type.

RDA terms for Extent of Still Image (singular or plural)

activity	painting	radiograph
chart	photograph	study print
collage	picture	technical drawing
drawing	postcard	wall chart
flash card	poster	*another concise term or terms*
icon	print	

If the exact number of units is not readily ascertainable, record an estimated number preceded by *approximately.*

Element	Example
Extent of Still Image	approximately 1,000 photographs

Extent » Extent of Three-Dimensional Form (RDA 3.4.6)

The number and type of units and/or subunits making up a resource consisting of one or more three-dimensional forms.

Application

For a resource consisting of one or more three-dimensional forms.

> **Related elements.** For globes and other cartographic resources in three-dimensional form, see *Extent of Cartographic Resource.*

Core element

Extent is a core element for three-dimensional resources only if the resource is complete or if the total extent is known.

> **Related elements.** For notes, see *Note on Carrier » Note on Extent of Manifestation, Note on Item-Specific Carrier Characteristic » Note on Extent of Item.*

Recording

Record by giving the number of units and an appropriate RDA term for Extent of Three-Dimensional Form. If the resource consists of more than one type of unit, record the number of each applicable type.

RDA terms for Extent of Three-Dimensional Form (singular or plural)

If the exact number of units is not readily ascertainable, record an estimated number preceded by *approximately*.

coin	jigsaw puzzle	sculpture
diorama	medal	specimen
exhibit	mock-up	toy
game	model	*another concise term or terms*

Element	Example
Extent of Three-Dimensional Form	approximately 400 specimens

When appropriate, specify the number and type or types of the component pieces, in parentheses, following the term for the type of unit.

Element	Example
Extent of Three-Dimensional Form	1 jigsaw puzzle (1,000 pieces)

Element	Example
Extent of Three-Dimensional Form	1 game (1 board, 50 cards, 5 role cards, 2 dice)

If the pieces cannot be named concisely or if their number cannot be readily ascertained, record *various pieces*.

Element	Example
Extent of Three-Dimensional Form	2 games (various pieces)

Extent » Extent of Text (RDA 3.4.5)

The number and type of units and/or subunits making up a resource consisting of text, with or without accompanying illustrations.

Application

For a printed or manuscript resource consisting of text (with or without accompanying illustrations). These instructions apply to text resources in volumes, sheets, portfolios or cases. These instructions also apply to volumes consisting primarily of still images.

> **Related elements.** Also apply these instructions to subunits in an atlas (see *Extent of Cartographic Resource*) or in a resource consisting of notated music (see *Extent of Notated Music*).
>
> For resources consisting of text in other media (e.g., microforms), see *Extent*.

Core element

Extent is a core element for text resources only if the resource is complete or if the total extent is known.

> **Related elements.** For notes, see *Note on Carrier » Note on Extent of Manifestation, Note on Item-Specific Carrier Characteristic » Note on Extent of Item*.

Recording

Apply the following instructions: for one volume or sheet, see *Extent of Text—Resource Consisting of a Single Unit* (p. 87); for more than one volume or sheet, see *Extent of Text—Resource Consisting of More Than One Unit* (p. 93).

Extent of Text—Resource Consisting of a Single Unit
(RDA 3.4.5.2–3.4.5.15)

Terminology

A **volume** is one or more sheets bound or fastened together to form a single unit.

A **sheet** is a unit of extent consisting of a single flat loose piece of paper or similar material.

A **page** is a unit of extent consisting of a single side of a leaf.

A **leaf** is a unit of extent consisting of a single bound or fastened sheet as a subunit of a volume; each leaf consists of two pages, one on each side, either or both of which may be blank.

A **column** is a unit of extent of text consisting of one of two or more vertical sections of text appearing on the same page or leaf.

A **plate** is a leaf, usually containing illustrative content, that does not form part of either the preliminary or the main sequence of pages or leaves.

Note on sequences. A sequence of pages, leaves, or columns is: a) a separately numbered group of pages; b) an unnumbered group of pages, etc., that stands apart from other groups in the resource; or c) a number of pages or leaves of plates distributed throughout the resource.

Single volume with numbered pages, leaves, or columns (RDA 3.4.5.2)

Record the number of pages, leaves, or columns in terms of the numbered or lettered sequences in the resource. Record the last numbered page, leaf, or column in each sequence and follow it with the appropriate term. Record pages, etc., that are numbered in words by giving the numeric equivalent.

Element	Example
Extent of Text	327 pages

Element	Example
Extent of Text	321 leaves

Element	Example
Extent of Text	381 columns

Element	Example
Extent of Text	xvii, 323 pages

Element	Example
Extent of Text	27 pages, 300 leaves

Record pages, etc., that are lettered inclusively in the form *A-K pages*, *a-d leaves*, etc.

Element	Example
Extent of Text	A-Z pages

Single volume with unnumbered pages, leaves, or columns (RDA 3.4.5.3)

Resource consists entirely of unnumbered pages, leaves, or columns

If the resource consists entirely of unnumbered pages, leaves, or columns, record the number of pages, leaves, or columns using one of the following methods:

a) Record the exact number of pages, leaves, or columns, if readily ascertainable.

Element	Example
Extent of Text	93 unnumbered pages

b) If the number is not readily ascertainable, record an estimated number of pages, leaves, or columns preceded by *approximately*.

Element	Example
Extent of Text	approximately 600 pages

c) Record:

Element	Example
Extent of Text	1 volume (unpaged)

When recording the number or estimated number of unnumbered pages or leaves, apply the following guidelines:

If the leaves are printed or written on both sides, record the extent in terms of *pages*.

If the leaves are printed or written on one side, record the extent in terms of *leaves*.

Numbered and unnumbered sequences

If the resource consists of both numbered and unnumbered sequences of pages, leaves, or columns, disregard the unnumbered sequences, unless: a) an unnumbered sequence constitutes a substantial part of the resource (see also instruction for complicated or irregular paging, etc.) *or* b) an unnumbered sequence includes pages, etc., that are referred to in a note.

When recording a sequence of unnumbered pages, etc., record *either* a) the exact number (if the number is readily ascertainable) followed by *unnumbered pages*, etc. or b) an estimated number preceded by *approximately, or* c) *unnumbered sequence of pages*, etc.

Element	Example
Extent of Text	33 leaves, 31 unnumbered leaves
Unnumbered sequence constitutes substantial part; exact number of leaves ascertainable.	

Element	Example
Extent of Text	8, vii, approximately 300, 73 pages
Unnumbered sequence constitutes substantial part; number of pages estimated.	

Element	Example
Extent of Text	27 pages, unnumbered sequence of leaves

Numbered pages and a sequence of unnumbered leaves.

Element	Example
Extent of Text	8 unnumbered pages, 155 pages

Bibliography referred to in a note appears on 6th preliminary page.

Inessential matter

Disregard unnumbered sequences of inessential matter (e.g., advertising, blank pages).

Changes in form of numbering within a sequence (RDA 3.4.5.4)

If the form of numbering within a sequence changes (e.g., from roman to arabic numerals), ignore the numbering of the first part of the sequence.

Misleading numbering (RDA 3.4.5.5)

In some cases, the numbering on the last page, leaf, or column of a sequence does not represent the total number in that sequence. When this occurs, do not correct it unless it gives a completely false impression of the extent of the resource (e.g., when only alternate pages are numbered or when the number on the last page, leaf, or column of the sequence is misprinted).

When correcting misleading numbering, record the numbering as it appears on the last page or leaf followed by *that is* and the correct number.

Element	Example
Extent of Text	329, that is, 392 pages

Incomplete volume (RDA 3.4.5.6)

If the last part of the volume is missing *and* the extent of the complete volume cannot be ascertained, *then* record the number of the last numbered page, leaf, or column using the appropriate term and add *(incomplete)*.

Element	Example
Extent of Text	xxiv, 179 pages (incomplete)

Pages, etc., numbered as part of a larger sequence (RDA 3.4.5.7)

If the pages, etc., are numbered as part of a larger sequence (e.g., as part of the continuous paging for a multivolume resource), record the first and last numbers of the pages, etc., preceded by the appropriate term.

Element	Example
Extent of Text	pages 713–797

If the resource has pagination of its own as well as pagination forming part of a larger sequence, record the pagination for the individual resource. Make a note on pagination forming part of the larger sequence.

Element	Example
Extent of Text	328 pages
Note on Extent of Manifestation	Pages also numbered 501–828

Complicated or irregular paging, etc. (RDA 3.4.5.8)

If the resource has complicated or irregular paging, etc., record the number of pages, leaves, or columns by using one of the following methods:

a) Record the total number of pages, leaves, or columns (excluding those that are blank or contain advertising or other inessential matter) followed by *in various pagings*, *in various foliations*, or *in various numberings*, as appropriate.

Element	Example
Extent of Text	1000 pages in various pagings

Element	Example
Extent of Text	1283 columns in various numberings

b) Record the number of pages, leaves, or columns in the main sequences of the pagination and add the total number of the remaining variously numbered or unnumbered sequences.

Element	Example
Extent of Text	560, 223 pages, 217 variously numbered pages

c) Record *1 volume (various pagings)*.

Leaves or pages of plates (RDA 3.4.5.9)

If the leaves or pages of plates in a resource are not included in the numbering for a sequence or sequences of pages or leaves of text, etc., record the extent of the sequence of leaves or pages of plates at the end of the sequence or sequences of pagination, etc. Record the extent of the sequence of leaves or pages of plates after the pagination, etc., whether the plates are found together or distributed throughout the resource.

Element	Example
Extent of Text	323 pages, 19 unnumbered pages of plates

> **Exception.** For complicated or irregular sequences of plates apply a method for recording complicated or irregular paging, etc.

Numbered leaves or pages of plates

Record the extent of the sequence or sequences of numbered plates in terms of leaves or pages, according to the type of sequence used in the resource. For each sequence, record the last numbered leaf or page with an appropriate term followed by *of plates*.

Element	Example
Extent of Text	xiv, 145 pages, 10 leaves of plates, xiii pages of plates

Record leaves or pages of plates that are lettered inclusively in the form *A-K pages of plates*, *a-d leaves of plates*, etc.

Record leaves or pages of plates that are numbered in words by giving the numeric equivalent, followed by *of plates*.

If the plates are numbered as leaves but have content on both sides: record the extent by following the instructions for misleading numbering *or* make an explanatory note (see *Note on Carrier » Note on Extent of Manifestation*).

Unnumbered leaves or pages of plates

Record the extent of the sequence of unnumbered leaves or pages of plates using the appropriate terms if: a) an unnumbered sequence constitutes a substantial part of the resource (see also instructions for complicated or irregular paging) *or* b) an unnumbered sequence includes plates that are referred to in a note, *or* c) this information is considered important for identification or selection.

When recording the extent of a sequence of unnumbered leaves or pages of plates, record: a) the exact number (if the number is readily ascertainable) followed by *unnumbered leaves of plates*, etc. *or* b) an estimated number preceded by *approximately*, followed by *leaves of plates*, etc.

Element	Example
Extent of Text	xvi, 249 pages, 12 unnumbered leaves of plates

Element	Example
Extent of Text	xvi, 504 pages, approximately 500 pages of plates

Folded leaves (RDA 3.4.5.10)

If leaves are folded, record that they are folded (e.g., *122 folded leaves*).

Duplicated paging, etc. (RDA 3.4.5.12)

If the paging is duplicated (e.g., in some books with parallel texts), record both pagings (e.g., *xii, 35, 35 pages*) and make an explanatory note (see *Note on Carrier » Note on Extent of Manifestation*).

Pages numbered in opposite directions (RDA 3.4.5.13)

If the resource has groups of pages numbered in opposite directions (e.g., in some books with texts in two languages), record all the pagings. Record the pagings of the various groups in order, starting from the title page selected for the description.

Element	Example
Extent of Text	ix, 155, 126, x pages

Updating loose-leafs (RDA 3.4.5.19)

If the resource is an updating loose-leaf, record: *1 volume (loose-leaf)*.

Single sheet (RDA 3.4.5.14)

Record the extent of a resource consisting of a single sheet as *1 sheet*. If the sheet is designed to be read in pages when folded, record the extent as *1 folded sheet* followed by the number of pages laid out on the sheet, in parentheses.

Element	Example
Extent of Text	1 folded sheet (8 pages)

Extent of Text—Resource Consisting of More Than One Unit (RDA 3.4.5.16–3.4.5.22)

More than one volume (RDA 3.4.5.16)

If the resource consists of more than one volume, record the extent by giving the number of volumes and the term *volumes*.

Element	Example
Extent of Text	3 volumes

Exception. *Completed serials.* For serials, record the extent by giving the number of bibliographic volumes as reflected in the numbering of the serial (see *Numbering of Serials elements*) instead of the number of physical volumes.

Continuously paged volumes (RDA 3.4.5.17)

If the volumes are continuously paged, specify the number of pages, leaves, or columns in parentheses, following the term for the type of unit. Ignore separately paged sequences of preliminary matter in volumes other than the first.

Element	Example
Extent of Text	2 volumes (xxxxi, 999 pages)

Optional omission. For multipart monographs and serials, omit the number of pages, etc.

Individually paged volumes (RDA 3.4.5.18)

If the volumes are individually paged, record the number of volumes and omit the pagination.

Optional addition. Specify the number of pages, leaves, or columns in each volume. Record this information in parentheses, following the term for the type of unit.

Element	Example
Extent of Text	2 volumes (xvi, 329; xx, 412 pages)

Updating loose-leafs (RDA 3.4.5.19)

If the resource is an updating loose-leaf, record the number of volumes followed by *loose-leaf*, in parentheses.

Element	Example
Extent of Text	3 volumes (loose-leaf)

More than one sheet (RDA 3.4.5.20)

If the resource consists of more than one sheet, record the extent by giving the number of sheets and the term *sheets*.

Dimensions

Dimensions (RDA 3.5)

The measurements of the carrier or carriers and/or the container of a resource. Dimensions include measurements of height, width, depth, length, gauge, and diameter.

Related elements. For instructions on specific types of resources, see *Dimensions of Map, Etc.* and *Dimensions of Still Image.*

Related elements. For notes, see *Note on Carrier » Note on Dimensions of Manifestation, Note on Item-Specific Carrier Characteristic » Note on Dimensions of Item.*

Recording

Unless instructed otherwise, record dimensions in centimeters to the next whole centimeters up and use the metric symbol *cm* (e.g., if the height measures 17.2 centimeters, record *18 cm*).

Alternative. Record dimensions in the system of measurement preferred by the agency preparing the description. Use symbols or abbreviate terms for units of measurement as applicable (RDA B.5.1).

Dimensions of volumes (RDA 3.5.1.4.14)

Record the height of the volume. If the volume measures less than 10 cm, record the height in mm.

Element	Example
Dimensions	22 cm

Exception. If the width of the volume is either less than half the height or greater than the height, record the height × width. See RDA 3.5.1.4.14 for additional exceptions.

Element	Example
Dimensions	20 × 8 cm

Dimensions of sheets (RDA 3.5.1.4.11)

Record height × width of the sheet, excluding any frame or mount.

Element	Example
Dimensions	28 × 22 cm

If the sheet is designed to be read in pages when folded, record only the height of the sheet when folded.

Element	Example
Dimensions	28 cm

For other folded sheets, record the height × width when extended followed by the height × width when folded.

Element	Example
Dimensions	48 × 30 cm folded to 24 × 15 cm

Related elements. For maps, etc. on sheets, see *Dimensions of Map, Etc.* For still images on sheets, see *Dimensions of Still Image.*

Dimensions of other carriers (RDA 3.5.1.4.1—3.5.1.4.10, 3.5.1.4.12—3.5.1.4.13)

Carrier	Instructions and syntax	Examples
cards	height × width	28 × 10 cm
audio cartridges	length × height of the face of the cartridge in cm followed by the width of the tape in mm	14 × 10 cm, 7 mm tape
computer cartridges	length of the side of the cartridge that is to be inserted into the machine	10 cm
film, filmstrip, and video cartridges	gauge (i.e., width) of the film or tape in mm For 8 mm, indicate whether the gauge is single, standard, super, or Maurer.	35 mm standard 8 mm
microfilm cartridges	width of the film in mm	35 mm
audiocassettes	length × height of the face of the cassette in cm followed by the width of the tape in mm	10 × 7 cm, 4 mm tape
computer cassettes	length × height of the face of the cassette	10 × 7 cm
film and videocassettes	gauge (i.e., width) of the film or tape in mm For 8 mm, indicate whether the gauge is single, standard, super, or Maurer.	13 mm standard 8 mm
microfiche cassettes	length × height of the face of the cassette	
microfilm cassettes	width of the film in mm	16 mm
discs	diameter of the disc	12 cm
filmstrips and filmslips	gauge (i.e., width) of the film in mm	35 mm

Carrier	Instructions and syntax	Examples
flipchart	height × width	11 × 15 cm
overhead transparencies	height × width, excluding any frame or mount	20 × 22 cm
audiotape reels	diameter of the reel in cm followed by the width of the tape in mm	18 cm, 13 mm tape
computer tape reels	diameter of the reel in cm followed by the width of the tape in mm	31 cm, 13 mm tape
film and videotape reels	diameter of the reel in cm followed by the gauge (i.e., width) of the film or tape in mm For 8 mm film, indicate whether the gauge is single, standard, super, or Maurer.	18 cm, 25.4 mm
microfilm reels	gauge (i.e., width) of the film in mm For 8 mm film, indicate whether the gauge is single, standard, super, or Maurer.	11 cm, 25.4 mm
film and microfilm rolls	gauge (i.e., width) of the film in mm For 8 mm film, indicate whether the gauge is single, standard, super, or Maurer.	105 mm super 8 mm
slides	height × width	5 × 5 cm
globes	diameter and indicate that it is the diameter	12 cm in diameter
other three-dimensional forms	dimensions of form itself If necessary, add a word to indicate which dimension is being given. If multiple dimensions are given, record them as height x width x depth.	110 cm high

Dimensions of container (RDA 3.5.1.5)

If the resource is in a container, name the container. Record the dimensions of the container (height × width × depth) if considered important for identification or selection *either* a) in addition to the dimensions of the carrier or carriers *or* b) as the only dimensions.

Element	Example
Dimensions	16 × 32 × 3 cm
Dimensions	case 17 × 34 × 6 cm
Dimensions of a model and its container.	

Element	Example
Dimensions	box 30 × 25 × 13 cm
Dimensions of container for a diorama; dimensions of diorama not recorded.	

Dimensions » Dimensions of Map, Etc. (RDA 3.5.2.)

Application

For a resource consisting of one or more sheets that contain one or more maps, diagrams, views, profiles, sections, etc.

> **Related elements.** *Note on Carrier » Note on Extent of Manifestation, Note on Item-Specific Carrier Characteristic » Note on Extent of Item.*

Recording

Record the dimensions of each map, etc., by giving the measurements of the face of the map, etc., measured within the neat line. Record the height × width or diameter, as appropriate. When recording diameter, indicate that it is the diameter. In addition, apply the basic instructions at Dimensions, as applicable.

Element	Example
Dimensions of Map, Etc.	25 × 35 cm

Element	Example
Dimensions of Map, Etc.	45 cm in diameter

Dimensions » Dimensions of Still Image (RDA 3.5.3)

Application

For a resource consisting of one or more sheets that contain one or more still images in the form of drawings, paintings, prints, photographs, etc.

> **Related elements.** For resources consisting of still images in other media (e.g., slides, transparencies), use *Dimensions.*
>
> For sheets containing maps, etc., use *Dimensions of Map, Etc.*

> **Related elements.** For notes, see *Note on Carrier » Note on Extent of Manifestation, Note on Item-Specific Carrier Characteristic » Note on Extent of Item.*

Recording

Record the height × width, diameter, or other dimensions, as appropriate, and give the dimensions with reference to the position in which the image is intended to be viewed. When recording dimensions other than height × width of a rectangle, indicate what is being measured. In addition, apply the basic instructions at Dimensions, as applicable.

Element	Example
Dimensions of Still Image	33 × 25 cm

Element	Example
Dimensions of Still Image	6 cm in diameter

Specialized Elements

RDA ESSENTIALS TIP

RDA provides instructions for recording terms and notes that describe specialized carriers. The following set of specialized elements covers characteristics such as base material, production method, generation of reproductions, and attributes of print and microform resources. Of interest to catalogers of print material is the Font Size element, in which is recorded the RDA term *large print*.

Base Material (RDA 3.6)

The underlying physical material of a resource.

Recording

Record one or more appropriate RDA terms, or if none is appropriate or sufficiently specific, use another concise term or terms.

Element	Example
Base Material	wood
Term for base material for a globe.	

Element	Example
Base Material	cellulose acetate

Details of Base Material (RDA 3.6.1.4)

Recording

Record a details note if considered important for identification or selection.

Element	Example
Details of Base Material	Paper watermarked: KS and a crown

Applied Material (RDA 3.7)

A physical or chemical substance applied to a base material of a resource.

Recording

Record one or more appropriate RDA terms, or if none is appropriate or sufficiently specific, use another concise term or terms. Record the predominant material first if there is more than one applied material.

Element	Example
Applied Material	oil paint
Applied material for a painting.	

Applied Material » Emulsion on Microfilm and Microfiche (RDA 3.7.2)

A suspension of light-sensitive chemicals used as a coating on a microfilm or microfiche (e.g., silver halide).

Recording

Record one or more appropriate RDA terms, or if none is appropriate or sufficiently specific, use another concise term or terms.

Element	Example
Emulsion on Microfilm and Microfiche	diazo

Details of Applied Material (RDA 3.7.1.4)

Recording

Record a details note if considered important for identification or selection.

Element	Example
Applied Material	tempera
Details of Applied Material	Egg tempera paint with tooled gold-leaf halos
A term and a details note for applied material for a painting.	

Details of Emulsion on Microfilm and Microfiche
(RDA 3.7.2.4)

Recording

Record a details note if considered important for identification or selection.

Mount (RDA 3.8)

The physical material used for the support or backing to which the base material of a resource has been attached.

Recording

Record one or more appropriate RDA terms, or if none is appropriate or sufficiently specific, use another concise term or terms.

Element	Example
Mount	Bristol board

Details of Mount (RDA 3.8.1.4)

Recording

Record a details note if considered important for identification or selection.

Element	Example
Details of Mount	On brass stand

Production Method (RDA 3.9)

The process used to produce a resource.

Recording

Record one or more appropriate RDA terms, or if none is appropriate or sufficiently specific, use another concise term or terms.

Element	Example
Production Method	engraving
A term for production method for an art print.	

Production Method » Production Method for Manuscript
(RDA 3.9.2)

The process used to produce an original manuscript or a copy.

Recording

Record an appropriate RDA term, or if none is appropriate or sufficiently specific, use another concise term.

Element	Example
Production Method for Manuscript	manuscript (transcript, handwritten)

Production Method » Production Method for Tactile Resource (RDA 3.9.3)

The process used to produce a tactile resource (e.g., embossing, thermoform).

Recording

Record an appropriate RDA term, or if none is appropriate or sufficiently specific, use another concise term.

Element	Example
Production Method for Tactile Resource	embossed

Details of Production Method (RDA 3.9.1.4)

Recording

Record a details note if considered important for identification or selection.

Element	Example
Details of Production Method	Finished using a gray wash technique

Details of Production Method for Manuscript (RDA 3.9.2.4)

Recording

Record a details note if considered important for identification or selection.

Details of Production Method for Tactile Resource (RDA 3.9.3.4)

Recording

Record a details note if considered important for identification or selection.

Generation (RDA 3.10)

The relationship between an original carrier and the carrier of a reproduction made from the original (e.g., a first-generation camera master, a second-generation printing master).

Generation » Generation of Audio Recording (RDA 3.10.2)

The relationship between an original audio carrier and the carrier of a reproduction made from the original (e.g., a tape duplication master, a test pressing).

Recording

Record an appropriate RDA term, or if none is appropriate or sufficiently specific, use another concise term.

Element	Example
Generation of Audio Recording	master tape

Generation » Generation of Digital Resource (RDA 3.10.3)

The relationship between an original carrier of a digital resource and the carrier of a reproduction from the original (e.g., a derivative master).

Recording

Record an appropriate RDA term, or if none is appropriate or sufficiently specific, use another concise term.

Element	Example
Generation of Digital Resource	original

Generation » Generation of Microform (RDA 3.10.4)

The relationship between an original microform carrier and the carrier of a reproduction made from the original (e.g., a printing master).

Recording

Record an appropriate RDA term, or if none is appropriate or sufficiently specific, use another concise term.

Element	Example
Generation of Microform	first generation

Generation » Generation of Motion Picture Film (RDA 3.10.5)

The relationship between an original carrier of a motion picture film resource and the carrier of a reproduction made from the original (e.g., a reference print).

Recording

Record an appropriate RDA term, or if none is appropriate or sufficiently specific, use another concise term.

Element	Example
Generation of Motion Picture Film	reference print

Generation » Generation of Videotape (RDA 3.10.6)

The relationship between an original carrier of a motion picture film resource and the carrier of a reproduction made from the original (e.g., a reference print).

Recording

Record an appropriate RDA term, or if none is appropriate or sufficiently specific, use another concise term.

Element	Example
Generation of Videotape	second generation, show copy

Details of Generation of Audio Recording (RDA 3.10.2.4)

Recording

Record a details note if considered important for identification or selection.

Details of Generation of Digital Resource (RDA 3.10.3.4)

Recording

Record a details note if considered important for identification or selection.

Details of Generation of Microform (RDA 3.10.4.4)

Recording

Record a details note if considered important for identification or selection.

Details of Generation of Motion Picture Film (RDA 3.10.5.4)

Recording

Record a details note if considered important for identification or selection.

Details of Generation of Videotape (RDA 3.10.6.4)

Recording

Record a details note if considered important for identification or selection.

Layout (RDA 3.11)

The arrangement of text, images, tactile notation, etc., in a resource.

Recording

Record one or more RDA terms, or if none is appropriate or sufficiently specific, use another concise term.

Element	Example
Layout	both sides
Layout of 3 maps printed on both sides of a single sheet.	

Details of Layout (RDA 3.11.1.4)

Recording

Record a details note if considered important for identification or selection.

Element	Example
Details of Layout	Alternate pages blank

Book Format (RDA 3.12)

The result of folding a printed sheet to form a gathering of leaves (e.g., a sheet folded once to form a folio, twice to form a quarto, three times to form an octavo).

Recording

Record an appropriate RDA term.

Element	Example
Book Format	4to

Details of Book Format (RDA 3.12.1.4)

Recording

Record a details note if considered important for identification or selection.

Font Size (RDA 3.13)

The size of the type used to represent the characters and symbols in a resource.

Recording

Record an appropriate RDA term, or if none is appropriate or sufficiently specific, use another concise term.

Element	Example
Font Size	large print

Details of Font Size (RDA 3.13.1.4)

Recording

Record a details note if considered important for identification or selection.

Element	Example
Details of Font Size	Font size varies from 18 point to 20 point

Polarity (RDA 3.14)

The relationship of the colors and tones in an image to the colors and tones of the object reproduced (e.g., positive, negative).

Recording

Record an appropriate RDA term.

Element	Example
Polarity	negative

Details of Polarity (RDA 3.14.1.4)

Recording

Record a details note if considered important for identification or selection.

Reduction Ratio (RDA 3.15)

The size of a micro-image in relation to the original from which it was produced.

Recording

Record one or more appropriate RDA terms.

Element	Example
Reduction Ratio	very high reduction

Details of Reduction Ratio (RDA 3.15.1.4)

Recording

Record a details note if considered important for identification or selection.

Element	Example
Details of Reduction Ratio	Reduction ratio varies

Elements for Sound, Projection, Video, and Digital File Characteristics

RDA ESSENTIALS TIP

RDA provides instructions to record terms and notes that describe carriers with sound, projection, video, or digital file characteristics.

Resources may be described by combinations of elements from the following set of specialized characteristics. For example, a DVD may have sound and video characteristics as well as digital file characteristics.

Sound Characteristic (RDA 3.16)

A technical specification relating to the encoding of sound in a resource.

Sound characteristics include type of recording, recording medium, playing speed, groove characteristics, track configuration, tape configuration, configuration of playback channels, and special playback characteristics.

Related elements. For instructions on recording additional characteristics of digitally encoded sound (e.g., audio encoding formats such as MP3), see *Digital File Characteristic*.

For details of any special equipment requirements for the playback of sound, see *Equipment or System Requirement*.

Sound Characteristic » Type of Recording (RDA 3.16.2)

The method used to encode audio content for playback (e.g., analog, digital).

Recording

Record an appropriate RDA term, or if none is appropriate or sufficiently specific, use another concise term.

Element	Example
Type of Recording	analog

Sound Characteristic » Recording Medium (RDA 3.16.3)

The type of medium used to record sound on an audio carrier (e.g., magnetic, optical).

Recording

Record an appropriate RDA term, or if none is appropriate or sufficiently specific, use another concise term.

Element	Example
Recording Medium	optical

Sound Characteristic » Playing Speed (RDA 3.16.4)

The speed at which an audio carrier must be operated to produce the sound intended.

Recording

Record using a measurement of speed appropriate to the type of recording.

Element	Example
Playing Speed	33 1/3 rpm
Analog disc speed recorded in rpm.	

Sound Characteristic » Groove Characteristic (RDA 3.16.5)

The groove width of an analog disc or the groove pitch of an analog cylinder.

Recording

Record an appropriate RDA term, or if none is appropriate or sufficiently specific, use another concise term.

Element	Example
Groove Characteristic	coarse groove
Groove width of an audio disc.	

Sound Characteristic » Track Configuration (RDA 3.16.6)

The configuration of the audio track on a sound-track film.

Recording

Record an RDA term: *centre track* or *edge track*.

Sound Characteristic » Tape Configuration (RDA 3.16.7)

The number of tracks on an audiotape.

Recording

Record tape configuration (i.e., number of tracks on the tape) for tape cartridges, cassettes, and reels.

Element	Example
Tape Configuration	12 track

Sound Characteristic » Configuration of Playback Channels (RDA 3.16.8)

The number of sound channels used to make a recording (e.g., one channel for a monophonic recording, two channels for a stereophonic recording).

Recording

Record one or more appropriate RDA terms, or if none is appropriate or sufficiently specific, use another concise term or terms.

Element	Example
Configuration of Playback Channels	mono
Configuration of Playback Channels	stereo
Terms for the two playback channels of an audio disc.	

Sound Characteristic » Special Playback Characteristic (3.16.9)

An equalization system, noise reduction system, etc., used in making an audio recording.

Recording

Record one or more appropriate RDA terms, or if none is appropriate or sufficiently specific, use another concise term or terms.

Element	Example
Special Playback Characteristic	Dolby-B encoded

Details of Sound Characteristic (RDA 3.16.1.4)

Recording

Record a details note if considered important for identification or selection.

Details of Type of Recording (RDA 3.16.2.4)

Recording

Record a details note if considered important for identification or selection.

Element	Example
Type of Recording	digital
Details of Type of Recording	Made from an analog original
A term and a details note for type of recording.	

Details of Recording Medium (RDA 3.16.3.4)

Recording

Record a details note if considered important for identification or selection.

Details of Playing Speed (RDA 3.16.4.4)

Recording

Record a details note if considered important for identification or selection.

Details of Groove Characteristic (RDA 3.16.5.4)

Recording

Record a details note if considered important for identification or selection.

Details of Track Characteristic (RDA 3.16.6.4)

Recording

Record a details note if considered important for identification or selection.

Details of Tape Characteristic (RDA 3.16.7.4)

Recording

Record a details note if considered important for identification or selection.

Details of Playback Channels (RDA 3.16.8.4)

Recording

Record a details note if considered important for identification or selection.

Details of Special Playback Characteristic (RDA 3.16.9.4)

Recording

Record a details note if considered important for identification or selection.

Projection Characteristic of Motion Picture Film (RDA 3.17)

A technical specification relating to the projection of a motion picture film.

> **Related elements.** For instructions on recording the aspect ratio of a motion picture film, see *Aspect Ratio.*
>
> For instructions on recording the color characteristics of a motion picture film, see *Colour Content.*
>
> For instructions on recording the sound characteristics of a motion picture film, see *Sound Characteristic and Sound Content.*
>
> For details of any special equipment requirements for projection, see *Equipment or System Requirement.*

Projection Characteristic of Motion Picture Film » Presentation Format (RDA 3.17.2)

The format used in the production of a projected image (e.g., Cinerama, IMAX).

Recording

Record one or more appropriate RDA terms, or if none is appropriate or sufficiently specific, use another concise term or terms.

Element	Example
Special Playback Characteristic	3D

Projection Characteristic of Motion Picture Film » Projection Speed (RDA 3.17.3)

The speed at which a projected carrier must be operated to produce the moving image intended.

Recording

Record in frames per second (fps).

Element	Example
Projection Speed	30 fps

Details of Projection Characteristic of Motion Picture Film (RDA 3.17.1.4)

Recording

Record a details note if considered important for identification or selection.

Details of Presentation Format (RDA 3.17.2.4)

Recording

Record a details note if considered important for identification or selection.

Details of Projection Speed (RDA 3.17.3 4)

Recording

Record a details note if considered important for identification or selection.

Video Characteristic (RDA 3.18)

A technical specification relating to the encoding of video images in a resource.

> **Related elements.** For instructions on recording the aspect ratio of a video, see *Aspect Ratio.*
>
> For instructions on recording the color characteristics of a video, see *Colour Content.*
>
> For instructions on recording the sound characteristics of a video, see Sound Characteristic and Sound Content.
>
> For instructions on recording additional characteristics of digitally encoded video, see Digital File Characteristic.
>
> For details of any special equipment requirements for video playback, see Equipment or System Requirement.

Video Characteristic » Video Format (RDA 3.18.2)

A standard, etc., used to encode the analog video content of a resource.

> **Related elements.** For instructions on recording the encoding format, etc., for digitally encoded video, see *Digital File Characteristic » Encoding Format*.

Recording

Record an appropriate RDA term or use another concise term, or if none is appropriate or sufficiently specific, use another concise term.

Element	Example
Video Format	VHS

Video Characteristic » Broadcast Standard (RDA 3.18.3)

A system used to format a video resource for television broadcast.

Recording

Record an appropriate RDA term or use another concise term, or if none is appropriate or sufficiently specific, use another concise term.

Element	Example
Broadcast Standard	NTSC

Details of Video Characteristic (RDA 3.18.1.4)

Recording

Record a details note on video characteristics (e.g., resolution (number of lines and frame rates), bandwidth, and other details) if considered important for identification or selection.

Element	Example
Details of Video Characteristic	Resolution: 1080i

Details of Video Format (RDA 3.18.2.4)

Recording

Record a details note if considered important for identification or selection.

Details of Broadcast Standard (RDA 3.18.3.4)

Recording

Record a details note if considered important for identification or selection.

Digital File Characteristic (RDA 3.19)

A technical specification relating to the digital encoding of text, image, audio, video, and other types of data in a resource.

> **Related elements.** For instructions on recording the color characteristics of a digital file, see *Colour Content*.
>
> For instructions on recording other sound characteristics of a digital file, see *Sound Characteristic*.
>
> For instructions on recording other video characteristics of a digital file, see *Video Characteristic*.
>
> For details of any special equipment requirements, see *Equipment or System Requirement*.

Digital File Characteristic » File Type (RDA 3.19.2)

A general type of data content encoded in a computer file.

> **Related elements.** *Extent* (used for subunits for number of audio, video, data files).

Recording

Record one or more appropriate RDA terms, or if none is appropriate or sufficiently specific, use another concise term or terms.

RDA terms for File Type

audio file	text file
data file	video file
image file	*another concise term or terms*
program file	

Digital File Characteristic » Encoding Format (RDA 3.19.3)

A schema, standard, etc., used to encode the digital content of a resource.

Recording

Record one or more appropriate RDA terms, or if none is appropriate or sufficiently specific, use another concise term or terms.

Element	Example
Encoding Format	CD audio

Element	Example
Encoding Format	JPEG

Element	Example
Encoding Format	PDF

Element	Example
Encoding Format	Daisy 3.0
Record the version of the encoding format if it affects or restricts the use of the resource.	

Digital File Characteristic » File Size (RDA 3.19.4)

The number of bytes in a digital file.

Recording

Record in *bytes*, *KB* (kilobytes), *MB* (megabytes), or *GB* (gigabytes), as appropriate.

Element	Example
File Size	182 KB

Digital File Characteristic » Resolution (RDA 3.19.5)

The clarity or fineness of detail in a digital image, expressed by the measurement of the image in pixels, etc.

Recording

Record if readily ascertained and considered important for identification or selection. Record by giving the measurement of the image in pixels.

Element	Example
Resolution	3.1 megapixels

Digital File Characteristic » Regional Encoding (RDA 3.19.6)

A code identifying the region of the world for which a videodisc has been encoded and preventing the disc from being played on a player sold in a different region.

Recording

Record if considered important for identification or selection.

Element	Example
Regional Encoding	region 4

Digital File Characteristic » Encoded Bitrate (RDA 3.19.7)

The speed at which streaming audio, video, etc., is designed to play.

Recording

Record encoded bitrate of file.

Element	Example
Encoded Bitrate	7.17 Mbps

Digital File Characteristic » Digital Representation of Cartographic Content (RDA 3.19.8)

A set of technical details relating to the encoding of geospatial information in a cartographic resource.

Recording

Record data type (e.g., raster, vector, point), term for object type (e.g., point, line, polygon, pixel), and/or number of objects (e.g., 5,000 x 5,000).

Details of Digital File Characteristic (RDA 3.19.1.4)

Recording

Record a details note (e.g., recording density, sectoring) if considered important for identification or selection.

Element	Example
Details of Digital File Characteristic	Single density

Element	Example
Details of Digital File Characteristic	Distributed as a Zip file

Element	Example
Details of Digital File Characteristic	Window media version streams at 700 kbps; Real Media version streams at 225 kbps

Element	Example
Details of Digital File Characteristic	Full audio structured by chapter

Details of File Type (RDA 3.19.2.4)

Recording

Record a details note if considered important for identification or selection.

Element	Example
File Type	video file
Details of File Type	Streaming video file
A term and a details note for file type.	

Details of Encoding Format (RDA 3.19.3.4)

Recording

Record a details note if considered important for identification or selection.

Details of Digital Representation of Cartographic Content (RDA 3.19.8.4)

Recording

Record a details note (e.g., topology level, compression) if considered important for identification or selection.

Equipment or System Requirement (RDA 3.20)

The equipment or system required for use, playback, etc., of an analog, digital, etc., resource.

Recording

Record any equipment or system requirements beyond what is normal and obvious for the type of carrier or type of file.

Record requirements such as the make and model of equipment or hardware, the operating system, the amount of memory, programming language, other necessary software, any plug-ins or peripherals required to play, view, or run the resource, etc.

Element	Example
Equipment or System Requirement	System requirements: Adobe Acrobat Reader

Element	Example
Equipment or System Requirement	Requires: Macintosh: power Macintosh/Power PC, OS9.1, OSX, 32 MB RAM, 14x CD-ROM drive

> **Alternative.** Record the equipment or system requirements as they are presented on the resource.

Notes

Note on Carrier (RDA 3.21)

A note providing information on attributes of the carrier or carriers of the manifestation.

> **Related elements.** For notes on identifying manifestation attributes other than those describing carriers, see *Note on Manifestation.*

Recording

For all Note on Carrier elements, apply guidelines: *Notes* (p. 269).

Note on Carrier » Note on Extent of Manifestation (RDA 3.21.2)

A note providing information on the extent of a manifestation that is not recorded as part of the Extent element or element sub-types.

Element	Example
Extent of Three-Dimensional Form	various pieces
Note on Extent of Manifestation	Includes headdress, beaded shirt, trousers, and moccasins

Element	Example
Extent of Text	3 volumes
Note on Extent of Manifestation	No more volumes published
Incomplete resource will not be continued.	

Element	Example
Extent of Text	328 pages
Note on Extent of Manifestation	Pages also numbered 501–828
Individual volume having pagination of its own as well as pagination forming a larger sequence.	

Element	Example
Extent of Text	5 volumes
Note on Extent of Manifestation	8 bibliographic volumes in 5 physical volumes
Multipart monograph where bibliographic volumes differ from physical volumes recorded in Extent of Text. For serials, the extent is recorded as the number of bibliographic volumes. For serials, use Note on Extent of Item for notes on the number of physical volumes in item being described.	

Note on Carrier » Note on Dimensions of Manifestation
(RDA 3.21.3)

A note providing information on the dimensions of a manifestation that is not recorded as part of the Dimensions element or element sub-types.

Element	Example
Note on Dimensions of Manifestation	Printed area measures 30 × 46 cm
Record dimensions in notes as instructed for Dimensions.	

Note on Carrier » Note on Changes in Carrier Characteristics (RDA 3.21.4)

A note on changes in the characteristics of the carrier that occur in subsequent issues or parts of a resource issued in successive parts or between iterations of an integrating resource.

Element	Example
Note on Changes in Carrier Characteristic	Some issues have audiocassette supplements, 1984–1997; compact disc supplements, 1998–

Note on Item-Specific Carrier Characteristic (RDA 3.22)

A note providing additional information about carrier characteristics that are specific to the item being described and are assumed not to apply to other items exemplifying the same manifestation.

> **Related elements.** For notes on identifying item-specific characteristics other than those describing carriers, see *Note on Item.*

Recording

For all Note on Item-Specific Carrier Characteristic elements, apply guidelines: *Notes* (p. 269).

Element	Example
Note on Item-Specific Carrier Characteristic	Library's copy has errata sheets inserted

Note on Item-Specific Carrier Characteristic » Note on Extent of Item (RDA 3.22.2)

A note providing information on the extent of the specific item being described that is not recorded as part of the Extent element or element sub-types.

Element	Example
Extent of Text	xxiv, 179 pages (incomplete)
Note on Extent of Item	Library's copy lacks pages after 179

Note on Item-Specific Carrier Characteristic » Note on Dimensions of Item (RDA 3.22.3)

A note providing information on the dimensions of the specific item being described that is not recorded as part of the Dimensions element or element sub-types.

Element	Example
Note on Dimensions of Item	Size when framed: 40 × 35 cm
Use instructions for Dimensions for recording dimensions in notes.	

3

Providing
Acquisition and
Access Information

MANIFESTATIONS AND ITEMS

Manifestation refers to the physical embodiment of an expression of a work.

Item refers to a single exemplar or instance of a manifestation.

Resource, in the context of this chapter, refers to a manifestation or an item.

SUPPORTING THE USER

When following the instructions in this chapter, a cataloger considers the resource in terms of the attributes that are most often used for acquisition and access.

By recording these attributes in separate elements, a cataloger supports a user in *obtaining* a resource (e.g., acquiring through purchase, loan, etc., or accessing a resource electronically through an online connection to a remote computer). The data recorded can also support users in *finding* resources that correspond to search criteria, and in *identifying* a resource (i.e., differentiating the resource from others with similar identifying information).

Elements

Elements for Manifestations		
Elements	**Sub-types**	**Core**
Terms of Availability		
Contact Information		
Restrictions on Access		
Restrictions on Use		
Uniform Resource Locator		

Elements for Items		
Elements	**Sub-types**	**Core**
Restrictions on Access		
Restrictions on Use		

Sources of information

Take acquisition and access information from any source.

Elements

Terms of Availability (RDA 4.2)

The conditions under which the publisher, distributor, etc., will normally supply a resource or the price of a resource.

Recording

Record the terms on which the resource is available. These terms consist of the price (recorded in numerals with standard symbols) if the resource is for sale *or* a brief statement of other terms if the resource is not for sale.

Element	Example
Terms of Availability	£8.99

Element	Example
Terms of Availability	Not for sale, for promotion only

Contact Information (RDA 4.3)

Information about an organization, etc., from which a resource may be obtained.

For published resources, contact information typically includes the name, address, etc., of the publisher, distributor, etc., of the resource.

Recording

Record contact information for a publisher, distributor, etc., if considered important for acquisition or access.

Element	Example
Contact Information	Diffusion Inter-Livres, 1701, rue Belleville, Lemoyne, Québec J4P 3M2

Element	Example
Contact Information	www.HaworthPress.com

Restrictions on Access (RDA 4.4)

Limitations placed on access to a resource.

Recording

Record all restrictions on access to the resource as specifically as possible. Include the nature and duration of the restriction.

If information affirming the absence of restrictions is considered important for access, record that there are no restrictions on access.

Element	Example
Restrictions on Access	Restricted to institutions with a subscription

Restrictions on Use (RDA 4.5)

Limitations placed on uses such as reproduction, publication, exhibition, etc.

Recording

Record all restrictions on use of the resource as specifically as possible. Include the nature and duration of the restriction.

Element	Example
Restrictions on Use	Donor permission is required for public screening of films in this collection

Uniform Resource Locator (RDA 4.6)

The address of a remote access resource.

Uniform Resource Locators include all resource identifiers intended to provide online access to a resource using a standard Internet browser.

Related elements. Record a Uniform Resource Locator for a related resource as part of the description of the related manifestation (see *Related Manifestation*).

Recording

Record the Uniform Resource Locator for the online resource being described. If there is more than one Uniform Resource Locator for the resource, record one or more according to the policy of the agency preparing the description.

Element	Example
Uniform Resource Locator	http://hdl.loc.gov/loc.rbc/jeff.16823

4

Identifying Works and Expressions

Terminology

Work refers to a distinct intellectual or artistic creation (i.e., the intellectual or artistic content).

Expression refers to the intellectual or artistic realization of a work in the form of alpha-numeric, musical or choreographic notation, sound, image, object, movement, etc., or any combination of such forms.

Resource, in the context of this chapter, refers to a work, expression, manifestation, or item.

SUPPORTING THE USER

When following instructions in this chapter, a cataloger considers the resource and seeks to identify its intellectual or creative content in terms of the attributes of works and expressions.

By recording these attributes in separate elements, a cataloger supports a user in *identifying* the work or expression (i.e., confirming that the work or expression represented is the one sought, or distinguishing between two or more works or expressions with the same or similar titles). The data recorded also supports users in *finding* works and expressions that correspond to the user's stated search criteria, and in *selecting* a work or expression that is appropriate to the user's requirements with respect to content characteristics (e.g., form of work, language).

Elements

Core designates a core element—see element instructions for more details; *AAP* designates an element that can be used in an Authorized Access Point; *VAP* designates an element that can be used in a Variant Access Point.

Elements for Works				
Elements	**Sub-types**	**Core**	**AAP**	**VAP**
Title of the Work				
	Preferred Title for the Work	X	X	X
	Variant Title for the Work			X
Form of Work		X	X	X
Date of Work		X	X	X
Place of Origin of Work		X	X	X
Other Distinguishing Characteristic of the Work		X	X	X
Medium of Performance		X	X	X
Numeric Designation of a Musical Work		X	X	X
Key		X	X	X
History of the Work				
Identifier for the Work		X		

Elements for Expressions				
Elements	**Sub-types**	**Core**	**AAP**	**VAP**
Content Type		X	X	X
Date of Expression		X	X	X
Language of the Expression		X	X	X
Other Distinguishing Characteristic of the Expression		X	X	X
Identifier for the Expression		X		

Record the following data as separate elements. These elements provide clarification or justification for the attributes recorded to identify works and expressions.

Status of Identification (RDA 5.7)

Source Consulted (RDA 5.8)

Cataloguer's Note (RDA 5.9)

Sources of information

Take information for all attributes from any source, and follow additional guidance for *Preferred Title for the Work*.

Determine the preferred title for a work from resources embodying the work or from reference sources.

Work Elements

Title of the Work (RDA 6.2)

A word, character, or group of words and/or characters by which a work is known.

For titles of musical works, legal works, religious works, official communications, and works created before 1501, use the Title of the Work element sub-types. Refer to RDA for additional instructions for these kinds of works.

Title of the Work » Preferred Title for the Work (RDA 6.2.2; see RDA 6.14.2 for musical works, RDA 6.19.2 for legal works, RDA 6.23.2 for religious work, and RDA 6.26.2 for official communications) **AAP VAP**

The title or form of title chosen to identify the work.

Core element

Choosing Preferred Title for the Work for works created after 1500

Choose the title or form of title in the original language by which the work is commonly identified either through use in resources embodying the work or in reference sources.

Element	Example
Preferred Title for the Work	Martin Chuzzlewit
Preferred title for work by Dickens published under various titles.	

No title or form of title in the original language established as the one by which the work is commonly identified or in case of doubt

Choose the Title Proper of the original edition as the preferred title.

Element	Example
Preferred Title for the Work	The little acorn
Preferred title from Title Proper The little acorn, *title of the only manifestation published. RDA has an option to omit the initial article (e.g.,* The).	

Work published simultaneously in different languages and the original language cannot be determined

Choose the Title Proper of the first resource received.

Language editions are in the same resource (e.g., a work issued with the same text in French and English)

Choose the Title Proper named on the preferred source of information.

Work published simultaneously in the same language under different titles

Choose the Title Proper of the first resource received.

Title proper of the original edition is not available or the original edition does not have a title proper and ***reference sources do not contain a title in the original language***

Choose (in this order of preference)

a) a well-established title from a modern reference source in the language preferred by the agency creating the data

b) a title devised by the agency creating the data

Recording

Apply guidelines: *Titles of Works* (p. 271) for individual works and for compilations of works.

Element	Example
Preferred Title for the Work	The sun also rises
Preferred title for work by Hemingway also published under the title: Fiesta.	

Do not include an alternative title as part of the preferred title.

Element	Example
Title Proper	The hobbit, or, There and back again
Preferred Title for the Work	The hobbit

If the title chosen as the preferred title includes introductory words, inaccuracies, words that vary from issue to issue or part to part, etc. apply the guidelines: *Titles Associated with a Manifestation* (p. 271).

Preferred title for a part or parts of a work (RDA 6.2.2.9)

Element	Example
Preferred Title for the Work	The two towers
Preferred title for a part of J.R.R. Tolkien's The lord of the rings.	

Part identified only by a generic term with or without a numeric or alphabetic designation (e.g., Preface; Book 1; Band 3)

Record the designation of the part as the preferred title for the part. Record the numeric designation as a numeral (e.g., *Book 1*).

> **Exception.** *Serials and integrating resources.* If the part is identified by both a designation and a title, record the designation first, followed by the title. Use a comma to separate the designation from the title.
>
> | Element | Example |
> |---|---|
> | Preferred Title for the Work | Series C, Traditional skills and practices |

Two or more consecutively numbered parts identified only by a general term and a number

Record the designation of the parts as the preferred title. Record the general term in the singular followed by the inclusive numbers of the parts. Record the numeric designations as numerals (e.g., *Book 1-6*).

Two or more unnumbered or nonconsecutively numbered parts

Record the preferred title for each of the parts.

Element	Example
Preferred Title for the Work	Gareth and Lynette
Preferred Title for the Work	Lancelot and Elaine
Preferred Title for the Work	The passing of Arthur
Three unnumbered parts of the work Idylls of the King *by Tennyson.*	

> **Alternative.** Identify the unnumbered or nonconsecutively-numbered parts collectively. Record the conventional collective title Selections as the preferred title for the parts. Apply this instruction instead of or in addition to recording the preferred title for each of the parts.
>
> | Element | Example |
> |---|---|
> | Preferred Title for the Work | Selections |

RDA ESSENTIALS **TIP**
(SEE ALSO *AUTHORIZED ACCESS POINT REPRESENTING A WORK*)

To identify a part of a work with an authorized access point, a preferred title for a part such as *Book 1* (or *Selections* if following the alternative) is added to the authorized access point representing the full work.

Access Point	Example
Authorized Access Point Representing a Work	Homer. Iliad. Book 1

or following the alternative for two or more parts:

Access point	Example
Authorized Access Point Representing a Work	Homer. Iliad. Selections

Preferred title for a compilation of works by one person, family, or corporate body (RDA 6.2.2.10)

Compilation of works commonly identified by a title or form of title in resources embodying that compilation or in reference sources

Choose the preferred title based upon the instructions for works created after 1500.

Compilation of works that consists of, or purports to be, the complete works of a person, family, or corporate body

Record the conventional collective title *Works*. Treat compilations that are complete at the time of publication as complete works.

Compilation of works that consists of, or purports to be, the complete works of a person, family, or corporate body, in one particular form

Record one of the following conventional collective titles:

Correspondence	Prose works	*If none of these terms is appropriate, record an appropriate specific collective title.*
Plays	Lyrics	
Essays	Short stories	
Poems	Novels	
Librettos	Speeches	

Compilation of two or more but not all works of one person, family, or corporate body in a particular form or two or more but not all the works of one person, family, or corporate body in various forms

Record the preferred title for each of the works.

> **Alternative.** When identifying two or more works in a compilation, identify the parts collectively by recording a conventional collective title followed by Selections. Apply this instruction instead of or in addition to recording the preferred title for each of the works in the compilation.

Element	Example
Preferred Title for the Work	Novels. Selections

Preferred title for a compilation of works by different persons, families, or corporate bodies (RDA 6.2.2.11)

Collective title. Compilation of works by different persons, families, or corporate bodies commonly identified by a collective title in resources embodying the compilation or in reference sources
Record the collective title as the preferred title of the compilation.

No collective title. Compilation of works by different persons, families, or corporate bodies not commonly identified by a collective title in resources embodying the compilation or in reference sources
Record the preferred title for each of the individual works.

> **Alternative.** Record a devised title (see instruction on devised titles for *Title » Title Proper*) for the compilation. Apply this instruction instead of or in addition to recording the preferred title for each of the works in the compilation.

Title of the Work » Variant Title for the Work (RDA 6.2.3; see RDA 6.14.3 for musical works, RDA 6.19.3 for legal works, RDA 6.23.3 for religious works, and RDA 6.26.3 for official communications) VAP

A title or form of title by which a work is known that differs from the title or form of title chosen as the preferred title for the work.

Recording

Apply guidelines: *Titles of Works* (p. 293).

Record a variant title for the work when it is different from the title recorded as the preferred title. Record as a variant title: a title or form of title under which the work has been issued or cited in reference sources *or* a title resulting from a different transliteration of the title.

Element	Example
Preferred Title for the Work	David Copperfield
Variant Title for the Work	The personal history of David Copperfield
RDA has an option to drop articles like The *in Title of the Work elements.*	

Element	Example
Preferred Title for the Work	The two towers
Variant Title for the Work	The 2 towers
Variant Title for the Work	The lord of the rings. The two towers

Element	Example
Preferred Title for the Work	Plays. Selections
Variant Title for the Work	Selected plays of Lady Gregory
Variant Title for the Work	Short plays of Lady Gregory
Variant Title for the Work	Seven short plays

Exception. Record a title appearing on a manifestation of the work as a variant title for the work only in the following case: if the title appearing on the manifestation differs significantly from the preferred title and if the work itself might reasonably be searched by that title.

If the title recorded as the preferred title for a work has one or more alternative linguistic forms (different language forms, scripts, spellings, or transliterations), record them as variant titles for the work.

Element	Example
Preferred Title for the Work	Chanson de Roland
Variant Title for the Work	Roland
Variant Title for the Work	Rolandslied
Variant Title for the Work	Song of Roland

Form of Work (RDA 6.3) AAP VAP

A class or genre to which a work belongs.

Core element

Form of Work is a core element when needed to differentiate a work from another work with the same title or from the name of a person, family, or corporate body.

Capitalization

Capitalize the first word of the term (RDA A.3.2).

Recording

Record the form of the work.

Element	Example
Form of Work	Play

Element	Example
Form of Work	Motion picture

Element	Example
Form of Work	Computer file

Date of Work (RDA 6.4; see RDA 6.20 for legal works) AAP VAP

The earliest date associated with a work. If no specific date can be identified as the date the work was created, treat the date of the earliest known manifestation embodying the work as the date of work.

Core element

Date of Work is a core element to identify a treaty. Date of Work is also a core element when needed to differentiate a work from another work with the same title or from the name of a person, family, or corporate body.

Recording

Record the year or years. See guidelines: *Dates Associated with Persons, Families, and Corporate Bodies* (p. 303) for the use of B.C. and A.D.

Element	Example
Date of Work	1960
Date of release of a motion picture titled Ocean's eleven.	

Place of Origin of the Work (RDA 6.5) AAP VAP

The country or other territorial jurisdiction from which a work originated.

Core element

Place of Origin of the Work is a core element when needed to differentiate a work from another work with the same title or from the name of a person, family, or corporate body.

Recording

Apply guidelines: *Places* (Group 2 elements) (p. 305).

Element	Example
Place of Origin of the Work	Boise, Idaho

Other Distinguishing Characteristic of the Work

(RDA 6.6; see RDA 6.21 for legal works) AAP VAP

A characteristic other than form of work, date of work, or place of origin of the work. It serves to differentiate a work from another work with the same title or from the name of a person, family, or corporate body.

Core element

Other Distinguishing Characteristic of the Work is a core element when needed to differentiate a work from another work with the same title or from the name of a person, family, or corporate body.

Capitalization

Capitalize the first word of the term (RDA A.3.2).

Recording

Record other distinguishing characteristics of the work.

Element	Example
Other Distinguishing Characteristic of the Work	Geological Survey (South Africa)
Issuing body of a work titled Bulletin.	

Element	Example
Other Distinguishing Characteristic of the Work	Anglo-Saxon poem
Other distinguishing characteristic of a work title Genesis *to distinguish it from other works with the same title.*	

Element	Example
Other Distinguishing Characteristic of the Work	Douglas
Surname of the director of a 1965 motion picture called Harlow, *to distinguish it from another motion picture with the same title.*	

Element	Example
Other Distinguishing Characteristic of the Work	Unnumbered
Other distinguishing characteristic of a work titled Caribbean *writers series.*	

Medium of Performance (RDA 6.15) AAP VAP

The instrument, instruments, voice, voices, etc., for which a musical work was originally conceived.

Core element

Medium of Performance is a core element when needed to differentiate a musical work from another work with the same title. It may also be a core element when identifying a musical work with a title that is not distinctive.

> **Related elements.** *Medium of Performance of Musical Content* for a details note.

Recording

Record appropriate terms for medium of performance.

Element	Example
Medium of Performance	soprano
	piano

Element	Example
Medium of Performance	flutes (2)
	clarinets (2)

Numeric Designation of a Musical Work (RDA 6.16) AAP VAP

A serial number, opus number, or thematic index number assigned to a musical work by a composer, publisher, or a musicologist.

Core element

Numeric Designation of a Musical Work is a core element when needed to differentiate a musical work from another work with the same title. It may also be a core element when identifying a musical work with a title that is not distinctive.

Recording

Record as many of the numeric designations of musical works as can readily be ascertained.

Element	Example
Numeric Designation of a Musical Work	op. 2, no. 1

Resource described: Piano sonata no. 1 in F minor, op. 2, no. 1 / Beethoven. *Preferred title:* Sonatas; *medium of performance:* piano; *serial number:* no. 1.

Key (RDA 6.17) AAP VAP

The set of pitch relationships that establishes the tonal center, or principal tonal center, of a musical work.

Key is indicated by its pitch name and its mode, when it is major or minor.

Core element

Key is a core element when needed to differentiate a musical work from another work with the same title. It may also be a core element when identifying a musical work with a title that is not distinctive.

Recording

Record the key.

Element	Example
Key	C minor

History of the Work (RDA 6.7)

Information about the history of a work.

Recording

Record information about the history of the work. Incorporate information associated with other identifying elements for the work.

Element	Example
History of the Work	Originally written as a serial and published in 19 issues over 20 months from March 1836 to October 1837. There was no issue in May 1837 as Dickens was in mourning for his sister-in-law.

Identifier for the Work (RDA 6.8)

A character string uniquely associated with a work, or with a surrogate for a work (e.g., an authority record).

The identifier serves to differentiate that work from other works.

Core element

Recording

Record an identifier for the work. Precede the identifier with the name or an identification of the agency, etc., responsible for assigning the identifier, if readily ascertainable.

Element	Example
Identifier for the Work	Library of Congress control number: n 79046204

Expression Elements

Content Type (RDA 6.9) AAP VAP

A categorization reflecting the fundamental form of communication in which the content is expressed and the human sense through which it is intended to be perceived.

For content expressed in the form of an image or images, content type also reflects the number of spatial dimensions in which the content is intended to be perceived and the perceived presence or absence of movement.

Core element

Recording

Record one or more RDA terms. Record as many terms as are applicable to the resource being described.

> **Alternative.** If the resource being described consists of more than one content type, record only a) the content type that applies to the predominant part of the resource (if there is a predominant part) or b) the content types that apply to the most substantial parts of the resource (including the predominant part, if there is one). Use one or more of the RDA terms for content type, as appropriate.

RDA terms for Content Type

cartographic dataset	notated movement	tactile three-dimensional form
cartographic image	notated music	text
cartographic moving image	performed music	three-dimensional form
cartographic tactile image	sounds	three-dimensional moving image
cartographic tactile three-dimensional form	spoken word	two-dimensional moving image
cartographic three-dimensional form	still image	other
computer dataset	tactile image	unspecified
computer program	tactile notated movement	
	tactile notated music	
	tactile text	

Examples of Content Type, Media Type, and Carrier Type for different resources

Element	Example
Content Type	text
Content Type	still image
Media Type	unmediated
Carrier Type	volume
A graphic novel.	

Element	Example
Content Type	two-dimensional moving image
Media Type	video
Carrier Type	videodisc
A DVD of a movie.	

Element	Example
Content Type	cartographic three-dimensional form
Media Type	unmediated
Carrier Type	object
A globe.	

Element	Example
Content Type	spoken word
Media Type	computer
Carrier Type	online resource
A downloadable e-audiobook.	

> **RDA ESSENTIALS TIP**
>
> Because content and carrier attributes are separated in RDA, catalogers can more easily provide categories to complex resources. All applicable Content Type and Carrier Type terms can be added to a description.
>
> ***Two-dimensional moving image*** content type includes motion pictures (using live action and/or animation), film and video recordings of performances, events, etc., video games, etc. Moving images may or may not be accompanied by sound.
>
> ***Computer program*** content type includes operating systems, application software, etc.
>
> ***Computer dataset*** content type includes numeric data, environmental data, etc. used by application software to calculate averages, correlations, etc., or to produce models, etc. For digital content (e.g., e-books, JPEG files, MP3 audio files, streaming video) intended to be perceived directly through human senses, use content types such as *text, still image, performed music, spoken word, and two-dimensional moving image.*

Date of Expression (6.10; see RDA 6.24 for expressions of religious works) AAP VAP

The earliest date associated with an expression.

The date of expression may represent the date a text was written, the date of final editing of a moving image work, the date of first broadcast for a television or radio program, the date of notation for a score, the date of the recording of an event, etc.

If no specific date can be identified as the date of expression, treat the date of the earliest known manifestation embodying the expression as the date of expression.

Core element

Date of expression is a core element when needed to differentiate an expression of a work from another expression of the same work.

Recording

Record the year or years.

Element	Example
Date of Expression	1992
Date of the director's cut of the 1982 motion picture Blade runner.	

Language of Expression (RDA 6.11) AAP VAP

A language in which a work is expressed.

Core element

> **Related elements.** *Language of the Content* for a details note.

Recording

Record the language or languages of the expression using an appropriate term or terms in a language preferred by the agency creating the data. Select terms from a standard list of names of languages, if available.

Element	Example
Language of Expression	English
Language of Expression	German
Language of Expression	French

Example of a single expression involving more than one language. A motion picture with some dialogue in English, some dialogue in German, and some dialogue in Russian.

Other Distinguishing Characteristic of the Expression

(RDA 6.12; see RDA 6.18 for expressions of musical works and RDA 6.25 for expressions of religious works) AAP VAP

A characteristic other than content type, language of expression, or date of expression. It serves to differentiate an expression from another expression of the same work.

Core element

Other distinguishing characteristic of the expression is a core element when needed to differentiate an expression of a work from another expression of the same work.

Recording

Record other distinguishing characteristics of the expression.

Element	Example
Other Distinguishing Characteristic of the Expression	2nd version

The second of three versions of Johann Gottlieb Fichte's Wissenschaftslehre 1804.

Element	Example
Other Distinguishing Characteristic of the Expression	Beck
An English translation by Tom Beck of Aleksandr Pushkin's Evgeniĭ Onegin.	

Element	Example
Other Distinguishing Characteristic of the Expression	Huber
Another audio recording of Victor Hugo's Notre-Dame de Paris *narrated by Élodie Huber.*	

Identifier for the Expression (RDA 6.13)

A character string uniquely associated with an expression, or with a surrogate for an expression (e.g., an authority record). The identifier serves to differentiate that expression from other expressions.

Core element

Recording

Record an identifier for the expression. Precede the identifier with the name or an identification of the agency, etc., responsible for assigning the identifier, if readily ascertainable.

Element	Example
Identifier for the Expression	Wolfgang's Vault ID: 20049774|1647
Identifier for a David Bowie concert recorded March 23, 1976.	

5

Describing Content

WORKS AND EXPRESSIONS

Terminology

Work refers to a distinct intellectual or artistic creation (i.e., the intellectual or artistic content).

Expression refers to the intellectual or artistic realization of a work in the form of alpha-numeric, musical or choreographic notation, sound, image, object, movement, etc., or any combination of such forms.

Resource, in the context of this chapter, refers to a work or an expression.

SUPPORTING THE USER

When following the instructions in this chapter, a cataloger continues to consider a resource and its intellectual or creative content in terms of attributes of works and expressions.

By recording these attributes in separate elements, a cataloger supports a user in *selecting* a resource that meets the user's needs (e.g., nature of the content, intended audience, language of the content). The data recorded can also support users in *finding* resources that correspond to the user's stated search criteria, and in *identifying* a resource (i.e., differentiating the resource from others with similar identifying information).

Elements

Core designates a core element—see element instructions for more details.

Elements for Works		
Elements	**Sub-types or Sub-elements**	**Core**
Nature of the Work		
Coverage of the Content		
Coordinates of Cartographic Content		
	Longitude and Latitude	
	Strings of Coordinate Pairs	
	Right Ascension and Declinations	
Equinox		
Epoch		
Intended Audience		
System of Organization		
Dissertation or Thesis Information	*Sub-elements*:	
	Academic Degree	
	Granting Institution or Faculty	
	Year Degree Granted	

Elements for Expressions		
Elements	**Sub-types or Sub-elements**	**Core**
Summarization of the Content		
Place and Date of Capture	*Sub-elements:*	
	Place of Capture	
	Date of Capture	
Language of the Content		
Form of Notation		
	Script	
	Form of Musical Notation	
	Form of Tactile Notation	
	Form of Notated Movement	
Details of Script		
Details of Form of Musical Notation		
Details of Form of Tactile Notation		

Elements for Expressions		
Elements	**Sub-types or Sub-elements**	**Core**
Details of Form of Notated Movement		
Accessibility Content		
Illustrative Content		
Details of Illustrative Content		
Supplementary Content		
Colour Content		
Details of Colour Content		
Sound Content		
Aspect Ratio		
Details of Aspect Ratio		
Format of Notated Music		
Details of Format of Notated Music		
Medium of Performance of Musical Content		
Duration		
Details of Duration		
Scale		
	Scale of Still Image or Three-Dimensional Form	
	Horizontal Scale of Cartographic Content	X
	Vertical Scale of Cartographic	X
	Additional Scale Information	
Projection of Cartographic Content		
Other Details of Cartographic Content		
Award		
Note on Expression		
	Note on Changes in Content Characteristics	

Sources of Information

Take information about the content from any source except for the following cases.

For the following elements take information from the resource first and then from any source.

> Coordinates of Cartographic Content element sub-types
>
> Colour Content
>
> Sound Content
>
> Aspect Ratio
>
> Scale » Horizontal Scale of Cartographic Content

For the following elements take information only from a source within the resource.

> *Source within the resource for these cartographic content elements:*
>
> Equinox
>
> Epoch
>
> Scale » Vertical Scale of Cartographic Content
>
> Scale » Additional Scale Information
>
> Projection of Cartographic Content

> *Source within the resource for these musical content elements:*
>
> Format of Notated Music
>
> Medium of Performance of Musical Content

Work Elements

Nature of the Content (RDA 7.2)

The specific character of the primary content of a resource (e.g., legal articles, interim report).

Recording

Record the nature of the content if considered important for identification or selection.

Element	Example
Nature of the Content	Field recording of birdsong

Element	Example
Nature of the Content	Singspiel in two acts

Coverage of the Content (RDA 7.3)

The chronological or geographic coverage of the content of a resource.

Recording

Record the coverage of the content if considered important for identification or selection.

Element	Example
Coverage of the Content	Based on 1981 statistics

Element	Example
Coverage of the Content	Shows all of western Europe and some of eastern Europe

Coordinates of Cartographic Content (RDA 7.4)

A mathematical system for identifying the area covered by the cartographic content of a resource. Coordinates may be expressed by means of longitude and latitude on the surface of planets or by the angles of right ascension and declination for celestial charts.

Coordinates of Cartographic Content » Longitude and Latitude (RDA 7.4.2)

A system for identifying the area covered by the cartographic content of a resource using longitude of the westernmost and easternmost boundaries and latitude of the northernmost and southernmost boundaries.

Longitude is the distance of a point on a planet or satellite measured east and west from a reference meridian. Latitude is the distance of a point on a planet or satellite measured north and south from the equator.

Recording

For terrestrial cartographic content, record the coordinates in the following order: westernmost extent of area covered (longitude), easternmost extent of area covered (longitude), northernmost extent of area covered (latitude), southernmost extent of area covered (latitude).

Element	Example
Longitude and Latitude	E 15°00'00"–E 17°30'45"/N 1°30'12"–S 2°30'35"

Coordinates of Cartographic Content » Strings of Coordinate Pairs (RDA 7.4.3)

A system for identifying the precise area covered by the cartographic content of a resource using coordinates for each vertex of a polygon.

Use strings of coordinate pairs for an indication of geographic coverage that is more precise than longitude and latitude coordinates.

Recording

Describe each closed polygon by using a string of coordinate pairs, in which each pair represents a vertex of the polygon.

Element	Example
Strings of Coordinate Pairs	W 114°/N 32° ; W 117°/N 33° ; W 121°/N 35° ; W 125°/N 43° ; W 120°/N 42° ; W 120°/N 39° ; W 115°/N 34° ; W 114°/N 32°

Coordinates of Cartographic Content » Right Ascension and Declination (RDA 7.4.4)

A system for identifying the location of a celestial object in the sky covered by the cartographic content of a resource using the angles of right ascension and declination.

Right ascension is the angular distance measured eastward on the equator from the vernal equinox to the hour circle through a celestial body, from 0 to 24 hours. Declination is the angular distance to a body on the celestial sphere measured north or south through 90° from the celestial equator along the hour circle of the body.

Recording

For celestial cartographic content, record as coordinates: a) the right ascension of the content, or the right ascensions of the western and eastern limits of its collective coverage *and* b) the declination of the center of the content, or the northern and southern limits of its collective coverage.

Element	Example
Right Ascension and Declination	Right ascension 16 hr. 30 min. to 19 hr. 30 min./ Declination -16° to -49°

Equinox (RDA 7.5)

One of two points of intersection of the ecliptic and the celestial equator, occupied by the sun when its declination is 0°.

Recording

When coordinates are recorded for celestial cartographic content, record also the statement of equinox. Record the equinox as a year.

Epoch (RDA 7.6)

An arbitrary moment in time to which measurements of position for a body or orientation for an orbit are referred.

Recording

When recording equinox for celestial cartographic content, record also a statement of the epoch when it is known to differ from the equinox.

Intended Audience (RDA 7.7)

The class of user for which the content of a resource is intended, or for whom the content is considered suitable. The class of user is defined by age group (e.g., children, young adults, adults), educational level (e.g., primary, secondary), type of disability, or another categorization.

Recording

Record the intended audience for the content if the information is stated on the resource or is readily available from another source.

Element	Example
Intended Audience	For children aged 7–9

Element	Example
Intended Audience	MPAA rating: PG-13

System of Organization (RDA 7.8)

A system of arranging materials in an archival resource or a collection.

Recording

Record information about the organization of component files or items in an archival resource or a collection.

Element	Example
System of Organization	This subseries is arranged alphabetically by the geographic location of the photograph and then by the item number assigned by the photographer

Dissertation or Thesis Information (RDA 7.9)

Information about a work presented as part of the formal requirements for an academic degree.

Element	Example
Academic Degree	1950
Granting Institution or Faculty	University College, London
Year Degree Granted	1969

Dissertation or Thesis Information » Academic Degree (RDA 7.9.2)

A rank conferred as a guarantee of academic proficiency.

Recording

Record a brief statement of the degree for which the author was a candidate.

Dissertation or Thesis Information » Granting Institution or Faculty (RDA 7.9.3)

An institution or faculty conferring an academic degree on a candidate.

Recording

Record the name of the granting institution or faculty.

Dissertation or Thesis Information » Year Degree Granted (RDA 7.9.4)

The calendar year in which a granting institution or faculty conferred an academic degree on a candidate.

Recording

Record the year in which the degree was granted. Apply guidelines: *Numbers Expressed as Numerals or as Words* (p. 267).

Expression Elements

Summarization of the Content (RDA 7.10)

An abstract, summary, synopsis, etc., of the content of a resource.

> **Related elements.** For instructions on recording contents as whole-part relationships, see *Related Work*.

Recording

Provide a brief objective summary of the content of the resource if: a) this information is considered important for identification or selection (e.g., for audiovisual resources or for resources designed for use by persons with disabilities) *and* b) sufficient information is not recorded in another part of the description.

Element	Example
Summarization of the Content	Toy medical kit designed to prepare children for hospital and medical procedures

Element	Example
Summarization of the Content	A brief historical account up to the introduction of wave mechanics

Place and Date of Capture (RDA 7.11)

The place and date associated with the capture (e.g., recording, filming) of the content of a resource.

Place and Date of Capture » Place of Capture (RDA 7.11.2)

The place associated with the capture (e.g., recording, filming) of the content of a resource.

Recording

Record by naming: a) the specific studio, concert hall, etc., if applicable and readily ascertainable *and* b) the city, etc.

Element	Example
Place of Capture	Paradise Studios, Sydney

Place and Date of Capture » Date of Capture (RDA 7.11.3)

A date or range of dates associated with the capture (e.g., recording, filming) of the content of a resource.

Recording

Record by giving the year, month, day, and time, as applicable.

Element	Example
Date of Capture	1997 April 22–23

Language of the Content (RDA 7.12)

A language used to express the content of a resource.

| **Related elements.** For instructions on recording programming language, see Equipment or *System Requirement.*

| **Related elements.** See *Language of the Expression* for language terms.

Recording

Record a details note if considered important for identification or selection.

Element	Example
Language of Expression	Latin
Language of Expression	English
Language of the Content	Latin text; parallel English translation
Language of the Expression is for language terms; Language of the Content is a details note.	

Element	Example
Language of Expression	Polish
Language of the Content	In Polish; tables of contents and summaries in Polish, Russian, and English

Form of Notation (RDA 7.13)

A set of characters and/or symbols used to express the content of a resource.

Form of Notation » Script (RDA 7.13.2)

A set of characters and/or symbols used to express the written language content of a resource.

Recording

Record an appropriate term or terms in a language preferred by the agency creating the data. Select terms from a standard list of names of scripts, if available. Record details in Details of Script if none of the terms is appropriate or sufficiently specific.

Element	Example
Script	Devanagari

Form of Notation » Form of Musical Notation (RDA 7.13.3)

A set of characters and/or symbols used to express the musical content of a resource.

Recording

Record one or more appropriate RDA terms. If more than one term applies to a single form of musical notation used in the resource, record the most specific term. Record details in Details of Form of Musical Notation if none of the terms is appropriate or sufficiently specific.

> **Related elements.** For recording tactile forms of musical notation, see *Form of Notation » Form of Tactile Notation*.
>
> For recording the encoding format, etc., for digitally encoded musical notation, see *Digital File Characteristic » Encoding Format*.

Element	Example
Form of Musical Notation	mensural notation

Form of Notation » Form of Tactile Notation (RDA 7.13.4)

A set of characters and/or symbols used to express the content of a resource in a form that can be perceived through touch.

Recording

Record one or more appropriate RDA terms. Record details in Details of Form of Tactile Notation if none of the terms is appropriate or sufficiently specific.

Element	Example
Form of Tactile Notation	braille code

Form of Notation » Form of Notated Movement
(RDA 7.13.5)

A set of characters and/or symbols used to express the movement content of a resource.

Recording

Record one or more appropriate RDA terms. Record details in Details of Form of Notated Movement if none of the terms is appropriate or sufficiently specific.

Element	Example
Form of Notated Movement	Beauchamp-Feuillet notation

Details of Script (RDA 7.13.2.4)

Recording

Record a details note if considered important for identification or selection.

Element	Example
Details of Script	Kazakh, Uighur (Cyrillic), and Chagatai (Cyrillic and Arabic script)

Details of Form of Musical Notation (RDA 7.13.3.4)

Recording

Record a details note if considered important for identification or selection.

Element	Example
Details of Form of Musical Notation	Melody in both staff and tonic sol-fa notation

Details of Form of Tactile Notation (RDA 7.13.4.4)

Recording

Record a details note if considered important for identification or selection.

Element	Example
Details of Form of Tactile Notation	Moon code (grade 2)
Details note recorded by adding level of contraction to a term for form of tactile notation.	

Element	Example
Details of Form of Tactile Notation	Contains braille and tactile images

Details of Form of Notated Movement (RDA 7.13.5.4)

Recording

Record a details note if considered important for identification or selection.

Element	Example
Details of Form of Notated Movement	Partly reconstructed from a video of the first performance

Accessibility Content (RDA 7.14)

Content that assists those with a sensory impairment in the greater understanding of content which their impairment prevents them fully seeing or hearing.

Accessibility content includes accessible labels, audio description, captioning, image description, sign language, and subtitles.

Related elements. Accessibility content does not include subtitles in a language different from the spoken content (see *Language of the Content*).

Recording

Record information about the accessibility content if the information is evident from the resource or is readily available from another source.

Element	Example
Accessibility Content	Closed captioning in German

Illustrative Content (RDA 7.15)

Content intended to illustrate the primary content of a resource.

Related elements. For instructions on recording the nature of the primary content of a resource, see *Nature of the Content*.

For instructions on recording color content of a resource, see *Colour Content*.

Recording

If the resource contains illustrative content, record *illustration* or *illustrations*, as appropriate. Tables containing only words and/or numerical data are not considered as illustrative content. Disregard illustrated title pages, etc., and minor illustrations.

Element	Example
Illustrative Content	illustrations

Alternative. Record the type of illustrative content in place of or in addition to the term illustration or illustrations if considered important for identification or selection. Use one or more appropriate terms from the following list (singular or plural). Record details in *Details of Illustrative Content* if none of the terms in the list is appropriate.

charts	graphs	plans
coats of arms	illuminations	portraits
facsimiles	maps	samples
forms	music	
genealogical tables	photographs	

Optional Addition. Record the number of illustrations if the number can be readily ascertained (e.g., when the illustrations are numbered).

Element	Example
Illustrative Content	100 maps

Details of Illustrative Content (RDA 7.15.1.4)

Recording

Record a details note if considered important for identification or selection.

Element	Example
Details of Illustrative Content	Map of Australia on endpapers

Supplementary Content (RDA 7.16)

Content (e.g., an index, a bibliography, an appendix) intended to supplement the primary content of a resource.

Related elements. For instructions on recording content that supplements the primary content of a resource as a related work, see *Related Work elements.*

Recording

If the resource contains supplementary content, record the nature of that content (e.g., its type, extent, location within the resource).

Element	Example
Supplementary Content	Includes index

Element	Example
Supplementary Content	Bibliography: pages 859–910

Colour Content (RDA 7.17)

The presence of color, tone, etc., in the content of a resource. Black, white, single color shades of black, single color tints of white, and single color tones of gray are considered to be single colors.

Related elements. For instructions on recording item-specific color information, see *Note on Item-Specific Carrier Characteristic.*

For instructions on recording illustrative content of a resource, see *Illustrative Content.*

Recording

Record by using one or more appropriate terms from the following list: *monochrome, polychrome.*

Element	Example
Colour Content	monochrome

Color content for a black and white photograph. Monochrome is color, content consisting of tones of one color, or black and white, or black and white and another color.

Element	Example
Colour Content	polychrome

Color content for a motion picture film in color. Polychrome is color content consisting of two colors (neither of which is black or white) or more than two colors.

Alternative. Record the color content by using one or more terms from a substitute vocabulary.

Element	Example
Colour Content	black and white
Color content for a motion picture film.	

Element	Example
Colour Content	black and white
Color content for a motion picture film.	

Element	Example
Colour Content	color
Color content for a map.	

Element	Example
Colour Content	multicolored
Color content for a booklet.	

Record details in Details of Colour Content if none of the terms in the list or in a substitute vocabulary is appropriate or sufficiently specific.

Details of Colour Content (RDA 7.17.1.4)

Recording

Record a details note if considered important for identification or selection.

Element	Example
Details of Colour Content	Color maps; black and white photographs

Element	Example
Details of Colour Content	Some color

Element	Example
Details of Colour Content	Chiefly color

Element	Example
Details of Colour Content	Illustrations (some color)

A monograph containing monochrome and polychrome illustrations.

Element	Example
Details of Colour Content	Tinted blue

A photograph in black and white, tinted blue.

Element	Example
Colour Content	monochrome
Colour Content	polychrome
Details of Colour Content	Black and white with color introductory sequences

A motion picture film.

Element	Example
Details of Colour Content	Various shades of pink

Element	Example
Details of Colour Content	Technicolor

Element	Example
Details of Colour Content	Colorized

Element	Example
Details of Colour Content	Gray scale

Element	Example
Details of Colour Content	Blue text on yellow background

A resource designed for person with visual impairments.

Sound Content (RDA 7.18)

The presence of sound in a resource other than one that consists primarily of recorded sound.

Recording

Record *sound* to indicate the presence of sound in a resource that does not consist primarily of recorded sound.

> **Exception.** For moving image resources (i.e., motion pictures and video recordings), record *sound* or *silent* to indicate the presence or absence of a sound track.

Aspect Ratio (RDA 7.19)

The ratio of the width to the height of a moving image.

Recording

Record one or more RDA terms: *full screen* (ratio less than 1.5:1), *wide screen* (ratio 1.5:1 or greater), *mixed* (for resources that include multiple aspect ratios within the same work).

In addition, record the numerical ratio in standard format with a denominator of 1, if known.

Element	Example
Aspect Ratio	wide screen (2.35:1)

Details of Aspect Ratio (RDA 7.19.1.4)

Recording

Record a details note on the aspect ratio if considered important for identification or selection.

Element	Example
Details of Aspect Ratio	Letterboxed

Format of Notated Music (RDA 7.20)

The musical or physical layout of the content of a resource that is presented in the form of musical notation.

> **Related elements.** *Extent » Extent of Notated Music* (RDA terms used as units of extent of notated music).

Recording

Record one or more appropriate RDA terms. Record details in Details of Format of Notated Music if none of the terms is appropriate or sufficiently specific.

Element	Example
Format of Notated Music	score

Details of Format of Notated Music (RDA 7.20.1.4)

Recording

Record a details note if considered important for identification or selection.

Medium of Performance of Musical Content (RDA 7.21)

The instrument, instruments, voice, voices, etc., used (or intended to be used) for performance of musical content.

❚ **Related elements.** *Medium of Performance* for musical terms.

Recording

Record a details note if considered important for identification or selection.

   If the musical content is for solo instruments, record all the instruments. If the work is for an orchestra, band, etc., do not list the instruments involved.

Element	Example
Medium of Performance of Musical Content	Reduction for clarinet and piano
Medium of Performance is for musical terms; Medium of Performance of Musical Content is a details note.	

Duration (RDA 7.22)

The playing time, running time, performance time, etc., of the content of a resource.

Abbreviations

Abbreviate terms for units of time (RDA B.5.3).

Recording

Record the duration in the form preferred by the agency creating the data.

Record the total duration using one of the following methods:

a) Record the exact time if readily ascertainable.

Element	Example
Duration	40 min.

b) If the exact time is not readily ascertainable, but an approximate time is stated or can be readily estimated, record that time preceded by *approximately*.

Element	Example
Duration	approximately 3 hr.

c) If the time cannot be readily ascertainable or estimated, omit it.

Duration of component parts

When recording duration of a resource consisting of more than one component part, record the duration of each component part.

Element	Example
Duration	17 min.
Duration	23 min.
Duration	9 min.
Duration of each act of a play.	

Alternative. Record the total duration of the resource. Apply this instruction instead of or in addition to recording the duration of the component parts.

Details of Duration (RDA 7.22.1.5)

Abbreviations

Abbreviate terms for units of time (RDA B.5.3).

Recording

Record a details note if considered important for identification or selection.

Element	Example
Details of Duration	A-side: 4:20; B-side: 4:03

Element	Example
Details of Duration	Running time given as 155 min. on container

Scale (RDA 7.25)

The ratio of the dimensions of an image or three-dimensional form contained or embodied in a resource to the dimensions of the thing it represents.

Scale applies to still images or three-dimensional forms *and* cartographic content (horizontal and vertical scale).

Scale can apply to horizontal, vertical, angular, and/or other measurements represented in the resource.

Core element

Scale is required only for cartographic content.

Recording Scale element sub-types

Record the scale of the resource as a representative fraction expressed as a ratio.

Element	Example
Horizontal Scale of Cartographic Content	1:32,500,000

Element	Example
Scale of Still Image or Three-Dimensional Form	4:1
Model of a human ear four times the actual size.	

> **Alternative.** For content that is not cartographic, record the scale using a term such as full size, life size, etc., as appropriate.

Record the scale even if it is already recorded as part of the title proper or other title information.

Element	Example
Title Proper	Italy 1:800 000
Horizontal Scale of Cartographic Content	1:800,000

Scale » Scale of Still Image or Three-Dimensional Form (RDA 7.25.2)

The ratio of the dimensions of a still image or three-dimensional form contained or embodied in a resource to the dimensions of the thing it represents.

Recording

Apply the common techniques for Scale.

If the still image or three-dimensional form is not to scale, and this fact is considered important for identification or selection, record *Not drawn to scale*.

Element	Example
Scale of Still Image or Three-Dimensional Form	1:2
Scale statement reads: Half the scale of the original.	

Scale » Horizontal Scale of Cartographic Content
(RDA 7.25.3)

The ratio of horizontal distances in the cartographic content of a resource to the actual distances they represent.

Core element

Recording

Apply the common techniques for Scale.

If the cartographic content is not drawn to scale, record *Not drawn to scale.* Do not estimate a scale.

Element	Example
Horizontal Scale of Cartographic Content	1:63,360

Scale » Vertical Scale of Cartographic Content (RDA 7.25.4)

The scale of elevation or vertical dimension of the cartographic content of a resource.

Core element

Recording

Apply the common techniques for Scale.

Record the vertical scale in addition to the horizontal scale when describing a relief model, other three-dimensional cartographic resource, or a two-dimensional cartographic representation of a three-dimensional feature (e.g., block diagram, profile). Indicate that it is the vertical scale.

Element	Example
Vertical Scale of Cartographic Content	Vertical scale 1:96,000

Scale » Additional Scale Information (RDA 7.25.5)

Supplemental information about scale such as a statement of comparative measurements or limitation of the scale to particular parts of the content of a resource.

Capitalization

Capitalize words as applicable (RDA appendix A).

Abbreviations

Use abbreviations or symbols for units of measurement (RDA appendix B).

Recording

Record additional scale information that appears on the resource. Substitute numerals for numbers expressed as words.

Element	Example
Horizontal Scale of Cartographic Content	1:250,000
Additional Scale Information	1 in. to 3.95 miles
Additional Scale Information	1 cm to 2.5 km

Element	Example
Hoizontal Scale of Cartographic Content	1:90,000
Additional Scale Information	not "1 inch to the mile"
In some cases enclose additional scale information in quotation marks.	

Projection of Cartographic Content (RDA 7.26)

The method or system used to represent the surface of the Earth or of a celestial sphere on a plane.

Recording

Record the projection of cartographic content if considered important for identification or selection.

Optional addition. Record phrases about meridians and/or parallels that are associated with the projection statement. Record information about ellipsoids as other details of cartographic content (see *Other Details of Cartographic Content*).

Element	Example
Projection of Cartographic Content	transverse Mercator projection, central meridian 35°13'30"E

Other Details of Cartographic Content (RDA 7.27)

Mathematical data and other features of the cartographic content of a resource not recorded in statements of scale, projection, and coordinates.

> **Related elements.** For instructions on recording technical details of the representation of cartographic content in digital form, see *Digital File Characteristic » Digital Representation of Cartographic Content.*

Recording

Record mathematical data that provides additional information not already recorded in statements of scale, projection, and coordinates.

Element	Example
Other Details of Cartographic Content	Oriented with north to right

Award (RDA 7.28)

A formal recognition of excellence, etc., given by an award- or prize-granting body, for the content of a resource.

Recording

Record information on awards if considered important for identification or selection.

Element	Example
Award	Academy Award: Best Documentary Feature

Note on Expression (RDA 7.29)

An annotation providing additional information about content recorded as an expression attribute.

Recording

For all Note on Expression elements, apply guidelines: *Notes* (p. 269).

Note on Expression » Note on Changes in Content Characteristics (RDA 7.29.2)

A note on changes in content characteristics that occur in subsequent issues or parts of a resource issued in successive parts or between iterations of an integrating resource.

Element	Example
Note on Changes in Content Characteristics	Volumes 1–3 in French, volumes 4–7 in German

6

Identifying Persons

Terminology

Person refers to an individual or an identity established by an individual (either alone or in collaboration with one or more individuals).

Persons include persons named in sacred scriptures or apocryphal books, fictitious and legendary persons, and real nonhuman entities.

SUPPORTING THE USER

When following the instructions in this chapter, a cataloger considers the attributes used to identify persons. By recording these attributes in separate elements and/or in access points, a cataloger supports a user in *identifying* the person represented by the data (i.e., confirming that the person represented is the one sought, or distinguishing between two or more persons with the same or similar names). The data recorded can also support users in *finding* persons that correspond to the user's stated search criteria.

Elements

Core designates a core element—see element instructions for more details; *AAP* designates an element that can be used in an Authorized Access Point; *VAP* designates an element that can be used in a Variant Access Point.

Elements for Persons				
Elements	**Sub-types**	**Core**	**AAP**	**VAP**
Name of the Person				
	Preferred Name for the Person	X	X	
	Variant Name for the Person			X
Date Associated with the Person				
	Date of Birth	X	X	X
	Date of Death	X	X	X
	Period of Activity of the Person	X	X	X
Title of the Person		X	X	X
Fuller Form of Name		X	X	X
Other Designation Associated with the Person		X	X	X
Profession or Occupation		X	X	X
Gender				
Place of Birth				
Place of Death				
Country Associated with the Person				
Place of Residence, Etc.				
Address of the Person				
Affiliation				
Language of the Person				
Field of Activity of the Person				
Biographical Information				
Identifier for the Person		X		

Record the following data as separate elements. These elements provide clarification or justification for the attributes recorded to identify persons.

Scope of Usage (RDA 8.8)

Date of Usage (RDA 8.9)

Status of Identification (RDA 8.10)

Undifferentiated Name Indicator (RDA 8.11)

Source Consulted (RDA 8.12)

Cataloguer's Note (RDA 8.13)

Sources of information

Take information for all attributes from any source, and follow additional guidance for Preferred Name for the Person.

Determine the preferred name for a person from the following sources (in order of preference):

a) the preferred sources of information in resources associated with the person
b) other formal statements appearing in resources associated with the person
c) other sources (including references sources)

Preferred Name for the Person

Name of the Person (RDA 9.2)

A word, character, or group of words and/or characters by which a person is known.

Name of the Person » Preferred Name for the Person
(RDA 9.2.2) AAP

The name or form of name chosen to identify the person.

Core element

Choosing Preferred Name for the Person

Generally choose the name, from the preferred sources of information, by which the person is commonly known. The name chosen can be the person's real name, pseudonym, title of nobility, nickname, initials, or other appellation.

Element	Example
Preferred Name for the Person	Griffith, D. W.
Not *David Wark Griffith*.	

Element	Example
Preferred Name for the Person	H. D.
Not Hilda Doolittle.	

Different forms of the same name

Forms vary in fullness

Choose the form most commonly found.

Forms vary in fullness; no one form predominates

Choose the latest form; in case of doubt about which is the latest form, choose the fuller or fullest form.

Name has appeared in different languages

Choose the form that corresponds to the language of most of the resources associated with the person.

> **Alternative.** Choose a well-accepted form in a language and script preferred by the agency creating the data.

Name has appeared in different languages; name does not appear in resources associated with the person, or in case of doubt

Choose the form most commonly found in reference sources of the person's country of residence or activity.

> **Exception.** For names in Greek or Latin versus other forms, choose the form most commonly found in reference sources.

Element	Example
Preferred Name for the Person	Grotius, Hugo
Not the form Hugo de Groot.	

> In case of doubt, choose the Greek or Latin form for persons who were active before, or mostly before, A.D. 1400. For persons active after that date, choose the form in the person's native or adopted language.

> **Exception.** If the first element of a person's name consists of a given name and/or a word or phrase associated with the person, determine the well-established form or forms in reference sources. If there is a well-established form of the name in a language preferred by the agency creating the data, choose that form of name as the preferred name.

Element	Example
Preferred Name for the Person	Francis of Assisi
Not Francesco d'Assisi.	

> In case of doubt, choose the form in the person's native or adopted language or the Latin form.

Variant spellings of a person's name are found and these variations are not the result of different transliterations

Choose the form of name found in the first resource received.

Different names for the same person

Person is known by more than one name

Choose the name by which the person is clearly most commonly known.

Person has changed his or her name

Choose the latest name or form of name as the preferred name.

> **Exception.** If there is reason to believe that an earlier name will persist as the name by which the person is better known, choose that name as the preferred name.

Individual has more than one identity

Choose the name associated with each identity as the preferred name for that identity.

a) Individual uses one or more pseudonyms (including joint pseudonyms): Consider the individual to have more than one identity. Choose the name associated with each pseudonym as the preferred name for that identity.

Element	Example
Preferred Name for the Person	Queen, Ellery
Joint pseudonym of Frederic Dannay and Manfred B. Lee.	

b) Individual uses his or her real name as well as one or more pseudonyms: Consider the individual to have more than one identity. Choose the name associated with the real identity and each pseudonym as the preferred names for those identities.

Element	Example
Preferred Name for the Person	Day Lewis, C.
Preferred Name for the Person	Blake, Nicholas
Real name C. Day Lewis *used in poetic and critical works; pseudonym* Nicholas Blake *used in detective novels.*	

> **Exception.** Individual uses only one pseudonym and does not use real name as a creator or contributor.
>
> Choose the pseudonym as the preferred name. Treat the real name as a variant name.

> **Related elements.** If an individual has more than one identity, record the relationships between these separate identities (see *Related Person*).

All other cases for different names for the same person

Choose in order of preference a) the name that appears most frequently in resources associated with the person, b) the name that appears most frequently in reference sources, c) the latest name.

Recording

Apply guidelines: *Names of Persons, Families, and Corporate Bodies* (p. 297).

   If the name consists of several parts, record as the first element that part of the name under which the person would normally be listed in authoritative alphabetic lists in the person's language, country of residence, or country of activity. Record the other part or parts of the name following the first element. See RDA appendix F for additional instructions for names in different languages.

> **Exception.** If a person's preference is known to be different from normal usage, follow that preference when choosing the part of the name to be recorded as the first element.

Recording names containing a surname (RDA 9.2.2.9)

Record the surname as the first element.

Element	Example
Preferred Name for the Person	Bernhardt, Sarah
Name: Sarah Bernhardt—*surname preceded by other parts of the name.*	

Element	Example
Preferred Name for the Person	Chiang, Kai-shek
Name: Chiang Kai-shek—*surname followed by other parts of the name.*	

Element	Example
Preferred Name for the Person	Mantovani
Names consists only of a surname.	

Element	Example
Preferred Name for the Person	G., Michael
Surname represented by an initial.	

Element	Example
Preferred Name for the Person	X, Malcolm
Part of the name that functions as a surname treated as a surname.	

Element	Example
Preferred Name for the Person	Seuss, Dr.
Variant Name for the Person	Dr. Seuss

Name consists of surname only, but word or phrase associated with the person or in reference sources treated as an integral part of the name.

Element	Example
Preferred Name for the Person	Davis, Maxwell, Mrs.

Married person identified only by a partner's name—term of address treated as an integral part of the name.

Element	Example
Preferred Name for the Person	Saur, Karl-Otto, Jr.

Word, etc. indicating relationship follow the person's given name or names (in Portuguese such words are part of the surname).

Element	Example
Preferred Name for the Person	More, Thomas
Other Designation Associated with the Person	Saint

The term Saint is not included as part of the name. Record Saint as a designation associated with the person.

Compound surnames (RDA 9.2.2.10)

Element	Example
Preferred Name for the Person	Day-Lewis, Daniel
Variant Name for the Person	Lewis, Daniel Day-

Compound surname consisting of two or more proper names separated by either a space or a hyphen.

Element	Example
Preferred Name for the Person	Brindle, Reginald Smith
Variant Name for the Person	Smith Brindle, Reginald

Family name Smith Brindle not used; author prefers to be listed under Brindle.

> ### *RDA ESSENTIALS* TIP
> Follow the preference of the person for recording a compound surname. If unknown, follow established usage in reference source, and if that is unknown, follow usage for the person's country of residence.

Surnames with separately written prefixes (RDA 9.2.2.11)

If a surname includes an article or preposition, or a combination of the two, record as the first element the part most commonly used as the first element.

Element	Example
Preferred Name for the Person	De la Mare, Walter
Variant Name for the Person	La Mare, Walter de
Variant Name for the Person	Mare, Walter de la

If the prefix is neither an article, nor a preposition, nor a combination of the two, record the prefix as the first element.

Element	Example
Preferred Name for the Person	Fitz Gerald, Gregory
Variant Name for the Person	Gerald, Gregory Fitz

Prefixes regularly or occasionally hyphenated or combined with surnames (RDA 9.2.2.12)

Record the prefix as the first element.

Element	Example
Preferred Name for the Person	Debure, Guillaume
Variant Name for the Person	Bure, Guillaume de

Names containing a title of nobility (RDA 9.2.2.14)

Record the proper name as the first element of the name if the person a) uses his or her title rather than a surname in resources with which he or she is associated *or* b) is listed under his or her title in reference sources.

Follow the proper name in the title by the personal name in direct order. Exclude unused given names.

Follow the personal name with the term of rank in the language in which it was conferred. Precede the personal name and the part of the title denoting rank by commas.

Omit the surname and term of rank if the person does not use a term of rank or a substitute for it.

Element	Example
Preferred Name for the Person	Bolingbroke, Henry St. John, Viscount
Variant Name for the Person	St. John, Henry, Viscount Bolingbroke
Preferred name uses proper name Bolingbroke *followed by personal name (*Henry St. John*) in direct order, followed by term of rank for* Viscount Bolingbroke*.*	

Element	Example
Preferred Name for the Person	Norwich, John Julius
Variant Name for the Person	Cooper, John Julius
For the preferred name, surname Cooper *and term of rank for* Viscount Norwich *not used;* Norwich *used as surname.*	

Names containing neither a surname nor a title of nobility (RDA 9.2.2.18)

Record as the first element the part of the name under which the person is listed in reference sources. In case of doubt, record the last part of the name, or part that functions as a surname, as the first element.

Element	Example
Preferred Name for the Person	Nelly

Element	Example
Preferred Name for the Person	Eric, the Red
Include words or phrases as an integral part of the name that indicate an association with a place of origin or domicile, an occupation, or other characteristics (in resources associated with the person or in reference sources).	

Element	Example
Preferred Name for the Person	Elizabeth I
Treat a roman numeral associated with a given name as an integral part of the name (e.g., in the case of some popes, royalty, and ecclesiastics).	

Names consisting of initials, or separate letters, or numerals (RDA 9.2.2.21)

Record the initials, letters, or numerals in direct order. Include any typographic devices when they appear as part of multi-letter abbreviations of a name, but omit them when they follow single-letter initials. Include any words or phrases associated with the initials, letters, or numerals as an integral part of the name.

Element	Example
Preferred Name for the Person	Q.E.D.

Names consisting of a phrase (RDA 9.2.2.22–9.2.2.26)

If a person is commonly identified by a) a phrase or appellation that does not contain a given name *or* b) a phrase that consists of a given name or names preceded by words other than a term of address or a title of position or office, *then* consider this phrase or appellation to be the preferred name for the person. Record the name in direct order.

Element	Example
Preferred Name for the Person	Miss Piggy
Variant Name for the Person	Piggy, Miss

A name consisting of a phrase sometimes has the appearance of a name consisting of a given name or initials, and a surname. When this occurs, record as the first element the word that has the appearance of a surname.

Element	Example
Preferred Name for the Person	Other, A. N.
Variant Name for the Person	A. N. Other

If a person is commonly identified by a phrase consisting of a given name preceded by a term of address or a title of position or office, consider this phrase to be the preferred name for the person. Record the given name as the first element. Record words or phrases commonly associated with the person (e.g., those denoting place of origin, domicile, occupation, or other characteristics).

Element	Example
Preferred Name for the Person	Jemima, Aunt
Variant Name for the Person	Aunt Jemima

If a person is commonly identified by a phrase that contains the name of another person, consider this phrase to be the preferred name for the person. Record the phrase in direct order.

Element	Example
Preferred Name for the Person	Pseudo-Brutus

If a person is commonly identified by a characterizing word or phrase in resources associated with the person and in reference sources, consider this word or phrase to be the preferred name for the person. Record the phrase in direct order.

Element	Example
Preferred Name for the Person	A Physician

Alternative. Omit an initial article when recording a characterizing word or phrase.

Element	Example
Preferred Name for the Person	Physician

Variant Names and Other Elements

Name of the Person » Variant Name for the Person
(RDA 9.3.2) **VAP**

A name or form of name by which is a person is known that differs from the name or form of name chosen as the preferred name.

Related elements. For persons who have two or more identities, use the instructions on recording relationships between related persons (see *Related Person*).

Recording

Apply guidelines: *Names of Persons, Families, and Corporate Bodies* (p. 297).
Record a variant name when it is different from the name recorded as the preferred name. Record as a variant name a name or form of name used by a person *or* a name or form of name found in reference sources *or* a form of name resulting from a different transliteration of the name.

Element	Example
Preferred Name for the Person	West, Morris
Variant Name for the Person	West, Morris L.
Most common form: Morris West.	

Element	Example
Preferred Name for the Person	Eliot, George
Variant Name for the Person	Cross, Marian Evans
Preferred name is pseudonym; variant name is real name which is not used as Creator or Contributor.	

Element	Example
Preferred Name for the Person	Brontë, Charlotte
Variant Name for the Person	Nicholls, Charlotte
Earlier name of person is preferred name; later name is variant name.	

Element	Example
Preferred Name for the Person	Hughes, Dorothy B.
Variant Name for the Person	Flanagan, Dorothy Belle
Name after author's marriage, before which the name used in works was Dorothy Belle Flanagan.	

Element	Example
Preferred Name for the Person	Ali, Muhammad
Variant Name for the Person	Clay, Cassius
Name changed from Cassius Clay.	

Variant names for persons include real names if only pseudonym is used, names not used by a person with a name in a religious vocation, and earlier or later names not used because of a name change.

If the name recorded as the preferred name for a person body has one or more alternative linguistic forms (different language form, different script, different spelling, different transliteration), record them as variant names.

Record other variant names and variant forms of the name if considered important for identification or access.

Date Associated with the Person (RDA 9.3)

A significant date associated with the history of a person (e.g., date of birth, date of death).

Core element

Date of Birth and Date of Death are core elements. Period of Activity of the Person is a core element only when needed to distinguish a person from another person with the same name.

Date Associated with the Person » Date of Birth
(RDA 9.3.2) AAP VAP

The year a person was born. Date of birth may also include the month or month and day of the person's birth.

Core element

Recording

Apply guidelines: *Dates Associated with Persons, Families, and Corporate Bodies* (p. 303).

Date Associated with the Person » Date of Death
(RDA 9.3.3) AAP VAP

The year a person died. Date of death may also include the month or month and day of the person's death.

Core element

Recording

Apply guidelines: *Dates Associated with Persons, Families, and Corporate Bodies* (p. 303).

Date Associated with the Person » Period of Activity of the Person (RDA 9.3.4) AAP VAP

A date or range of dates indicative of the period in which a person was active in his or her primary field of endeavor.

Core element

Period of Activity of the Person is a core element when needed to distinguish a person from another person with the same name.

Recording

Apply guidelines: *Dates Associated with Persons, Families, and Corporate Bodies* (p. 303).

Record a date or range of dates indicative of the period in which the person was active if a person's date of birth and date of death are both unknown.

If it is not possible to establish specific years of activity, record the century or centuries in which the person was active.

Title of the Person (RDA 9.4) AAP VAP

A word or phrase indicative of royalty, nobility, ecclesiastical rank or office, or a term of address for a person or religious vocation.

Title of the Person includes other terms indicative of rank, honor, or office, including initials and/or abbreviations representing an academic degree, or membership in an organization.

Title of the Person excludes terms of address that simply indicate gender or marital status (e.g., Mr., Mrs.).

Core element

Title of the person is a core element when it is a word or phrase indicative of royalty, nobility, or ecclesiastical rank or office, or a term of address for a person of religious vocation. Any other term indicative of rank, honor, or office is a core element when needed to distinguish a person from another person with the same name.

Capitalization

Capitalize title or term as applicable to the language involved (RDA A.2.4).

Recording

Record an appropriate term for title of the person.

Categories of Title of the Person

a) Titles of royalty (core element)

Element	Example
Title of the Person	Queen of Great Britain

Element	Example
Title of the Person	Empress, consort of Akihito, Emperor of Japan

Element	Example
Title of the Person	Princess, daughter of Juliana, Queen of the Netherlands

b) Titles of nobility (core element)

Element	Example
Title of the Person	marchese
For a nobleman or noblewoman whose title has not been recorded as the first element in the preferred name, record the title of nobility in the language in which it was conferred.	

c) Popes (core element)

Element	Example
Title of the Person	Pope

d) Bishops, etc. (core element)

Element	Example
Title of the Person	Cardinal

e) Other persons of religious vocations (core element)

Element	Example
Title of the Person	Rabbi

f) Other term of rank, honor, or office (core element if needed to distinguish persons with the same name)

Element	Example
Title of the Person	Captain

Element	Example
Title of the Person	Sir

Element	Example
Title of the Person	Ph. D.

Fuller Form of Name (RDA 9.5) AAP VAP

The full form of a part of a name represented only by an initial or abbreviation in the form chosen as the preferred name *or* a part of the name not included in the form chosen as the preferred name.

Core element

A fuller form of name is a core element when needed to distinguish a person from another person with the same name.

Recording

Apply guidelines: *Names of Persons, Families, and Corporate Bodies* (p. 297).

Record a fuller form of a person's name if it is known and the preferred name does not include all of that fuller form. Record the name in its fuller form as a variant name, when appropriate (see *Variant Name for the Person*).

Examples

Preferred Name for the Person: Known given names (spelled out or initials) *or* known surname (spelled out or initials) not used.

Fuller Form of Name: All of the known given names (spelled out or initials) *or* all of the known surname (spelled out or initials).

Element	Example
Preferred Name for the Person	King, Mrs.
Fuller Form of Name	Annie Liddon
Variant Name for the Person	King, Annie Liddon

Element	Example
Preferred Name for the Person	Smith, Nancy E.
Fuller Form of Name	Nancy Elizabeth
Variant Name for the Person	Smith, Nancy Elizabeth

Element	Example
Preferred Name for the Person	Johnson, Barbara
Fuller Form of Name	Barbara A.
Variant Name for the Person	Johnson, Barbara A.

Element	Example
Preferred Name for the Person	Rodríguez L., Oswaldo
Fuller Form of Name	Rodríguez Larralde
Variant Name for the Person	Rodríguez Larralde, Oswaldo
Fuller form of surname known but not used in Preferred Name for the Person.	

Preferred Name for the Person: Known given names (spelled out or initials) *and* known surname (spelled out or initials) not used.

Fuller Form of Name: All of the known given names (spelled out or initials) *and* all of the known surname (spelled out or initials).

Element	Example
Preferred Name for the Person	H. D.
Fuller Form of Name	Hilda Doolittle
Variant Name for the Person	Doolittle, Hilda

Element	Example
Preferred Name for the Person	Rodríguez V., Manuel G.
Fuller Form of Name	Manuel Guillermo Rodríguez Valbuena
Variant Name for the Person	Rodríguez Valbuena, Manuel Guillermo

Other Designation Associated with the Person (RDA 9.6)
AAP VAP

A term other than a title that is associated with a person's name.

Core element
Other Designation Associated with the Person is a core element for a Christian saint, a spirit, a person named in a sacred scripture or an apocryphal book, a fictitious or legendary person, or a real nonhuman entity. For other persons, Other Designation Associated with the Person is a core element when needed to distinguish a person from another person with the same name.

Capitalization
Capitalize the first word and any proper names (RDA A.2.4).

Recording
Record an appropriate term for designation associated with the person.

Categories of Other Designation Associated with the Person

a) For a Christian saint, record *Saint* (core element).
b) For a spirit, record *Spirit* (core element).
c) For a person named in a sacred scripture or an apocryphal book, record an appropriate designation (core element).
   Examples: *Angel, Biblical figure, Demon, Talmudic figure*
d) For a fictitious or legendary person, record *Fictitious character, Legendary character*, or another appropriate designation (core element).
   Examples: *Greek deity, Mythical animal, Vampire*
e) For a real nonhuman entity, record a designation for type, species, or breed (core element).
   Examples: *Chimpanzee, Portuguese water dog, Whale*
f) Record an appropriate designation if none of the following attributes are sufficient or appropriate for distinguishing between two or more persons with the same name: Date of Birth, Date of Death, Fuller Form of Name, Period of Activity of the Person, Profession or Occupation, Title of the Person (other term of rank, honor, or office). (core element if needed to distinguish persons with the same name).
   Examples: *Brother of Andrew Lang, Cree Indian, Ship captain's wife*

Profession or Occupation (RDA 9.16) AAP VAP

A person's vocation or avocation.

Core element

Profession or occupation is a core element for a person whose name consists of a phrase or appellation not conveying the idea of a person. For other persons, profession or occupation is a core element when needed to distinguish a person from another person with the same name.

Capitalization

Capitalize the first word and any proper names (RDA A.2.4).

Recording

Record an appropriate term for class of persons engaged in the profession or occupation.

Element	Example
Profession or Occupation	Architect

Gender (RDA 9.7)

The gender with which a person identifies.

Recording

Record the gender of the person using an appropriate term in a language preferred by the agency creating the data. Select a term from a standard list, if available.

Place of Birth (RDA 9.8)

The town, city, province, state, and/or country in which a person was born.

Recording

Apply guidelines: *Places* (Group 2 elements) (p. 305).

Element	Example
Place of Birth	N.Z.
Place of birth of filmmaker Peter Jackson.	

Place of Death (RDA 9.9)

The town, city, province, state, and/or country in which a person died.

Recording

Apply guidelines: *Places* (Group 2 elements) (p. 305).

Country Associated with the Person (RDA 9.10)

A country with which a person is identified.

Recording

Apply guidelines: *Places* (Group 2 elements) (p. 305).

Element	Example
Country Associated with the Person	Russia
Country Associated with the Person	France
Country Associated with the Person	U.S.
Countries associated with the composer Igor Stravinsky.	

Place of Residence, Etc. (RDA 9.11)

A town, city, province, state and/or country in which a person resides or has resided, or another significant place associated with the person other than place of birth, place of death, or residence (e.g., a place where a person has worked or studied).

Recording

Apply guidelines: *Places* (Group 2 elements) (p. 305).

Element	Example
Place of Residence, Etc.	Jackson, Miss.
Place of residence, etc., of author Eudora Welty.	

Address of the Person (RDA 9.12)

The address of a person's place of residence, business, or employer and/or an e-mail or Internet address.

Recording

Record the address of the person's place of residence, business, or employer, and/or an e-mail or Internet address.

Element	Example
Address of the Person	www.rodneysharman.com

Affiliation (RDA 9.13)

A group with which a person is affiliated or has been affiliated through employment, membership, cultural identity, etc.

Recording

Record the preferred name for the group by applying the instructions for Preferred Name for the Corporate Body.

Element	Example
Affiliation	New York State College of Agriculture. Department of Entomology

Language of the Person (RDA 9.14)

A language a person uses when writing for publication, broadcasting, etc.

Recording

Record an appropriate term or terms in a language preferred by the agency creating the data. Select terms from a standard list of names of languages, if available.

Field of Activity of the Person (RDA 9.15)

A field of endeavor, area of expertise, etc., in which a person is engaged or was engaged.

Capitalization

Capitalize the first word and any proper names (RDA A.2.4).

Recording

Record an appropriate term for field of activity.

Element	Example
Field of Activity of the Person	Mathematics

Biographical Information (RDA 9.17)

Information about the life or history of a person.

Recording

Record information about the life or history of the person. Incorporate information associated with other identifying elements for the person.

Identifier for the Person (RDA 9.18)

A character string uniquely associated with a person, or with a surrogate for a person (e.g., an authority record). The identifier serves to differentiate that person from other persons.

Core element

Recording

Record an identifier for the person. Precede the identifier with the name or an identification of the agency, etc., responsible for assigning the identifier, if readily ascertainable.

7
Identifying Families

Family refers to two or more persons related by birth, marriage, adoption, civil union, or similar legal status, or who otherwise present themselves as a family.

SUPPORTING THE USER

When following the instructions in this chapter, a cataloger considers the attributes used to identify families. By recording these attributes in separate elements and/or access points, a cataloger supports a user in *identifying* the family represented by the data (i.e., confirming that the family represented is the one sought, or distinguishing between two or more families with the same or similar names). The data recorded can also support users in *finding* families that correspond to the user's stated search criteria.

Elements

Core designates a core element—see element instructions for more details; *AAP* designates an element that can be used in an Authorized Access Point; *VAP* designates an element that can be used in a Variant Access Point.

Elements for Families				
Elements	**Sub-types**	**Core**	**AAP**	**VAP**
Name of the Family				
	Preferred Name for the Family	X	X	
	Variant Name for the Family			X
Type of Family		X	X	X
Date Associated with the Family		X	X	X
Place Associated with the Family		X	X	X
Prominent Member of the Family		X	X	X
Hereditary Title				X
Language of the Family				
Family History				
Identifier for the Family		X		

Record the following data as separate elements. These elements provide clarification or justification for the attributes recorded to identify families.

Scope of Usage (RDA 8.8)

Status of Identification (RDA 8.10)

Source Consulted (RDA 8.12)

Cataloguer's Note (RDA 8.13)

Sources of information

Take information for all attributes from any source, and follow additional guidance for Preferred Name for the Family.

Determine the preferred name for a family from the following sources (in order of preference):

a) the preferred sources of information in resources associated with the family

b) other formal statements appearing in resources associated with the family

c) other sources (including references sources)

Preferred Name for the Family

Name of the Family (RDA 10.2)

A word, character, or group of words and/or characters by which a family is known.

Name of the Family » Preferred Name for the Family
(RDA 10.2.2) AAP

The name or form of name chosen to identify the family.

Core element

Choosing Preferred Name for the Family

Generally choose the name, from the preferred sources of information, by which the family is commonly known. The name chosen can be the surname (or equivalent) used by members of the family, the name of a royal house or dynasty, or the name of a clan, etc.

Element	Example
Preferred Name for the Family	Van den Bergh

Element	Example
Preferred Name for the Family	Windsor

Different forms of the same name

If a family is known by more than one form of the same name, apply the same instructions used for choosing the preferred name for a person (for fullness, language, names found in a nonpreferred script, and spelling).

Different names for the same family

Family known by more than one name

Choose in order of preference a) the name that appears most frequently in resources associated with the family, b) the name that appears most frequently in reference sources.

Family has changed its name (including changes from one language to another)

Choose the earlier name as the preferred name for use with resources associated with the earlier name. Choose the later name as the preferred name for use with resources associated with the later name.

> **Related elements.** If a family has changed its name, record the relationships between the earlier form and the later form (see *Related Family*).

Recording

Apply guidelines: *Names of Persons, Families, and Corporate Bodies* (p. 297).

If the name consists of several parts, record as the first element that part of the name under which the family would normally be listed in authoritative alphabetic lists in its language, country of residence, or country of activity. Record the other part or parts of the name following the first element. See RDA appendix F for additional instructions for names in different languages.

> **Exception.** If a family's preference is known to be different from normal usage, follow that preference when choosing the part of the name to be recorded as the first element.

If the name chosen as the preferred name consists of a surname, or a name that functions as a surname, record that name as the family name. Apply the same instructions on recording surnames that are used for the surnames of persons.

Element	Example
Preferred Name for the Family	Giroux

Apply the same additional instructions on recording surnames that are used for the surnames of persons, as applicable: compound surnames, surnames with separately written prefixes, and prefixes with hyphenated or combined with surnames.

If the name chosen as the preferred name consists of the name of a royal house, a dynasty, a clan, etc., record that name as the family name.

Element	Example
Preferred Name for the Family	Windsor

Variant Names and Other Elements

Name of the Family » Variant Name for the Family
(RDA 10.2.3) VAP

A name or form of name by which a family is known that differs from the name or form of name chosen as the preferred name.

> **Related elements.** For families who have changed their name, use the instructions on recording relationships between related families (see *Related Family*).

Recording

Apply guidelines: *Names of Persons, Families, and Corporate Bodies* (p. 297).

Record a variant name when it is different from the name recorded as the preferred name. Record as a variant name: a name or form of name used by a family *or* a name or form of name found in reference sources *or* a form of name resulting from a different transliteration of the name.

Record as a variant name a form using a different part of the name as the first element if the name might reasonably be searched by that part.

If the name recorded as the preferred name for a family has one or more alternative linguistic forms (different language form, different script, different spelling, different transliteration) record them as variant names.

Element	Example
Preferred Name for the Family	DiPietro
Variant Name for the Family	Di Pietro

If a family has a hereditary title associated with its name, record this title as a variant name. Record the proper name in the title as the first element, followed by a comma and the term of rank in the plural.

Element	Example
Preferred Name for the Family	Chandos
Variant Name for the Family	Chandos, Dukes of

Type of Family (RDA 10.3) AAP VAP

A categorization or generic descriptor for the type of family.

Core element

Capitalization

Capitalize first word of the term (RDA A.2.6).

Recording

Record an appropriate term for type of family (e.g., *Family, Clan, Royal house, Dynasty*).

Date Associated with the Family (RDA 10.4) AAP VAP

A significant date associated with the history of a family.

Core element

Recording

Apply guidelines: *Dates Associated with Persons, Families, and Corporate Bodies* (p. 303).

Element	Example
Date Associated with the Family	1802–1945

Element	Example
Date Associated with the Family	4th century–9th century

Place Associated with the Family (RDA 10.5) AAP VAP

A place where a family resides or has resided or has some connection.

Core element

A place associated with the family is a core element when needed to distinguish a family from another family with the same name.

Recording

Apply guidelines: *Places* (Group 2 elements) (p. 305).

Element	Example
Place Associated with the Family	Sydney, N.S.W.

Element	Example
Place Associated with the Family	Wis.

Prominent Member of the Family (RDA 10.6) AAP VAP

A well-known individual who is a member of a family.

Core element

The name of a prominent member of the family is a core element when needed to distinguish a family from another family with the same name.

Recording

Record the name of a prominent member or members of the family in the form used for Authorized Access Point Representing a Person (p. 315).

Element	Example
Prominent Member of the Family	Peale, Norman Vincent, 1898–1993

Hereditary Title (RDA 10.7) VAP

A title of nobility, etc., associated with a family.

Recording

Record a hereditary title associated with the family in direct order in the plural form.

Record hereditary titles as separate elements and/or as variant names (see *Variant Name for the Family*).

Element	Example
Hereditary Title	Dukes of Chandos

Element	Example
Variant Name for the Family	Chandos, Dukes of

Language of the Family (RDA 10.8)

A language a family uses in its communications.

Recording

Record an appropriate term or terms in a language preferred by the agency creating the data. Select terms from a standard list of names of languages, if available.

Family History (RDA 10.9)

Biographical information about the family and/or its members.

Recording

Record biographical information about the family and/or its members. Incorporate information associated with other identifying elements for the family.

Element	Example
Family History	Italian rulers, bankers, merchants, collectors, and patrons of the arts, active in Florence particularly from 15th through mid-18th centuries

Identifier for the Family (RDA 10.10)

A character string uniquely associated with a family, or with a surrogate for a family (e.g., an authority record). The identifier serves to differentiate that family from other families.

Core element

Recording

Record an identifier for the family. Precede the identifier with the name or an identification of the agency, etc., responsible for assigning the identifier, if readily ascertainable.

8

Identifying
Corporate Bodies

Corporate body refers to an organization or group of persons and/or organizations that is identified by a particular name and that acts, or may act, as a unit.

A body is considered to be a corporate body only if it is identified by a particular name and if it acts, or may act, as a unit. A particular name consists of words that are a specific appellation rather than a general description.

Typical examples of corporate bodies are associations, institutions, business firms, non-profit enterprises, governments, government agencies, projects and programs, religious bodies, local church groups identified by the name of the church, and conferences.

Ad hoc events (e.g., athletic contests, exhibitions, expeditions, fairs, and festivals) and vessels (e.g., ships and spacecraft) are considered to be corporate bodies.

SUPPORTING THE USER

When following the instructions in this chapter, a cataloger considers the attributes used to identify corporate bodies. By recording these attributes in separate elements and/or access points, a cataloger supports a user in *identifying* the corporate body represented by the data (i.e., confirming that the corporate body represented is the one sought, or distinguishing between two or more corporate bodies with the same or similar names). The data recorded can also support users in *finding* corporate bodies that correspond to the user's stated search criteria.

Elements

Core designates a core element—see element instructions for more details; *AAP* designates an element that can be used in an Authorized Access Point; *VAP* designates an element that can be used in a Variant Access Point.

Elements for Corporate Bodies				
Elements	**Sub-types**	**Core**	**AAP**	**VAP**
Name of the Corporate Body				
	Preferred Name for the Corporate Body	X	X	
	Variant Name for the Corporate Body			X
Place Associated with the Corporate Body				
	Location of Conference, Etc.	X	X	X
	Other Place Associated with the Corporate Body	X	X	X
Date Associated with the Corporate Body				
	Date of Conference, Etc.	X	X	X
	Date of Establishment	X	X	X
	Period of Activity of the Corporate Body	X	X	X
Associated Institution		X	X	X
Number of a Conference, Etc.		X	X	X
Other Designation Associated with the Corporate Body				
	Type of Corporate Body	X	X	X
	Type of Jurisdiction	X	X	X
	Other Designation	X	X	X
Language of the Corporate Body				
Address of the Corporate Body				
Field of Activity of the Corporate Body				
Corporate History				
Identifier for the Corporate Body		X		

Record the following data as separate elements. These elements provide clarification or justification for the attributes recorded to identify corporate bodies.

Scope of Usage (RDA 8.8)

Status of Identification (RDA 8.10)

Source Consulted (RDA 8.12)

Cataloguer's Note (RDA 8.13)

Sources of information

Take information for all attributes from any source, and follow additional guidance for Preferred Name for the Corporate Body.

Determine the preferred name for a corporate body from the following sources (in order of preference):

a) the preferred sources of information in resources associated with the corporate body
b) other formal statements appearing in resources associated with the corporate body
c) other sources (including references sources)

Preferred Name for the Corporate Body

Name of the Corporate Body (RDA 11.2)

A word, character, or group of words and/or characters by which a corporate body is known.

Name of the Corporate Body » Preferred Name for the Corporate Body (RDA 11.2.2.) AAP

The name or form of name chosen to identify the corporate body.

Core element

Choosing Preferred Name for the Corporate Body

Choose the name, from the preferred sources of information, by which the corporate body is commonly identified.

Element	Example
Preferred Name for the Corporate Body	British Museum

Element	Example
Preferred Name for the Corporate Body	Voltamp Electric Mfg. Co.

Different forms of the same name

Variant forms found in resources associated with the body

Choose the name that appears in the preferred sources of information.

Variant forms appear in the preferred source of information

Choose the form that is presented formally. If no form is presented formally, or if all forms are presented formally, choose the most commonly found form of the name.

No most commonly found form of the name

Choose a brief form of the name. The brief form may be an initialism or an acronym. The brief form must be sufficiently specific to differentiate the body from others with the same or similar brief names.

No brief form of the name that is specific enough to differentiate two or more bodies with the same or similar names

Prefer a form found in reference sources over the official form.

Variant spellings of the name appear in resources associated with the body

Choose the form of name found in the first resource received.

Name has appeared in different languages

Choose the form in the official language of the body.

Alternative. Choose a form in a language preferred by the agency creating the data.

Name has appeared in different languages; more than one official language

Choose the form in an official language that is a language preferred by the agency creating the data. If the official language is not one preferred by the agency, or the language is not known, choose the form in the language used predominantly in resources associated with the corporate body. In case of doubt, choose the form presented first in the first resource received. Apply these instructions also to names of international bodies (RDA 11.2.2.5.3).

Element	Example
Preferred Name for the Corporate Body	European Economic Community
Not Communauté économique européenne *or Europese Economische Gemeenschap if English is a preferred language of the agency creating the data.*	

Corporate body is frequently identified by a conventional name rather than its real or official name in reference sources in its own language

Generally, choose the conventional name. Exceptions are made in some cases (see RDA 11.2.2.5.4), such as for the names of religious orders and societies which are recorded in a language preferred by the agency creating the data. For governments, generally choose the conventional name but choose the official name if it is in common use.

Element	Example
Preferred Name for the Corporate Body	York Minster
Not Metropolitan Church of St. Peter York. *Choose the conventional name.*	

Change of name (including changes from one language to another)

Choose the earlier name as the preferred name for use with resources associated with the earlier name. Choose the later name as the preferred name for use with resources associated with the later name.

> **Related elements.** Record the relationships between the earlier and later names of the body (see *Related Corporate Body*).

Element	Example
Preferred Name for the Corporate Body	Pennsylvania State University
Preferred Name for the Corporate Body	Pennsylvania State College
Name changed from earlier form: Pennsylvania State College.	

Recording

Apply guidelines: *Names of Persons, Families, and Corporate Bodies* (p. 297) and *Places* (Group 1 elements) (p. 305) for names of governments.

Record the name of a corporate body as it appears in resources associated with the body. If the name does not appear in resources associated with the body, or in case of doubt, record it in the form most commonly found in reference sources.

Names consisting of or containing initials (RDA 11.2.2.7)

If the name of a corporate body consists of or contains initials, omit or include full stops and other marks of punctuation according to the most commonly found usage of the body. In case of doubt, omit the full stops, etc.

Element	Example
Preferred Name for the Corporate Body	L.I.F.E. Choir

Initial articles (RDA 11.2.2.8)

When recording the preferred name of a corporate body, include an initial article, if present.

Element	Example
Preferred Name for the Corporate Body	The Library Association

Alternative. Omit an initial article unless the name is to be accessed under the article (e.g., a corporate name that begins with an article that is the first part of the name of a person or place).

Element	Example
Preferred Name for the Corporate Body	Library Association

Omitting terms (RDA 11.2.2.9—11.2.2.11)

Omit the following from the preferred name for the corporate body: citations of honors; terms indicating incorporation, state ownership, or type of incorporated entity (but transpose term to end of name if needed to make it clear that the name is that of a corporate body); abbreviations occurring before the name of a ship; and the number or year of convocation of a conference, etc.

Element	Example
Preferred Name for the Corporate Body	Royal Ulster Constabulary
Phrase citing an honor or order dropped: Royal Ulster Constabulary George Cross.	

Element	Example
Preferred Name for the Corporate Body	American Cancer Society
Term indicating incorporation dropped: American Cancer Society, Inc.	

Element	Example
Preferred Name for the Corporate Body	Arizona
Type of Corporate Body	Battleship
Abbreviation before name of a ship dropped: U.S.S. Arizona.	

Element	Example
Preferred Name for the Corporate Body	Schweizerische Grönland-Expedition
Year dropped from expedition: Schweizerische Grönland-Expedition 1912/13.	

Element	Example
Preferred Name for the Corporate Body	San Francisco Art Association. Annual Drawing and Print Exhibition
Number dropped from exhibition treated as a subordinate body: San Francisco Art Association. Twenty-second Annual Drawing and Print Exhibition.	

Recording names of subordinate and related bodies (RDA 11.2.2.13)

Record the name of a subordinate body or a related body by applying the basic instructions for recording the preferred name of the corporate body, unless its name belongs to one or more of the types of corporate bodies listed below. For these types record the name of the subordinate or related body as a subdivision of the higher or related body. Record it in the form of a subdivision of the authorized access point representing the higher or related body. Follow the instructions for direct or indirect subdivision.

Omit from the subdivision the name (or abbreviation of the name) of the higher or related body in noun form unless the omission would result in a name that does not make sense.

Element	Example
Preferred Name for the Corporate Body	Stanford University. Archives
Not Stanford University. Stanford University Archives; *name is presented as* Stanford University Archives	

In case of doubt about whether the corporate body is subordinate or whether it falls within the scope of a specific instruction, record the name of the body directly.

Element	Example
Preferred Name for the Corporate Body	Governor's Fellowship Program (Ind.)
Not Indiana. Governor's Fellowship Program.	

Types of subordinate and related corporate bodies recorded subordinately, with examples (RDA 11.2.2.14)

Body whose name implies it is a part of another (e.g., Department, Division, Section, Branch)

> Bangalore University. Department of Botany
> Kent (England). Land Use and Transport Policy Unit

Body whose name implies administrative subordination (e.g., Committee, Commission)

> Apply only if the name of the higher body is required for the identification of the subordinate body.
>
> > International Dairy Congress (22nd : 1986 : The Hague, Netherlands). Organizing Committee
> > Canada. Royal Commission on Banking and Finance
> > *but* Honolulu Committee on Aging

Body whose name is general in nature (e.g., contains neither distinctive proper nouns or adjectives, nor subject words) or simply indicates a geographic, chronological, or numbered or lettered subdivision of a parent body

> American Dental Association. Research Institute
> United States. National Labor Relations Board. Library
> Canadian Jewish Congress. Central Region
> Knights of Labor. District Assembly No. 3

Body whose name does not convey the idea of a corporate body and does not contain the name of the higher body

> Illinois. Bureau of Employment Security. Research & Analysis
> *but* BC Fisheries

University faculty, school, college, institute, laboratory, etc., with name that simply indicates a particular field of study

> Princeton University. Bureau of Urban Research
> *but* Harvard Law School

Non-governmental body with name that includes the entire name of the higher or related body

Distinguish cases in which the subordinate body's name includes the names of higher bodies from cases in which the names of higher bodies appear only in association with the subordinate body's name.

> American Legion. Auxiliary
> (*Name:* American Legion Auxiliary)
> United Methodist Church (U.S.). General Conference
> (*Name:* General Conference of the United Methodist Church)
> *but* BBC Symphony Orchestra
> *but* Utah Museum of Fine Arts
> (*not* University of Utah. Museum of Fine Art)

Ministry or similar major executive agency (i.e., one that has no other agency above it) as defined by official publications of the government in question

> United States. National Aeronautics and Space Administration

Examples of other categories (RDA 11.2.2.18–11.2.2.29)

Government official or a religious official

> Indonesia. President
> Germany. Chancellor (2005– : Merkel)

Legislative body

> Idaho. Legislature
> Australia. Parliament. Senate. Legal and Constitutional References Committee

Constitutional convention

> New Hampshire. Constitutional Convention (1902)

Court

> Vermont. Court of Chancery
> United States. District Court (Delaware)

Principal service of the armed forces of a government

> United States. Marine Corps
> Great Britain. Army. Army, Third
> New York (State). National Guard

Embassy, consulate, etc.

> India. High Commission (Trinidad and Tobago)
> United States. Consulate (Port Louis, Mauritius)

Delegation to an international or intergovernmental body

> United States. Delegation (International Monetary Conference (1892 : Brussels, Belgium))

Direct or indirect subdivision (RDA 11.2.2.15)

Unless instructed otherwise, record the name of the body as a subdivision of the authorized access point representing the lowest organizational unit in the hierarchy that is recorded directly under its own name.

Element	Example
Preferred Name for the Corporate Body	Public Library Association. Audiovisual Committee
Hierarchy: American Library Association—Public Library Association—Audiovisual Committee. Public Library Association *is the lowest organizational unit recorded directly under its own name.*	

Omit intervening units in the hierarchy, unless the name of the subordinate or related body has been, or is likely to be, used by another body recorded as a subdivision of the authorized access point representing the same higher or related body. In that case, interpose the name of the lowest unit in the hierarchy that will distinguish between the bodies.

Element	Example
Preferred Name for the Corporate Body	University of Texas at Austin. Petroleum Extension Service
Hierarchy: University of Texas at Austin - Division of Continuing Education - Petroleum Extension Service. *Intervening units omitted.*	

Element	Example
Preferred Name for the Corporate Body	California. Department of Corrections. Research Division
Hierarchy: California Health and Welfare Agency Department of Corrections - Research Division. *Other California departments have units called* Research Division.	

Record other forms of direct or indirect subdivision as variant names (see *Variant Name for the Corporate Body*).

Joint committees, commissions, etc. (RDA 11.2.2.16)

Omit the names of the parent bodies in these cases a) when the names of the parent bodies occur within or at the end of the name *and* b) when the name of the joint unit is distinctive without them.

Element	Example
Preferred Name for the Corporate Body	Joint Committee on Insulator Standards
Name: Joint Committee on Insulator Standards of the Edison Electric Institute and the National Electrical Manufacturers Association.	

Element	Example
Preferred Name for the Corporate Body	Joint Committee of the American Library Association and the Rural Sociological Society
Name of joint committee is not distinctive without names of parent bodies.	

If the names of the parent bodies are recorded as subdivisions of a common higher body, record the name of the joint unit as a subordinate body of the common higher body.

Element	Example
Preferred Name for the Corporate Body	American Library Association. Joint Committee to Compile a List of International Subscription Agents
A joint committee of the Acquisitions and Serials sections of the American Library Association's Resources and Technical Services Division.	

Conventionalized names for state and local units of United States political parties (RDA 11.2.2.17)

Record the name of a state or local unit of a political party in the United States as a subdivision of the party. Record it in the form of a subdivision of the authorized access point representing the party. Omit from the name of the unit any indication of the name of the party or the state or locality.

Element	Example
Preferred Name for the Corporate Body	Democratic Party (Mo.). State Committee
Name: Missouri Democratic State Committee.	

Variant Names and Other Elements

Name of the Corporate Body » Variant Name for the Corporate Body (RDA 11.2.3) VAP

A name or form of name by which a corporate body is known that differs from the name or form of name chosen as the preferred name.

> **Related elements.** For corporate bodies that have changed their name, use the instructions on recording relationships between related corporate bodies (see *Related Corporate Body*).

Recording

Apply guidelines: *Names of Persons, Families, and Corporate Bodies* (p. 297) and *Places* (Group 1 elements) (p. 305) for names of governments.

Record a variant name when it is different from the name recorded as the preferred name. Record as a variant name a name or form of name used by the corporate body *or* a name or form of name found in reference sources *or* a form of name resulting from a different transliteration of the name.

Record these forms as variant names only if the name might reasonably be searched in that form:

Direct form of name if the preferred name is recorded as a subdivision of a higher or related body

Element	Example
Preferred Name for the Corporate Body	American Library Association. Joint Committee to Compile a List of International Subscription Agents
Variant Name for the Corporate Body	Joint Committee to Compile a List of International Subscription Agents

Name as a subdivision of a higher or related body if preferred name is recorded in direct form

Element	Example
Preferred Name for the Corporate Body	Bodleian Library
Variant Name for the Corporate Body	University of Oxford. Bodleian Library

Variant names for corporate bodies include expanded forms of acronyms, abbreviations, and initialisms; acronym, initialism, or abbreviated form for a full form; and if access is affected, forms with or without full stops and forms with numbers expressed as words or numerals.

If the name recorded as the preferred name for a corporate body has one or more alternative linguistic forms (different language form, different script, different spelling, different transliteration) record them as variant names.

Record other variant names and variant forms of the name if considered important for identification or access.

Element	Example
Preferred Name for the Corporate Body	IBM Canada
Variant Name for the Corporate Body	International Business Machines Canada

Element	Example
Preferred Name for the Corporate Body	Abbey of St. Peter and St. Paul
Variant Name for the Corporate Body	Abbey of Saint Peter and Saint Paul

Element	Example
Preferred Name for the Corporate Body	European Economic Community
Variant Name for the Corporate Body	EEC

Element	Example
Preferred Name for the Corporate Body	North Atlantic Treaty Organization
Variant Name for the Corporate Body	NATO
Variant Name for the Corporate Body	N.A.T.O.

Element	Example
Preferred Name for the Corporate Body	African Centre for Fertilizer Development
Variant Name for the Corporate Body	African Center for Fertilizer Development
Resource received first has spelling Centre; *resource received second has spelling* Center.	

Place Associated with the Corporate Body (RDA 11.3)

A significant location associated with a corporate body.

Place Associated with the Corporate Body » Location of Conference, Etc. (RDA 11.3.2) AAP VAP

A local place in which a conference, congress, meeting, exhibition, fair, festival, etc., was held.

Core element

Recording

Apply guidelines: *Places* (Group 2 elements) (p. 305).

Element	Example
Location of Conference, Etc.	Columbia Falls, Me.

If the conference was held in more than one place, record the names of each of the places in which the conference was held.

Element	Example
Location of Conference, Etc.	Mailing, England
Location of Conference, Etc.	Dundee, Scotland
Conference held in two locations.	

> **Exception.** Record the name of an associated institution (see *Associated Institution*) instead of the local place name if: the name of the associated institution provides better identification or the local place is not known or the local place name cannot be readily determined.

> **Exception.** Record *Online* for a conference that was held online.

> | Element | Example |
> |---|---|
> | Location of Conference, Etc. | Online |

Place Associated with the Corporate Body » Other Place Associated with the Corporate Body (RDA 11.3.3) AAP VAP

A place associated with a corporate body other than location of a conference, etc.

Other place associated with the corporate body includes a country, state, province, local place, etc., associated with a corporate body and the location of headquarters of a corporate body.

Core element

Other Place Associated with the Corporate Body is a core element when needed to distinguish a corporate body from another corporate body with the same name.

Recording

Apply guidelines: *Places* (Group 2 elements) (p. 305).

If a corporate body has a character that is national, state, provincial, etc., record the name of the country, state, province, etc., in which it is located.

Element	Example
Other Place Associated with the Corporate Body	Fla.

> **Exception.** If the name of a country, state, province, etc., in which a body is located does not provide sufficient identification or is inappropriate, record the local place name (e.g., in the case of national, state, provincial, etc., universities of the same name serving the same country, state, province).

For other bodies, record the name of the place that is commonly associated with the name of the body.

Element	Example
Preferred Name for the Corporate Body	Newport High School
Other Place Associated with the Corporate Body	Newport, Ky.

Element	Example
Preferred Name for the Corporate Body	Universität Duisburg-Essen
Other Place Associated with the Corporate Body	Duisberg, Germany
Other Place Associated with the Corporate Body	Essen, North Rhine-Westphalia, Germany
Corporate body has headquarters in two locations.	

Element	Example
Preferred Name for the Corporate Body	Gianni Versace S.p.A.
Other Place Associated with the Corporate Body	Italy

If more precise identification is necessary, add the name of a particular area within the local place. Add it before the name of the local place.

Element	Example
Other Place Associated with the Corporate Body	Lafayette Square, Washington, D.C.

Change of name of jurisdiction or locality

If the name of the local jurisdiction or geographic locality changes during the lifetime of the corporate body, record the latest name in use during the lifetime of the corporate body.

Element	Example
Other Place Associated with the Corporate Body	Harare, Zimbabwe
Place name changed from Salisbury *to* Harare *in 1982.*	

> **Optional addition.** Record earlier names of the local jurisdiction or geographic locality if considered important for identification.

Date Associated with the Corporate Body (RDA 11.4)

A significant date associated with the history of a corporate body, including date of conference, date of establishment, date of termination, and period of activity.

Date Associated with the Corporate Body » Date of Conference, Etc. (RDA 11.4.2) AAP VAP

The date or range of dates on which a conference, congress, meeting, exhibition, fair, festival, etc., was held.

Core element

Recording

Apply guidelines: *Dates Associated with Persons, Families, and Corporate Bodies* (p. 303).

Record the year or years in which the conference, etc., was held. Record specific dates if necessary to distinguish between two or more conferences, etc., with the same name held in the same year.

Element	Example
Date of Conference, Etc.	2010

Element	Example
Date of Conference, Etc.	1911–1912

Element	Example
Date of Conference, Etc.	1978 November 27–29
Two conferences with the same name held in 1978.	

Date Associated with the Corporate Body » Date of Establishment (RDA 11.4.3) AAP VAP

The date on which a corporate body was established or founded.

Core element

Date of Establishment is a core element when needed to distinguish a corporate body from another corporate body with the same name.

Recording

Apply guidelines: *Dates Associated with Persons, Families, and Corporate Bodies* (p. 303).

Element	Example
Preferred Name for the Corporate Body	Double Image
Date of Establishment	1989
Date of Establishment is a core element when needed to distinguish corporate bodies with the name.	

If two or more governments claim jurisdiction over the same area (e.g., as with occupying powers and insurgent governments), record the applicable year of establishment of the government.

Date Associated with the Corporate Body » Date of Termination (RDA 11.4.4) AAP VAP

The date on which a corporate body was terminated or dissolved.

Core element

Date of Termination is a core element when needed to distinguish a corporate body from another corporate body with the same name.

Recording

Apply guidelines: *Dates Associated with Persons, Families, and Corporate Bodies* (p. 303).

If two or more governments claim jurisdiction over the same area (e.g., as with occupying powers and insurgent governments), record the applicable year of termination of the government.

Element	Example
Preferred Name for the Corporate Body	France
Date of Establishment	1940
Date of Termination	1944
Dates of establishment and termination for the territory under German occupation from 1940 to 1944.	

Date Associated with the Corporate Body » Period of Activity of the Corporate Body (RDA 11.4.5) AAP VAP

A date or range of dates indicative of the period in which a corporate body was active.

Core element

Period of Activity of the Corporate Body is a core element when needed to distinguish a corporate body from another corporate body with the same name.

Recording

Apply guidelines: *Dates Associated with Persons, Families, and Corporate Bodies* (p. 303).

Record a date or range of dates indicative of the period in which the corporate body was active if a corporate body's date of establishment and date of termination are both unknown. If it is not possible to establish specific years of activity, record the century or centuries in which the corporate body was active.

Element	Example
Period of Activity of the Corporate Body	1810–1818

Associated Institution (RDA 11.5) AAP VAP

An institution commonly associated with a corporate body.

Core element

Associated Institution is a core element for conferences, etc., if the institution's name provides better identification than the local place name or if the local place name is unknown or cannot be readily determined. Associated Institution is a core element for other corporate bodies if the institution's name provides better identification than the local place name or if the local place name is unknown or cannot be readily determined, and it is needed to distinguish the corporate body from another corporate body with the same name.

Recording

Record the name of an associated institution by applying the instructions for Preferred Name for the Corporate Body.

Element	Example
Preferred Name for the Corporate Body	Center for Biodiversity and Conservation
Associated Institution	American Museum of Natural History

Number of a Conference, Etc. (RDA 11.6) AAP VAP

A designation of the sequencing of a conference, etc., within a series of conferences, etc.

Core element

Recording

If a conference, etc., is stated or inferred to be one of a series of numbered meetings of the same name, record the number of the conference. Record an ordinal number in form preferred by the agency creating the data.

Element	Example
Preferred Name for the Corporate Body	International Conference on Georgian Psalmody
Number of Conference, Etc.	1st

Other Designation Associated with the Corporate Body (RDA 11.7)

A word, phrase, or abbreviation indicating incorporation or legal status of a corporate body, or any term serving to differentiate the body from other corporate bodies, persons, etc.

Core element

Other Designation Associated with the Corporate Body is a core element for a body with a name that does not convey the idea of a corporate body. For other corporate bodies, Other Designation Associated with the Corporate Body is a core element when needed to distinguish a corporate body from another corporate body with the same name.

Other Designation Associated with the Corporate Body » Type of Corporate Body (RDA 11.7.1.4) AAP VAP

Core element

Type of Corporate Body is a core element for a body with a name that does not convey the idea of a corporate body.

Capitalization

Capitalize first word of the term and capitalize other words as applicable to the language involved (RDA A.2.6).

Recording

Record the type of corporate body in a language preferred by the agency creating the data. Select terms from a standard list of names of types of corporate body, if available. If there is no equivalent term for the type of corporate body in a language preferred by the agency, or in case of doubt, record the type of corporate body in the official language of the corporate body.

Element	Example
Preferred Name for the Corporate Body	Red Hot Chili Peppers
Type of Corporate Body	Musical group

Element	Example
Preferred Name for the Corporate Body	Johann Traeg
Type of Corporate Body	Firm

Other Designation Associated with the Corporate Body » Type of Jurisdiction (RDA 11.7.1.5) AAP VAP

Core element

Core element when needed to distinguish a corporate body from another corporate body with the same name.

Capitalization

Capitalize first word of the term and capitalize other words as applicable to the language involved (RDA A.2.6).

Recording

For a government, record the type of jurisdiction in a language preferred by the agency creating the data. If there is no equivalent term for the type of jurisdiction in a language preferred by the agency, or in case of doubt, record it in the official language of the jurisdiction.

Element	Example
Preferred Name for the Corporate Body	New York
Type of Corporate Body	State

Other Designation Associated with the Corporate Body » Other Designation (RDA 11.7.1.6) AAP VAP

Core element

Core element when needed to distinguish a corporate body from another corporate body with the same name.

Capitalization

Capitalize first word of the term and capitalize other words as applicable to the language involved (RDA A.2.6).

Recording

Record a suitable designation if none of the following attributes is sufficient or appropriate for distinguishing between two or more corporate bodies with the same name:

> Place Associated with the Corporate Body
> Date Associated with the Corporate Body
> Associated Institution
> Type of Corporate Body
> Type of Jurisdiction

Record the designation in a language preferred by the agency creating the data.

Exception. If a body has a name that does not convey the idea of a corporate body *and* Type of Corporate Body is not recorded, *then* record a suitable designation.

Element	Example
Preferred Name for the Corporate Body	Church of God
Other Designation	Seventh Day

Element	Example
Preferred Name for the Corporate Body	World Cup
Other Designation	Cricket

Language of the Corporate Body (RDA 11.8)

A language a corporate body uses in its communications.

Recording

Record an appropriate term or terms in a language preferred by the agency creating the data. Select terms from a standard list of names of languages, if available.

Element	Example
Preferred Name for the Corporate Body	Canadian Standards Association
Language of the Corporate Body	English
Language of the Corporate Body	French
Languages used by the corporate body.	

Address of the Corporate Body (RDA 11.9)

The address of a corporate body's headquarters or offices, or an e-mail or Internet address for the body.

Recording

Record the address of the corporate body's place of business and/or an e-mail or Internet address for the body.

Element	Example
Address of the Corporate Body	www.cleo.on.ca

Field of Activity of the Corporate Body (RDA 11.10)

A field of business in which a corporate body is engaged and/or the body's area of competence, responsibility, jurisdiction, etc.

Recording

Record the field or fields of activity of the corporate body by recording a term indicating the field.

Element	Example
Preferred Name for the Corporate Body	Amnesty International
Field of Activity of the Corporate Body	Human rights

Element	Example
Preferred Name for the Corporate Body	Selden Society
Field of Activity of the Corporate Body	English legal history
Field of Activity of the Corporate Body	Publishing

Corporate History (RDA 11.11)

Historical information about the corporate body.

Recording

Record historical information about the corporate body. Incorporate information associated with other identifying elements for the corporate body.

Element	Example
Corporate History	The company was incorporated in 1911 as the Computing-Tabulating-Recording Corporation. It adopted the current name in 1924. The company headquarters are located at 1 New Orchard Road, Armonk, NY 10504-1722 United States.

Identifier for the Corporate Body (RDA 11.12)

A character string uniquely associated with a corporate body, or with a surrogate for a corporate body (e.g., an authority record). The identifier serves to differentiate that corporate body from other corporate bodies.

Core element

Recording

Record an identifier for the corporate body. Precede the identifier with the name or an identification of the agency, etc., responsible for assigning the identifier, if readily ascertainable.

Element	Example
Identifier for the Corporate Body	AMG Artist ID: P 435023
AMG Data Solutions identifier for Coldplay.	

9

Relationships between Entities

BY FOLLOWING RDA'S sequence of instructions step-by-step, a cataloger records the attributes of the bibliographic entities of interest: manifestations, items, works, expressions, persons, families, and corporate bodies.

Illustration of an Entity of Interest (the Work) and One of its Attributes (Preferred Title for the Work)

The next step in RDA is to record relationships between those bibliographic entities to support users in finding resources. The following illustrations each show two entities joined by a relationship element.

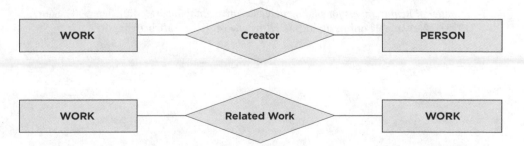

A cataloger records a relationship by choosing a relationship element (e.g., Creator or Related Work). RDA provides several techniques, such as authorized access points representing works or persons, to identify the two entities connected by the relationship element.

For each resource, a cataloger records *primary relationships* (RDA 17). These relationships are inherent in the FRBR definitions for work, expression, manifestation, and item.[1] The primary relationships are reciprocal:

> A work is realized through one or more expressions/an expression realizes one work.
>
> An expression is embodied in one or more manifestations/a manifestation embodies one or more expressions.
>
> A manifestation is exemplified by one or more items/an item exemplifies one manifestation.

Depending on the design of the encoding standards used, a cataloger may record data where the primary relationships are inferred rather than explicitly recorded in the primary relationship elements listed in RDA 17. For example, a catalog user would infer the work that is manifested by the presence of the authorized access point representing the work in a composite description of the manifestation.

SUPPORTING THE USER

By recording primary relationships, a cataloger supports a user in *finding* all resources that embody the same work or expression, and in *finding* all items that exemplify a particular manifestation. How this is accomplished in a catalog varies based upon system design.

While there are different ways of recording this data, at a minimum a cataloger records data sufficient to identify the work manifested, or if more than one, the predominant or first-named work embodied in the manifestation.

While describing a resource a cataloger may learn that one or more expressions have been manifested more than once (e.g., a specific translation published more than once). In that case, at a minimum, a cataloger records data identifying the expression manifested, or if more than one, the predominant or first-named expression embodied in the manifestation.

NOTE

1. *Functional Requirements for Bibliographic Records: Final Report* (München: K. G. Saur, 1998), 12. Available online at: http://archive.ifla.org/VII/s13/frbr/frbr.pdf.

10

Relationships to Persons, Families, and Corporate Bodies Associated with a Resource

Terminology

Person refers to an individual or an identity established by an individual (either alone or in collaboration with one or more other individuals).

Family refers to two or more persons related by birth, marriage, adoption, civil union, or similar legal status, or who otherwise present themselves as a family.

Corporate body refers to an organization or group of persons and/or organizations that is identified by a particular name and that acts, or may act, as a unit.

Work refers to a distinct intellectual or artistic creation (i.e., the intellectual or artistic content).

Expression refers to the intellectual or artistic realization of a work in the form of alpha-numeric, musical or choreographic notation, sound, image, object, movement, etc., or any combination of such forms.

Manifestation refers to the physical embodiment of an expression of a work.

Item refers to a single exemplar or instance of a manifestation.

Resource, in the context of this chapter, refers to a work, expression, manifestation, or item.

SUPPORTING THE USER

A cataloger records data that reflects all significant relationships to persons, families, and corporate bodies associated with the resource being described. By recording this data in relationship elements, a cataloger supports a user in *finding* all resources associated with a particular person, family, or corporate body.

Elements

Core designates a core element—see element instructions for more details.

Relationship elements from a work to a person, family, or corporate body	
Elements	**Core**
Creator	X
Other Person, Family, or Corporate Body Associated with a Work	X

Relationship elements from an expression to a person, family, or corporate body	
Elements	**Core**
Contributor	

Relationship elements from a manifestation to a person, family, or corporate body	
Elements	**Core**
Producer of an Unpublished Resource	
Publisher	
Distributor	
Manufacturer	
Other Person, Family, or Corporate Body Associated with a Manifestation	

Relationship elements from an item to a person, family, or corporate body	
Elements	**Core**
Owner	
Custodian	
Other Person, Family, or Corporate Body Associated with an Item	

If the relationship to a person, family, or corporate body associated with a resource requires explanation (e.g., in a case where an attribution of authorship is dubious), make one or more notes using the following related elements, as applicable (RDA 18.6).

Manifestation elements

Note on Manifestation » Note on Statement of Responsibility

Note on Manifestation » Note on Edition Statement

Note on Manifestation » Note on Production Statement

Note on Manifestation » Note on Publication Statement

Note on Manifestation » Note on Distribution Statement

Note on Manifestation » Note on Manufacture Statement

Element associated with a work or expression

Cataloguer's Note (RDA 5.9)

Relationship Designators (RDA 18.5, RDA appendix I)

Relationship designators provide more specific information about the nature of the relationship between a resource and a person, family, or corporate body associated with the resource (e.g., author, donor) than the relationship elements under which designators are organized.

If any of the eleven relationship elements (Creator; Other Person, Family, or Corporate Body Associated with a Work; Contributor; Producer of an Unpublished Resource; Publisher; Distributor; Manufacturer; Other Person, Family, or Corporate Body Associated with a Manifestation; Owner; Custodian; Other Person, Family, or Corporate Body Associated with an Item) is considered sufficient for the purposes of the agency creating the data, do not use a relationship designator.

Recording

Record a relationship designator with the identifier and/or authorized access point representing the person, family, or corporate body associated with a resource.

Some relationship designators are organized by levels of specificity. Record a relationship designator at the level of specificity considered appropriate for the purposes of the agency creating the data.

Another concise term for a relationship designator can be used if none of the listed terms is appropriate or sufficiently specific.

Sources of Information (RDA 19.1.1, 20.1.1, 21.1.1, 22.1.1)

Sources of information for relationships to a work, expression, or manifestation

Take information from statements appearing on the preferred sources of information in the resource.

If those statements are ambiguous or insufficient, use the following sources of information, in order of preference:

a) other statements appearing prominently in the resources
b) information appearing only in the content of the resources (e.g., the text of a book, the sound content of an audio recording)
c) other sources

Sources of information for relationships to an item

Take information from any source.

Relationship Elements

Creator (RDA 19.2)

A person, family, or corporate body responsible for the creation of a work.

Core element

If there is more than one creator responsible for the work, only the creator having principal responsibility named first in resources embodying the work or in reference sources is required.

If principal responsibility is not indicated, only the first-named creator is required.

Scope

Joint responsibility for the creation of a work

Creators include persons, families, or corporate bodies jointly responsible for the creation of a work. There are two types of joint responsibility:

a) creators who perform the same role (e.g., as in a collaboration between two writers)
b) creators who perform different roles (e.g., as in a collaboration between a composer and a lyricist)

Compilation resulting in a new work

In some cases, the selection, arrangement, editing, etc., of content for a compilation effectively results in the creation of a new work. When this occurs, the person, family, or corporate body responsible for compiling the aggregate work may be considered to be the creator of the compilation.

Modification of a previously existing work resulting in a new work

In some cases, the modification of a previously existing work substantially changes the nature or content of the original and results in a new work. When this occurs, the person, family, or corporate body responsible for modifying the previously existing work is considered to be the creator of the new work.

Corporate bodies considered to be creators

Corporate bodies are considered to be creators when they are responsible for originating, issuing, or causing to be issued, works that fall into one or more of the following categories:

a) works of an administrative nature dealing with any of the following aspects of the body itself
   i)   its internal policies, procedures, finances, and/or operations, or
   ii) its officers, staff, and/or membership (e.g., directories), or
   iii) its resources (e.g., catalogs, inventories)
b) works that record the collective thought of the body (e.g., reports of commissions, committees; official statements of position on external policies, standards)

    c) works that record hearings conducted by legislative, judicial, governmental, and other corporate bodies

    d) works that report the collective activity of
        i) a conference (e.g., proceedings, collected papers), or
        ii) an expedition (e.g., results of exploration, investigation), or
        iii) an event (e.g., an exhibition, fair, festival) falling within the definition of a corporate body (i.e., an organization or group identified by a particular name and that acts, or may act, as a unit) provided that the conference, expedition, or event is named in the resource being described

    e) works that result from the collective activity of a performing group as a whole where the responsibility of the group goes beyond that of mere performance, execution, etc.

    f) cartographic works originating with a corporate body other than a body that is merely responsible for their publication or distribution

    g) legal works of the following types
        i) laws
        ii) decrees of a head of state, chief executive, or ruling executive body
        iii) bills and drafts of legislation
        iv) administrative regulations, etc.
        v) constitutions, charters, etc.
        vi) court rules
        vii) charges to juries, indictments, court proceedings, and court decisions

    h) named individual works of art by two or more artists acting as a corporate body

Government and religious officials considered to be creators

Government and religious officials are considered to be creators when they are responsible for the following types of official communications:

    a) official communications by heads of state, heads of government, heads of dependent or occupied territories, or heads of international bodies (e.g., messages to legislatures, proclamations, executive orders)

    b) official communications from popes, patriarchs, bishops, etc. (e.g., orders, decrees, pastoral letters, bulls, encyclicals; official messages to councils, synods)

Persons or families considered to be creators of serials

A person or family is considered to be the creator of a serial if it is responsible for the serial as a whole, not an individual issue or a few issues.

  Indications that a person or family may be considered responsible for the serial as a whole include the following:

    a) the name or part of the name of the person is in the title proper

    b) the person or family is the publisher of the serial

    c) content consists of personal opinions, etc.

    d) lack of another person, another family, or a corporate body involved with the serial

If different issues of the serial are likely to be created by different persons or families, do not consider a person or family to be the creator.

If it is likely that the serial would continue without that person's or family's responsibility for the serial, do not consider the person or family to be the creator. In case of doubt, do not consider the person or family to be the creator.

Recording

Technique 1. Provide an identifier for the person, family, or corporate body.

Technique 2. Provide an authorized access point representing the person, family, or corporate body.

Element	Example
Creator	Hemingway, Ernest, 1899–1961
Authorized access point representing the creator for: The sun also rises / by Ernest Hemingway.	

Element	Example
Creator	Kaufman, Moisés
Creator	Tectonic Theater Project
Authorized access points representing the creators for the script of a play: The Laramie project / by Moisés Kaufman and the members of Tectonic Theater Project	

RDA ESSENTIALS TIP

The authorized access point representing a work's creator that is identified as having principal responsibility or named first is generally used as the first part in constructing the authorized access point representing the work (RDA 6.27-31).

Creators other than those with principal responsibility or named first may be used as the first part in constructing a variant access point representing the work.

Element	Example
Creator	Hamill, Dorothy
Creator	Amelon, Deborah
Creators of: A skating life / Dorothy Hamill with Deborah Amelon.	

Access point	Example
Authorized Access Point Representing a Work	Hamill, Dorothy. A skating life

Element	Example
Creator	Snoopy, Dr.
Creator	Schultz, Charles M. (Charles Monroe), 1922–2000
Creators of: Dr. Snoopy's advice to pet owners / by Dr. Snoopy ; illustrations by Charles M. Schultz.	

Access point	Example
Authorized Access Point Representing a Work	Snoopy, Dr. Dr. Snoopy's advice to pet owners
Variant Access Point Representing a Work	Schultz, Charles M. (Charles Monroe), 1922–2000. Dr. Snoopy's advice to pet owners

Relationship Designators for Creators of a Work (RDA I.2.1)

architect
    landscape architect

artist
    book artist
    calligrapher
    sculptor

author
    librettist
    lyricist
    rapporteur
    screenwriter

cartographer

choreographer

compiler

composer

designer

enacting jurisdiction

filmmaker

interviewee

inventor

photographer

praeses

programmer

respondent

Other Person, Family, or Corporate Body Associated with a Work (RDA 19.3)

A person, family, or corporate body associated with a work in a relationship other than that of creator. Includes persons, etc., to whom correspondence is addressed, persons, etc., honored by a festschrift, directors, cinematographers, etc., sponsoring bodies, production companies, etc., institutions, etc., hosting an exhibition or event, etc.

The scope for this element excludes persons, families, or corporate bodies who are the subject of a work.

Core element

Other person, family, or corporate body associated with a work is a core element if the access point representing that person, family, or corporate body is used to construct the authorized access point representing the work.

Recording

Technique 1. Provide an identifier for the person, family, or corporate body.

Technique 2. Provide an authorized access point representing the person, family, or corporate body.

Element	Example
Other Person, Family, or Corporate Body Associated with a Work	American Geological Institute
Authorized access point representing the corporate body associated with the work: Dictionary of mining, mineral, and related terms / compiled by the American Geological Institute.	

RDA ESSENTIALS TIP

The authorized access point representing a person, family, or corporate body associated with a work (other than a creator) is in some cases used as the first part in constructing the authorized access point representing the work. For example, authorized access points representing legal works can include the defendant or the plaintiff (who are not "creators" but are associated with the work).

Access point	Example
Authorized Access Point Representing a Work	Riel, Louis, 1844–1885. Queen vs. Louis Riel

The authorized access point representing a person, family, or corporate body associated with a work other than that of creator is used in some cases as the first part in constructing a variant access point representing the work. For example, variant access points representing legal works can include courts and countries associated with the work. (RDA 6.29.3)

Relationship Designators for Other Persons, Families, and Corporate Bodies Associated with a Work (RDA I.2.2)

addressee

appellant

appellee

commissioning body

consultant

court governed

dedicatee

dedicator

defendant

degree committee member

degree granting institution

degree supervisor

director

  film director

  radio director

  television director

director of photography

honouree

host institution

issuing body

judge

jurisdiction governed

medium

organizer

participant in a treaty

plaintiff

producer

  film producer

  radio producer

  television producer

production company

sponsoring body

Contributor (RDA 20.2)

A person, family, or corporate body contributing to an expression. Contributors include editors, translators, arrangers of music, performers, etc.

Scope

In some cases, an expression consists of a primary work accompanied by commentary, etc., illustrations, additional musical parts, etc. When this occurs, the writers of commentary, etc., illustrators, composers of additional parts, etc., are considered to be contributors.

Persons, families, or corporate bodies responsible for compilations of data, information, etc., that result in new works are not treated as contributors but as creators of the new work.

Recording

Technique 1. Provide an identifier for the person, family, or corporate body.
Technique 2. Provide an authorized access point representing the person, family, or corporate body.

Element	Example
Contributor	Weir, Harrison, 1824-1906
Contributor	Greenaway, John, 1816–1890

Authorized access points representing the illustrators of the expression: Three hundred and fifty Aesop's fables / literally translated from the Greek by Geo. Fyler Townsend ; with one hundred and fourteen illustrations, designed by Harrison Wier, and engraved by J. Greenaway.

Element	Example
Contributor	Streep, Meryl
Contributor	Chieftains

Authorized access points representing the performers of the expression: Meryl Streep reads The Tailor of Gloucester / written by Beatrix Potter ; music by the Chieftains.

Relationship Designators for Contributors to an Expression (RDA I.3.1)

abridger

animator

arranger of music

art director

cartographer (expression)

choreographer (expression)

composer (expression)

costume designer

court reporter

draftsman

editor

editor of moving image work

illustrator

   letterer

interviewee (expression)

interviewer (expression)

lighting designer

minute taker

musical director

on-screen participant

performer

   actor

     voice actor

   commentator

   conductor

   dancer

   host

   instrumentalist

   moderator

   narrator

   on-screen presenter

   panelist

   puppeteer

   singer

   speaker

   storyteller

   teacher

presenter

production designer

recording engineer

recordist

software developer

sound designer

special effects provider

stage director

surveyor

transcriber

translator

visual effects provider

writer of supplementary textual content

   writer of added commentary

   writer of added text

     writer of added lyrics

   writer of afterword

   writer of foreword

   writer of introduction

   writer of postface

   writer of preface

Producer of an Unpublished Resource (RDA 21.2)

A person, family, or corporate body responsible for inscribing, fabricating, constructing, etc., a resource in an unpublished form.

Recording

Technique 1. Provide an identifier for the person, family, or corporate body.

Technique 2. Provide an authorized access point representing the person, family, or corporate body.

Publisher (RDA 21.3)

A person, family, or corporate body responsible for publishing, releasing, or issuing a resource.

Recording

Technique 1. Provide an identifier for the person, family, or corporate body.

Technique 2. Provide an authorized access representing the person, family, or corporate body.

Relationship Designators for Publishers of a Manifestation (RDA I.4.2)

broadcaster

Distributor (RDA 21.4)

A person, family, or corporate body responsible for distributing a resource.

Recording

Technique 1. Provide an identifier for the person, family, or corporate body.
Technique 2. Provide an authorized access point representing the person, family, or corporate body.

Relationship Designators for Distributors of a Manifestation (RDA I.4.3)

film distributor

Manufacturer (RDA 21.5)

A person, family, or corporate body responsible for printing, duplicating, casting, etc., a resource in a published form.

Recording

Technique 1. Provide an identifier for the person, family, or corporate body.
Technique 2. Provide an authorized access point representing the person, family, or corporate body.

Relationship Designators for Manufacturers of a Manifestation (RDA I.4.1)

book designer	engraver	platemaker
braille embosser	etcher	printer
caster	lithographer	printmaker
collotyper	papermaker	

Other Person, Family, or Corporate Body Associated with a Manifestation (RDA 21.6)

A person, family, or corporate body other than a producer, publisher, distributor, or manufacturer associated with a manifestation. Includes book designers, platemakers, etc.

Recording

Technique 1. Provide an identifier for the person, family, or corporate body.
Technique 2. Provide an authorized access point representing the person, family, or corporate body.

Owner (RDA 22.2)

A person, family, or corporate body having legal possession of an item.

Recording

Technique 1. Provide an identifier for the person, family, or corporate body.
Technique 2. Provide an authorized access point representing the person, family, or corporate body.

Relationship Designators for Owners of an Item (RDA I.5.1)

current owner
    depositor

former owner
    donor
    seller

Custodian (RDA 22.3)

A person, family, or corporate body having legal custody of an item.

Recording

Technique 1. Provide an identifier for the person, family, or corporate body.
Technique 2. Provide an authorized access point representing the person, family, or corporate body.

Other Person, Family, or Corporate Body Associated with an Item (RDA 22.4)

A person, family, or corporate body other than an owner or custodian associated with an item. Includes curators, binders, restorationists, etc.

Recording

Technique 1. Provide an identifier for the person, family, or corporate body.
Technique 2. Provide an authorized access point representing the person, family, or corporate body.

Relationship Designators for Other Persons, Families, or Corporate Bodies Associated with and Item (RDA I.5.2)

annotator

autographer

binder

curator
    collection registrar
    collector

dedicatee (item)

honouree (item)

illuminator

restorationist (item)

11

Relationships between Works and Subjects

Terminology

Work refers to a distinct intellectual or artistic creation (i.e., the intellectual or artistic content). The term work can refer to an individual work, an aggregate work, or a component of a work.

Subject refers to a term, phrase, classification number, etc., that indicates what the work is about.

SUPPORTING THE USER

A cataloger records data that reflects all significant subject relationships to a work. By recording this data in relationship elements, a cataloger supports a user in *finding* all works about a particular subject.

Elements

Core designates a core element—see element instructions for more details.

Relationship elements between a work and its subject	
Elements	**Core**
Subject	X

Relationship Designators (RDA 23.5, RDA appendix M)

Relationship designators provide more specific information about the nature of the relationship between a work and its subject (e.g., commentary in, evaluation of).

If the relationship element Subject is considered sufficient for the purposes of the agency creating the data, do not use a relationship designator.

Recording

Record one or more appropriate relationship designators with the identifier, authorized access point and/or description representing the subject of the work.

Another concise term for a relationship designator can be used if none of the listed terms is appropriate or sufficiently specific.

Sources of information

For relationship designators, take information on the nature of the subject relationship from any source.

Relationship Elements

Subject (RDA 23)

The relationship between a work and an identifier, an authorized access point, and/or a description that indicates what the work is about.

Core element

When recording relationships between a work and its subject, include as a minimum at least one subject relationship element that is applicable and readily ascertainable.

Recording

Technique 1. Provide an identifier for the subject.

Technique 2. Provide an authorized access point representing the related subject.
   The access point may be a controlled subject term or a combination of terms, or a classification number, as specified in an identifiable subject system.

Technique 3. Provide a description of the related subject by using either a structured description or an unstructured description (e.g., keywords), as appropriate.

Element	Example
Subject	Library of Congress control number: sh 85040737
Example of an identifier.	

Element	Example
Subject	Economic policy

Example of an authorized access point in the Library of Congress Subject Headings.

Element	Example
Subject	Wright, Frank Lloyd, 1867–1959

Example of an authorized access point representing a person (from the Library of Congress/NACO authority file).

Element	Example
Subject	349.73

Example of an authorized access point in the Dewey Decimal Classification system for the subject of a work.

Element	Example
Subject	"An exegesis of Mark 11:15:19"

Example of an unstructured description of the related subject.

Element	Example
Subject	knitting; patterns; sweaters; Fair Isle

Example of keywords describing related subjects.

Relationship Designators (RDA M.2)

Work as subject of a work, with reciprocal designators

description of (work)	described in (work)
analysis of (work)	analysed in (work)
commentary on (work)	commentary in (work)
critique of (work)	critiqued in (work)
evaluation of (work)	evaluated in (work)
review of (work)	reviewed in (work)

Expression as subject of a work, with reciprocal designators

description of (expression)	described in (expression)
analysis of (expression)	analysed in (expression)
commentary on (expression)	commentary in (expression)
critique of (expression)	critiqued in (expression)
evaluation of (expression)	evaluated in (expression)
review of (expression)	reviewed in (expression)

Manifestation as subject of a work, with reciprocal designators

description of (manifestation)	described in (manifestation)
analysis of (manifestation)	analysed in (manifestation)
commentary on (manifestation)	commentary in (manifestation)
critique of (manifestation)	critiqued in (manifestation)
evaluation of (manifestation)	evaluated in (manifestation)
review of (manifestation)	reviewed in (manifestation)

Item as subject of a work, with reciprocal designators

description of (item)	described in (item)
analysis of (item)	analysed in (item)
commentary on (item)	commentary in (item)
critique of (item)	critiqued in (item)
evaluation of (item)	evaluated in (item)
review of (item)	reviewed in (item)

12

Relationships between Works, Expressions, and Items

Work refers to a distinct intellectual or artistic creation (i.e., the intellectual or artistic content).

Expression refers to the intellectual or artistic realization of a work in the form of alpha-numeric, musical or choreographic notation, sound, image, object, movement, etc., or any combination of such forms.

Manifestation refers to the physical embodiment of an expression of a work.

Item refers to a single exemplar or instance of a manifestation.

Resource, in the context of this chapter, refers to a work, expression, manifestation, or item.

> **SUPPORTING THE USER**
>
> A cataloger records data that reflects all significant relationships to works, expressions, manifestations, and items related from the resource being described. By recording this data in relationship elements, a cataloger supports a user in *finding* works, expressions, manifestations, and items that are related to the resource being described.

Elements

Relationship elements between works		
Elements	**Sub-types**	**Core**
Related Work		
	Numbering of Part	

Relationship elements between expressions		
Elements	**Sub-types**	**Core**
Related Expression		

Relationship elements between manifestations		
Elements	**Sub-types**	**Core**
Related Manifestation		

Relationship elements between manifestations		
Elements	**Sub-types**	**Core**
Related Manifestation		

Record the following separate elements to provide clarification or justification for the data recorded to reflect relationships.

Source Consulted (RDA 24.7)

Cataloguer's Note (RDA 24.8)

Explanation of Relationship (RDA 25.2, 26.2)

Relationship Designators (RDA 24.5, RDA appendix J)

Relationship designators provide more specific information about the nature of the relationship between works, expressions, manifestations, and items (e.g., parody of, facsimile of) than the relationship elements under which designators are organized.

If any of the four relationship elements (Related Work, Related Expression, Related Manifestation, Related Item) is considered sufficient for the purposes of the agency creating the data, do not use a relationship designator.

Recording

Record a relationship designator with the identifier, authorized access point and/or structured description representing the related resource.

Many relationship designators are organized by levels of specificity. Record a relationship designator at the level of specificity considered appropriate for the purposes of the agency creating the data.

Another concise term for a relationship designator can be used if none of the listed terms is appropriate or sufficiently specific.

RDA ESSENTIALS TIP

The list of relationship designators provides clues for determining if a resource contains a new work, the same work, or a different expression of a work.

For example, if a resource states that it is an adaptation then there is likely a Related Work relationship to record, along with a designator such as *adaptation of (work)*. However, if the resource is an edition of a previously existing work, then the relationship is a primary relationship, and the same Authorized Access Point Representing a Work is used for both resources.

Related Expression elements are recorded when there is a need to relate two distinct expressions, such as the specific language source used for a translation. However, if that level of detail is not needed, the primary relationships are still recorded, and the two language expressions are linked by the same Authorized Access Point Representing a Work.

Structured descriptions

Applicable to Related Work, Related Expression, Related Manifestation, and Related Item.

A *structured description* is a full or partial description of the related resource using the same data that would be recorded in RDA elements for a description of that related resource. The data is presented in the order specified by a recognized display standard (e.g., ISBD presentation). A relationship designator may be recorded with the structured description.

Unstructured descriptions

Applicable to Related Work, Related Expression, Related Manifestation, and Related Item.

An *unstructured description* is a full or partial description of the related resource written as a sentence or paragraph. Include information about the nature of the relationship as part of the unstructured description rather than record a separate relationship designator.

Sources of information

Take information for all elements from any source.

Relationship Elements

Related Work (RDA 25)

A work, represented by an identifier, an authorized access point, or a description, that is related to the work being described (e.g., an adaptation, commentary, supplement, sequel, part of a larger work).

Relationships between works can be derivative, whole-part, accompanying, or sequential.

Recording

Technique 1. Provide an Identifier for the Work.
Technique 2. Provide an Authorized Access Point Representing a Work.
Technique 3. Provide a structured description.
Technique 4. Provide an unstructured description.

Element	Example
Related Work	Shakespeare, William, 1564–1616. Taming of the shrew
Authorized Access Point Representing a Work used to identify a related work.	

Element	Example
Related Work	ISWC T-010.304.108-2
Identifier for the Work used to identify a related work.	

Element	Example
Related Work	Also contains two short prose pieces dated 1937
Unstructured description used to identify related works.	

Element	Example
Related Work	Split into: Children & libraries; and: Young adult library services
Unstructured description used to identify related works.	

Relationship Designators (RDA J.2)

DERIVATIVE WORK RELATIONSHIPS, WITH RECIPROCAL DESIGNATORS (RDA J.2.2)

Related Work	Related Work
based on (work)	derivative (work)
abridgement of (work)	abridged as (work)
abstract of (work)	abstracted as (work)
abstracts for (work)	abstracted in (work)
adaptation of (work)	adapted as (work)
choreographic adaptation of (work)	adapted as choreography (work)
dramatization of (work)	dramatized as (work)
graphic novelization of (work)	adapted as graphic novel (work)
libretto based on (work)	adapted as libretto (work)
motion picture adaptation of (work)	adapted as motion picture (work)
musical theatre adaptation of (work)	adapted as musical theatre (work)
novelization of (work)	adapted as novel (work)
opera adaptation of (work)	adapted as opera (work)
oratorio adaptation of (work)	adapted as oratorio (work)
radio adaptation of (work)	adapted as radio program (work)
radio script based on (work)	adapted as radio script (work)
screenplay based on (work)	adapted as screenplay (work)
motion picture screenplay based on (work)	adapted as motion picture screenplay for (work)
television screenplay based on (work)	adapted as television screenplay for (work)
video screenplay based on (work)	adapted as video screenplay (work)
television adaptation of (work)	adapted as television program (work)
verse adaptation of (work)	adapted in verse as (work)
video adaptation of (work)	adapted as video (work)
video game adaptation of (work)	adapted as video game (work)
digest of (work)	digested as (work)
expanded version of (work)	expanded as (work)
free translation of (work)	freely translated as (work)
imitation of (work)	imitated as (work)
parody of (work)	parody as (work)

Related Work	Related Work
indexing for (work)	indexed in (work)
inspired by	inspiration for
musical setting of (work)	set to music as (work)
paraphrase of (work)	paraphrased as (work)
remake of (work)	remade as (work)
summary of (work)	summarized as (work)
variations based on (work)	modified by variation as (work)

WORK RELATIONSHIPS, WITH RECIPROCAL DESIGNATORS (RDA J.2.4)

Related Work	Related Work
contained in (work)	container of (work)
in series	series container of
subseries of	subseries

ACCOMPANYING WORK RELATIONSHIPS, WITH RECIPROCAL DESIGNATORS (RDA J.2.5)

Related Work	Related Work
augmentation of (work)	augmented by (work)
addenda to (work)	addenda (work)
appendix to (work)	appendix (work)
cadenza composed for (work)	cadenza (work)
catalogue of (work)	catalogue (work)
concordance to (work)	concordance (work)
errata to (work)	errata (work)
finding aid for (work)	finding aid (work)
guide to (work)	guide (work)
illustrations for (work)	illustrations (work)
index to (work)	index (work)
supplement to (work)	supplement (work)
complemented by (work)	complemented by (work)
choreography (work)	choreography for (work)
libretto (work)	libretto for (work)

Related Work	Related Work
music (work)	music for (work)
incidental music (work)	incidental music for (work)
motion picture music (work)	music for motion picture (work)
radio program music (work)	music for radio program (work)
television program music (work)	music for television program (work)
video music (work)	music for video (work)
radio script (work)	script for radio program (work)
screenplay (work)	screenplay for (work)
motion picture screenplay (work)	screenplay for motion picture (work)
television screenplay (work)	screenplay for television program (work)
video screenplay (work)	screenplay for video (work)

SEQUENTIAL WORK RELATIONSHIPS, WITH RECIPROCAL DESIGNATORS (RDA J.2.6)

Related Work	Related Work
preceded by (work)	succeeded by (work)
absorption in part of (work)	absorbed in part by (work)
absorption of (work)	absorbed by (work)
continuation in part of (work)	split into (work)
continuation of (work)	continued by (work)
merger of (work)	merged to form (work)
prequel	prequel to
replacement in part of (work)	replaced in part by (work)
replacement of (work)	replaced by (work)
separated from (work)	continued in part by (work)
sequel to	sequel

Examples

Element	Example
Related Work	Scarlett : the sequel to Margaret Mitchell's Gone with the wind / by Alexandra Ripley. — New York, NY : Warner Books, 1991
Relationship Designator	sequel

Structured description used to identify a related work, recorded with a relationship designator.

Element	Example
Related Work	'Til death do us plots / by Julianne Bernstein -- Class act / by Michael Elkin -- Where's your stuff? / by Daniel Brenner -- Foot peddler / by Vivian Green -- Smoke / by Louis Greenstein -- Single Jewish female / by Julianne Bernstein -- In spite of everything / by Hindi Brooks -- Ger (the convert) / by Leslie B. Gold and Louis Greenstein -- Golden opportunity / by Julianne Bernstein -- Interview with a scapegoat / by Louis Greenstein
Relationship Designator	container of (work)

The contents represented by a structured description of works in a whole-part relationship to a container work.
Resource being described: Voices from Ariel : ten-minute plays reflecting the Jewish experience : a collection of ten short plays / compiled and edited by Julianne Bernstein and Deborah Baer Mozes.

Element	Example
Related Work	Davis, Jack, 1917–2000. The dreamers
Relationship Designator	container of (work)
Related Work	Johnson, Eva. Murras
Relationship Designator	container of (work)
Related Work	Maza, Bob, 1939–2000. The keepers
Relationship Designator	container of (work)

The contents represented by authorized access points related to a container work. Resource being described: Plays from Black Australia / Jack Davis, Eva Johnson, Richard Walley, Bob Maza ; with an introduction by Justine Saunders.

Numbering of Part (RDA 24.6)

A designation of the sequencing of a part or parts within a larger work. Element sub-type of Related Work.

Numbering of part may include a numeral, a letter, any other character, or the combination of these with or without an accompanying caption (e.g., volume, number) and/or a chronological designation.

Abbreviations

Use appropriate abbreviations (RDA B.7–B.10). Examples: *bk., no., pt., v.*

Recording

Record numbering as it appears on the source. Apply guidelines: *Numbers Expressed as Numerals or as Words* (p. 267).

Element	Example
Related Work	Synopses of the British fauna
Relationship Designator	in series
Numbering of Part	new series, no. 21
Numbering of Part used in a series relationship from the work: Brinkhurst, Ralph O. British and other marine and estuarine oligochaetes.	

Related Expression (RDA 26)

An expression, represented by an identifier, an authorized access point, or a description, that is related to the expression being described (e.g., a revised version, a translation).

Relationships between expressions can be derivative, whole-part, accompanying, or sequential.

Recording

Technique 1. Provide an Identifier for the Expression.
Technique 2. Provide an Authorized Access Point Representing an Expression.
Technique 3. Provide a structured description.
Technique 4. Provide an unstructured description.

Relationship Designators (RDA J.3)

DERIVATIVE EXPRESSION RELATIONSHIPS, WITH RECIPROCAL DESIGNATORS (RDA J.3.2)

Related Expression	Related Expression
based on (expression)	derivative (expression)
abridgement of (expression)	abridged as (expression)
abstract of (expression)	abstracted as (expression)
abstracts for (expression)	abstracted in (expression)
adaptation of (expression)	adapted as (expression)
choreographic adaptation of (expression)	adapted as choreography (expression)
dramatization of (expression)	dramatized as (expression)
graphic novelization of (expression)	adapted as graphic novel (expression)
libretto based on (expression)	adapted as libretto (expression)
motion picture adaptation of (expression)	adapted as motion picture (expression)
musical theatre adaptation of (expression)	adapted as musical theatre (expression)

Related Expression	Related Expression
novelization of (expression)	adapted as novel (expression)
opera adaptation of (expression)	adapted as opera (expression)
oratorio adaptation of (expression)	adapted as oratorio (expression)
radio adaptation of (expression)	adapted as radio program (expression)
radio script based on (expression)	adapted as radio script (expression)
screenplay based on (expression)	adapted as screenplay (expression)
motion picture screenplay based on (expression)	adapted as motion picture screenplay for (expression)
television screenplay based on (expression)	adapted as television screenplay for (expression)
video screenplay based on (expression)	adapted as video screenplay (expression)
television adaptation of (expression)	adapted as television program (expression)
verse adaptation of (expression)	adapted in verse as (expression)
video adaptation of (expression)	adapted as video (expression)
arrangement of	arranged as
digest of (expression)	digested as (expression)
expanded version of (expression)	expanded as (expression)
free translation of (expression)	freely translated as (expression)
imitation of (expression)	imitated as (expression)
parody of (expression)	parody as (expression)
indexing for (expression)	indexed in (expression)
musical setting of (expression)	musical setting (expression)
paraphrase of (expression)	paraphrased as (expression)
remake of (expression)	remade as (expression)
revision of	revised as
summary of (expression)	summary (expression)
translation of	translated as
dubbed version of	dubbed version
variations based on (expression)	modified by variation of (expression)

WHOLE-PART EXPRESSION RELATIONSHIPS, WITH RECIPROCAL DESIGNATORS (RDA J.3.4)

Related Expression	Related Expression
contained in (expression)	container of (expression)

ACCOMPANYING EXPRESSION RELATIONSHIPS, WITH RECIPROCAL DESIGNATORS (RDA J.3.5)

Related Expression	Related Expression
augmentation of (expression)	augmented by (expression)
addenda to (expression)	addenda (expression)
appendix to (expression)	appendix (expression)
cadenza composed for (expression)	cadenza (expression)
catalogue of (expression)	catalogue (expression)
concordance to (expression)	concordance (expression)
errata to (expression)	errata (expression)
finding aid for (expression)	finding aid (expression)
guide to (expression)	guide (expression)
illustrations for (expression)	illustrations (expression)
index to (expression)	index (expression)
supplement to (expression)	supplement (expression)
complemented by (expression)	complemented by (expression)
choreography (expression)	choreography for (expression)
libretto (expression)	libretto for (expression)
music (expression)	music for (expression)
incidental music (expression)	incidental music for (expression)
motion picture music (expression)	music for motion picture (expression)
radio program music (expression)	music for radio program (expression)
television program music (expression)	music for television program (expression)
video music (expression)	music for video (expression)
radio script (expression)	script for radio program (expression)
screenplay (expression)	screenplay for (expression)
motion picture screenplay (expression)	screenplay for motion picture (expression)
television screenplay (expression)	screenplay for television program (expression)
video screenplay (expression)	screenplay for video (expression)

SEQUENTIAL EXPRESSION RELATIONSHIPS, WITH RECIPROCAL DESIGNATORS (RDA J.3.6)

Related Expression	Related Expression
preceded by (expression)	succeeded by (expression)
absorption in part of (expression)	absorbed in part by (expression)
absorption of (expression)	absorbed by (expression)

Related Expression	Related Expression
continuation in part of (expression)	split into (expression)
continuation of (expression)	continued by (expression)
merger of (expression)	merged to form (expression)
replacement in part of (expression)	replaced in part by (expression)
replacement of (expression)	replaced by (expression)
separated from (expression)	continued in part by (expression)

Examples

Element	Example
Related Expression	Biology of fishes / Carl E. Bond. — Second edition. — Fort Worth : Saunders College Publishing, [1996]
Relationship Designator	revision of
Structured description of an earlier expression in a derived relationship, recorded with a relationship designator. Resource being described: Bond's Biology of fishes / Michael Barton. — Third edition — Belmont, CA : Thomson, [2007].	

Related Manifestation (RDA 27)

A manifestation, represented by an identifier or a description, that is related to the manifestation being described (e.g., a manifestation in a different format).

Relationships between manifestations can be equivalent, whole-part, or accompanying.

Recording

Technique 1. Provide an Identifier for the Manifestation.
Technique 2. Provide a structured description.
Technique 3. Provide an unstructured description.

Element	Example
Related Manifestation	Issued also in Blu-ray Disc format
Unstructured description for a related manifestation.	

Relationship Designators (RDA J.4)

EQUIVALENT MANIFESTATION RELATIONSHIPS, WITH RECIPROCAL DESIGNATORS (RDA J.4.2)

Related Manifestation	Related Manifestation
equivalent (manifestation)	equivalent (manifestation)
also issued as	also issued as
mirror site	mirror site
reproduced as (manifestation)	reproduction of (manifestation)
digital transfer (manifestation)	digital transfer of (manifestation)
electronic reproduction (manifestation)	electronic reproduction of (manifestation)
facsimile (manifestation)	facsimile of (manifestation)
preservation facsimile (manifestation)	preservation facsimile of (manifestation)
reprinted as (manifestation)	reprint of (manifestation)

WHOLE-PART MANIFESTATION RELATIONSHIPS, WITH RECIPROCAL DESIGNATORS (RDA J.4.4)

Related Manifestation	Related Manifestation
contained in (manifestation)	container of (manifestation)
facsimile contained in	facsimile container of
inserted in	insert
special issue of	special issue

ACCOMPANYING MANIFESTATION RELATIONSHIPS, WITH RECIPROCAL DESIGNATORS (RDA J.4.5)

Related Manifestation	Related Manifestation
accompanied by (manifestation)	accompanied by (manifestation)
issued with	issued with
filmed with (manifestation)	filmed with (manifestation)
on disc with (manifestation)	on disc with (manifestation)

Related Item (RDA 28)

An item, represented by an identifier or a description, that is related to the item being described (e.g., an item used as the basis for a microform reproduction).

   Relationships between items can be equivalent, whole-part, or accompanying.

Recording

   Technique 1. Provide an Identifier for the Item.
   Technique 2. Provide a structured description.
   Technique 3. Provide an unstructured description.

Relationship Designators (RDA J.5)

EQUIVALENT ITEM RELATIONSHIPS, WITH RECIPROCAL DESIGNATORS (RDA J.5.2)

Related Item	Related Item
equivalent (item)	equivalent (item)
reproduced as (item)	reproduction of (item)
digital transfer (item)	digital transfer of (item)
electronic reproduction (item)	electronic reproduction of (item)
facsimile (item)	facsimile of (item)
preservation facsimile (item)	preservation facsimile of (item)
reprinted as (item)	reprint of (item)

WHOLE-PART ITEM RELATIONSHIPS, WITH RECIPROCAL DESIGNATORS (RDA J.5.4)

Related Item	Related Item
contained in (item)	container of (item)

ACCOMPANYING ITEM RELATIONSHIPS, WITH RECIPROCAL DESIGNATORS (RDA J.5.5)

Related Item	Related Item
accompanied by (item)	accompanied by (item)
bound with	issued with
filmed with (item)	filmed with (item)
on disc with (item)	on disc with (item)

13

Relationships between Persons, Families, and Corporate Bodies

Terminology

The term **person** refers to an individual or an identity established by an individual (either alone or in collaboration with one or more other individuals).

The term **family** refers to two or more persons related by birth, marriage, adoption, civil union, or similar legal status, or who otherwise present themselves as a family.

The term **corporate body** refers to an organization or group of persons and/or organizations that is identified by a particular name and that acts, or may act, as a unit.

SUPPORTING THE USER

A cataloger records data that reflects all significant relationships between persons, families, and corporate bodies. By recording this data in relationship elements, a cataloger supports a user in *finding* persons, families, or corporate bodies related to the person, family, or corporate body recorded for the resource being described.

Elements

Relationship elements to a person from a person, family, or corporate body		
Elements	Sub-types	Core
Related Person		

Relationship elements to a family from a person, family, or corporate body		
Elements	Sub-types	Core
Related Family		

Relationship elements to a corporate body from a person, family, or corporate body		
Elements	Sub-types	Core
Related Corporate Body		

Record the following separate elements to provide clarification or justification for the data recorded to reflect relationships.

Source Consulted (RDA 29.6)

Cataloguer's Note (RDA 29.7)

Explanation of Relationship (RDA 30.2, 31.2, 32.2)

Relationship Designators (RDA 29.5, RDA K)

Relationship designators provide more specific information about the nature of the relationship between persons, families, or corporate bodies (e.g., alternate identity, predecessor) than the relationship elements under which the designators are organized.

If any of the three relationship elements (Related Person, Related Family, Related Corporate Body) is considered sufficient for the purposes of the agency creating the data, do not use a relationship designator.

Recording

Record a relationship designator with the identifier and/or authorized access point representing the related person, family, or corporate body.

Some relationship designators are organized by levels of specificity. Record a relationship designator at the level of specificity considered appropriate for the purposes of the agency creating the data.

Another concise term for a relationship designator can be used if none of the listed terms is appropriate or sufficiently specific.

Sources of information

Take information for relationships from any source.

Relationship Elements

Related Person (RDA 30)

A person who is associated with the person, family, or corporate body being identified (e.g., a collaborator, a member of a family, a founder of a corporate body). Related persons include separate identities established by an individual (either alone or in collaboration with one or more other individuals).

Recording

Technique 1. Provide an Identifier for the Person.
Technique 2. Provide an Authorized Access Point Representing a Person.

Relationship Designators (RDA K.2)

PERSONS RELATED TO OTHER PERSONS, WITH RECIPROCAL DESIGNATORS

Related Person	Related Person
alternate identity	real identity
real identity	alternate identity

PERSONS RELATED TO FAMILIES, WITH RECIPROCAL DESIGNATORS

Related Person	Related Family
family member	family
progenitor	descendants

PERSONS RELATED TO CORPORATE BODIES, WITH RECIPROCAL DESIGNATORS

Related Person	Related Corporate Body
employee	employer
founder	founded corporate body
graduate	graduate of
officer	officer of
member	corporate body
sponsor	

Examples

Element	Example
Related Person	Will, 1904–1974
Relationship Designator	alternate identity
Relationship between a person, Lipkind, William, 1904-1974, *and an identity established by that person.*	

Element	Example
Related Person	Lipkind, William, 1904–1974
Relationship Designator	real identity
Relationship between an identity established by a person, Will, 1904-1974, *and that person.*	

Related Family (RDA 31)

A family that is associated with the person, family, or corporate body being identified (e.g., a person's family, a family that owns the controlling interest in a corporate body).

Recording

> *Technique 1.* Provide an Identifier for the Family.
> *Technique 2.* Provide an Authorized Access Point Representing a Family.

Relationship Designators (RDA K.3)

FAMILIES RELATED TO PERSONS, WITH RECIPROCAL DESIGNATORS

Related Family	Related Person
family	family member
descendants	progenitor

FAMILIES RELATED TO OTHER FAMILIES

Related Family
descendant family

FAMILIES RELATED TO CORPORATE BODIES, WITH RECIPROCAL DESIGNATORS

Related Family	Related Corporate Body
founding family	founded corporate body
sponsoring family	sponsored corporate body

Related Corporate Body (RDA 32)

A corporate body that is associated with the person, family, or corporate body being identified (e.g., a musical group to which a person belongs, a subsidiary company). Related corporate bodies include corporate bodies that precede or succeed the corporate body being identified as the result of a change of name.

Recording

Technique 1. Provide an Identifier for the Corporate Body.
Technique 2. Provide an Authorized Access Point Representing a Corporate Body.

Relationship Designators (RDA K.4)

CORPORATE BODIES RELATED TO PERSONS, WITH RECIPROCAL DESIGNATORS

Related Corporate Body	Related Person
corporate body	member
employer	employee
founded corporate body	founder
graduate of	graduate
officiated corporate body	incumbent

CORPORATE BODIES RELATED TO FAMILIES, WITH RECIPROCAL DESIGNATORS

Related Corporate Body	Related Family
founded corporate body	founding family
sponsored corporate body	sponsoring family

CORPORATE BODIES RELATED TO OTHER CORPORATE BODIES, WITH RECIPROCAL DESIGNATORS

Related Corporate Body	Related Corporate Body
absorbed corporate body	absorbing corporate body
absorbing corporate body	absorbed corporate body
broader affiliated body	local affiliate
component of merger	product of merger
corporate member	membership corporate body
founded corporate body	founding corporate body
founding corporate body	founded corporate body
hierarchical subordinate	hierarchical superior
hierarchical superior	hierarchical subordinate
jointly held conference	jointly held conference
local affiliate	broader affiliated body
membership corporate body	corporate member
mergee	mergee
predecessor	successor
predecessor of split	product of split
product of merger	component of merger
product of split	predecessor of split
sponsored corporate body	sponsoring corporate body
sponsoring corporate body	sponsored corporate body
successor	predecessor

Examples

Element	Example
Related Corporate Body	National Library of Canada
Relationship Designator	component of a merger
Related Corporate Body	National Archives of Canada
Relationship Designator	component of a merger
Relationships from a corporate body, Library and Archives Canada, *which was the product of a merger.*	

Element	Example
Related Corporate Body	National Archives of Canada
Relationship Designator	mergee
Related Corporate Body	Library and Archives Canada
Relationship Designator	product of a merger
Relationships from a corporate body, National Library of Canada, *which was a mergee in a merger.*	

Element	Example
Related Corporate Body	National Library of Canada
Relationship Designator	mergee
Related Corporate Body	Library and Archives Canada
Relationship Designator	product of a merger
Relationships from a corporate body, National Library of Canada, *which was a mergee in a merger.*	

14

Transcription
(RDA 1.7)

THESE GUIDELINES APPLY to the elements checked as *Transcribed*. Transcribe these elements as they appear on the source of information. The instructions and examples for transcribed elements in *RDA Essentials* reflect the RDA guidelines on transcription of capitalization, punctuation, diacritical marks, symbols, spacing of initials and acronyms, letters or words intended to be read more than once, abbreviations, and inaccuracies.

Capitalization (RDA 1.7.2)

Apply the instructions for capitalization in RDA appendix A.

Punctuation (RDA 1.7.3)

Transcribe punctuation as it appears on the source.

Element	Example
Title Proper	...and then there were none

Element	Example
Title Proper	What is it?...what is it not?

Exception. *Punctuation separating different elements.*

Omit punctuation that separates data to be recorded as one element from data to be recorded as a different element.

Element	Example
Title Proper	DDC 21
Other Title Information	international perspectives
Title appears on the source of information with punctuation separating it from the other title information: DDC 21: international perspectives.	

Element	Example
Place of Publication	Nashville
Publisher's Name	Vanderbilt University
Publisher's name appears on the source of information with punctuation separating it from the place of publication: Vanderbilt University, Nashville.	

Exception. *Punctuation separating instances of the same element.*

Omit punctuation that separates data to be recorded as one element from data recorded as a second or subsequent instance of the same element.

Element	Example
Place of Publication	Ottawa
Place of Publication	Dakar
Place of publication appears on the source of information with punctuation separating each place: Ottawa – Dakar – Montevideo – Nairobi – New Delhi – Singapore.	

Add punctuation, as necessary, for clarity:

Element	Example
Title Proper	Travailler mieux, vivez mieux
Title appears on the source of information with each word on a separate line. Comma added for clarity.	

Diacritical marks (RDA 1.7.4)

Transcribe diacritical marks such as accents as they appear on the source of information.

> **Optional addition.** Add diacritical marks that are not present on the source of information in accordance with standard usage for the language of the data.
>
> | Element | Example |
> | --- | --- |
> | Title Proper | Les misérables |
>
> *Source of information reads:* LES MISERABLES.

Symbols (RDA 1.7.5)

Replace symbols and other characters, etc., that cannot be reproduced by the facilities available, with a description of the symbol. Indicate that this description was taken from a source outside the resource itself (e.g., by using square brackets). Make an explanatory note if necessary (see *Note on Manifestation* element sub-types).

Element	Example
Title Proper	My name is Brain [crossed out] Brian
Note on Title	The word "Brain" in the title appears with an X through it

Ignore typographical devices that are used as separators, etc.

Spacing of initials and acronyms (RDA 1.7.6)

If separate letters or initials appear on the source of information without full stops between them, transcribe the letters without spaces between them, regardless of spacing on the source. If such letters or initials have full stops between them, omit any internal spaces.

Element	Example
Title Proper	ALA rules for filing catalog cards

Element	Example
Publisher's Name	W.W. Norton & Company

Letters or words intended to be read more than once (RDA 1.7.7)

If a letter or word appears only once but the design of the source of information makes it clear that it is intended to be read more than once, repeat the letter or word.

Element	Example
Title Proper	Canadian citations
Parallel Title Proper	Citations canadiennes
Source of information reads: Canadian CITATIONS canadiennes.	

Abbreviations (RDA 1.7.8, B.4)

For transcribed elements, use only those abbreviations found in the sources of information for the element. If supplying all or part of a transcribed element, generally do not abbreviate words.

Inaccuracies (RDA 1.7.9)

When instructed to transcribe an element as it appears on the source, transcribe an inaccuracy or a misspelled word unless the instructions for a specific element indicate otherwise (e.g., exception at *Title Proper* for a serial or integrating resource). See guidelines: *Titles Associated with a Manifestation* (p. 271).

Make a note correcting the inaccuracy if considered important for identification or access (see *Note on Manifestation* element sub-types).

If the inaccuracy appears in a title and a corrected form of the title is considered important for identification or access, record a corrected form of the title as a variant title (see *Title » Variant Title*).

Element	Example
Title Proper	Heirarchy in organizations
Variant Title	Hierarchy in organizations
Note on Title	Title should read: Hierarchy in organizations

Numbers expressed as numerals or as words (RDA 1.8.1)

When recording numbers expressed as numerals or as words in a transcribed element, transcribe them in the form in which they appear on the source of information.

15

Numbers Expressed as Numerals or as Words

(RDA 1.8)

THESE GUIDELINES APPLY to the following elements:

- **Numbering of Serials element sub-types:**

    Numeric and/or Alphabetic Designation of First Issue or Part of Sequence

    Chronological Designation of First Issue or Part of Sequence

    Numeric and/or Alphabetic Designation of Last Issue or Part of Sequence

    Chronological Designation of Last Issue or Part of Sequence

    Alternative Numeric and/or Alphabetic Designation of First Issue or Part of Sequence

    Alternative Chronological Designation of First Issue or Part of Sequence

    Alternative Numeric and/or Alphabetic Designation of Last Issue or Part of Sequence

    Alternative Chronological Designation of Last Issue or Part of Sequence

    Production Statement » Date of Production

- **Publication Statement » Date of Publication**
- **Distribution Statement » Date of Distribution**
- **Manufacture Statement » Date of Manufacture**
- **Copyright Date**
- **Series Statement » Numbering within Series**
- **Series Statement » Numbering within Subseries**
- **Dissertation or Thesis Information » Year Degree Granted**

Form of Numerals (RDA 1.8.2)

Record numerals in the form preferred by the agency creating the data, unless the substitution would make the numbering less clear.

Element	Example
Numbering within Series	tome 3
Numbering within series on source of information reads: tome III.	

Alternative. Record numerals in the form in which they appear on the source of information.

Element	Example
Numbering within Series	tome III

Alternative. Record the numerals in the form in which they appear on the source. Add the equivalent numerals in the form preferred by the agency creating the data. Indicate that the information was taken from a source outside the resource itself.

Element	Example
Numbering within Series	tome 3 [3]
Numbering within series on source of information reads: tome III.	

Numbers expressed as words (RDA 1.8.3)

Substitute numerals for numbers expressed as words.

Inclusive numbers (RDA 1.8.4)

When recording inclusive dates and other inclusive numbers, record both the first and last number in full.

Element	Example
Date of Publication	1967–1972
Source of information reads: 1967–72.	

Ordinal numbers (RDA 1.8.5)

When recording ordinal numbers (expressed either as numerals or as words), record them as numerals and indicate that they are ordinal numbers following standard usage for the language:

English language source

When recording ordinal numbers from an English-language source, record them as numerals in the form *1st, 2nd, 3rd, 4th,* etc.

16

Notes
(RDA 1.10)

THESE GUIDELINES APPLY to instructions that specify making a note.

Capitalization (RDA 1.10.2, appendix A.8–A.9)

Capitalize the first word or abbreviation in a note.

If a note consists of more than one sentence, capitalize the first word of each subsequent sentence.

Capitalize a title as instructed in the guidelines: *Titles Associated with a Manifestation* (p. 271). Capitalize other words as applicable to the language involved (RDA A.10–A.55).

Quotations (RDA 1.10.3)

Record quotations from the resource or from other sources in quotation marks. Follow the quotation by an indication of its source, unless that source is the preferred source of information for the identification of the resource.

Element	Example
Intended Audience	"A textbook for 6th form students"—Preface

References (RDA 1.10.4)

Refer to passages in the resource, or in other sources, if: a) the references support assertions made in the description *or* b) the references save repetition of information readily available from other sources.

Element	Example
Note on Statement of Responsibility	Introduction (page xxix) refutes attribution to John Bodenham

Applicability of the information recorded in a note (RDA 1.10.5)

If it is known that the note does not apply to the entire resource, identify the applicable part or iteration.

17

Titles Associated with a Manifestation

(RDA 2.3.1)

THESE GUIDELINES APPLY to the following elements:

- **Title element sub-types:**

  Title Proper

  Parallel Title Proper

  Other Title Information

  Parallel Other Title Information

  Variant Title

  Earlier Title Proper

  Later Title Proper

- **Series Statement sub-elements:**

  Title Proper of Series

  Parallel Title Proper of Series

  Other Title Information of Series

  Parallel Other Title Information of Series

  Title Proper of Subseries

  Parallel Title Proper of Subseries

  Other Title Information of Subseries

  Parallel Other Title Information of Subseries

RDA ESSENTIALS TIP

Titles associated with a manifestation may also be recorded in other elements such as notes or descriptions used to record Related Work, Related Expression, Related Manifestation, and Related Item.

Titles associated with a manifestation are particular to each manifestation. The work, which may be embodied in many manifestations, is also identified by a title but that title is unique and used to identify the work across all resources and in relationships between works. For recording the titles or forms of the title by which a work has become known, see *Title of the Work*.

Transcribe a title as it appears on the source of information. Apply guidelines: *Transcription* (p. 263).

Optional omission. Abridge a long title only if it can be abridged without loss of essential information. Use a mark of omission (...) to indicate such an omission. Never omit any of the first five words.

Exception. *Introductory words.* Do not transcribe words that serve as an introduction and are not intended to be part of the title.

Element	Example
Title Proper	Sleeping Beauty
Source of information reads: Disney presents Sleeping Beauty.	

Optional addition. If considered important for identification or access, record the form in which the title appears on the source of information (i.e., with the introductory words) as a variant title (see *Title » Variant Title*).

Exception. *Inaccuracies.* For a serial or an integrating resource, correct obvious typographic errors in Title Proper. Make a note recording the title as it appears on the source of information (see *Note on Manifestation » Note on Title*). In case of doubt about whether the spelling of a word is incorrect, transcribe the spelling as found. Record as a variant title (see *Title » Variant Title*) the title of a serial or an integrating resource as it appears on the source of information, if considered important for access.

Element	Example
Title Proper	Housing starts
Source of information on v. 1, no. 1 reads: Housing sarts.	

Exception. *Date, name, number, etc., that varies from issue to issue or from part to part.* If a title of a serial or multipart monograph includes a date, name, number, etc., that varies from issue to issue or from part to part, omit this date, name, number, etc. Use a mark of omission (...) to indicate such an omission.

Element	Example
Title Proper	Supply estimate for the year ending ...
Source of information reads: Supply estimates for the year ending 1997.	

Names of persons, families, and corporate bodies

If a title consists solely of the name of a person, family, or corporate body, record the name as the title.

Element	Example
Title Proper	Woody Guthrie
Source of information 1 for title has only: Woody Guthrie.	

If the title includes a name that would normally be treated either as part of a statement of responsibility or as the name of a publisher, distributor, etc. *and* the name is an integral part of the title (e.g., connected by a case ending), *then* record the name as part of the title.

Element	Example
Title Proper	Marlowe's plays

Titles of parts, sections, and supplements

If the title of a separately issued part, section, or supplement appears on the source of information without the title that is common to all parts or sections, record the title of the part, section, or supplement as Title Proper.

When a common title is not recorded with the title of a part, section, or supplement, record it in any of the following ways that are applicable:

a) as part of a Series Statement
b) as a title in a Related Work element

Element	Example
Title Proper	British journal of applied physics
Title Proper of Series	Journal of physics
Title of part recorded as Title Proper. Common title, which does not appear on the same source, recorded as Title Proper of Series in a Series Statement.	

If the title of a separately issued part, section, or supplement appears on the source of information with the title that is common to all parts or sections, apply these instructions, as applicable.

Title of part, section, or supplement insufficient to identify the resource

If the title of the separately issued part, section, or supplement appears on the same source of information with the title common to all parts or sections (or the title of the larger resource) *and* the title of the part, section, or supplement alone is insufficient to identify the resource, *then* record the common title followed by the title of the part, section, or supplement.

Element	Example
Title Proper	Advanced calculus. Student handbook

If the title of the part, section, or supplement has a numeric and/or alphabetic designation, record (in this order):

a) the common title
b) the designation of the part, section, or supplement
c) the title of the part, section, or supplement.

Element	Example
Title Proper	Journal of polymer science. Part A, General papers

Treat a phrase such as *new series*, *second series*, etc., that appears on the same source of information with the title proper of an unnumbered monographic series as the title of a part, section, or supplement (see *Series Statement » Title Proper of Subseries*).

Element	Example
Title Proper	Journal of polymer science. Part A, General papers
Title Proper of Subseries	New series

If such a phrase differentiates a new sequence of numbering of a numbered monographic series or serial, treat it as part of numbering within the series (Series Statement » Numbering within Series) or numbering within the serial (Numbering of Serials » Numeric and/or Alphabetic Designation of First Issue or Part of Sequence).

Element	Example
Numbering within Series	new series, v. 3

Element	Example
Numeric and/or Alphabetic Designation of First Issue or Part of Sequence	new series, v. 1, no. 1

Title of part, section, or supplement sufficient to identify the resource

If the title of a separately issued part, section, or supplement appears on the same source of information with the title common to all parts or sections (or the title of the larger resource), *and* the title of the part, section, or supplement alone is sufficient to identify the resource, then record the title of the part, section, or supplement as the title.

Element	Example
Title Proper	Structured settlements
Title Proper of Series	Art of advocacy
Title of part recorded as Title Proper. Common title recorded as Title Proper of Series.	

Exception. For serials and integrating resources, record the common title followed by the title of the part, section, or supplement even if the title of the part, section, or supplement alone is sufficient to identify the resource.

Element	Example
Title Proper	Key abstracts. Industrial power and control systems

Capitalization (RDA A.4)

Capitalize the first word or the abbreviation of the first word in a title, or in a title of a part, section, or supplement. Capitalize other words within titles by applying the guidelines at RDA A.10–A.55, as applicable to the language involved.

Element	Example
Title Proper	Journal of polymer science

Element	Example
Title Proper of Series	Communications of the Dublin Institute for Advanced Studies
Title Proper of Subseries	Series D, Geophysical bulletin
Title of section in subseries capitalized.	

Exception. *Other title information.* In general, do not capitalize the first word or the abbreviation of the first word in other title information. Capitalize the first word or abbreviation if otherwise specified in RDA (RDA A.10–A.55, RDA appendix B).

Element	Example
Title Proper	Quo vadis?
Other Title Information	a narrative from the time of Nero

Exception. For titles with unusual capitalization, follow the capitalization of the title as found on the source of information.

Element	Example
Title Proper	eBay bargain shopping for dummies

Titles preceded by punctuation indicating incompleteness

Do not capitalize the first word of a title if it is preceded by punctuation indicating that the beginning of the phrase from which the title was derived has been omitted.

Element	Example
Title Proper	... and master of none

18

Statements of Responsibility

(RDA 2.4.1)

THESE GUIDELINES APPLY to the following elements:

- **Statement of Responsibility element sub-types:**

    Statement of Responsibility Relating to Title Proper

    Parallel Statement of Responsibility Relating to Title Proper

- **Edition Statement sub-elements:**

    Statement of Responsibility Relating to the Edition

    Parallel Statement of Responsibility Relating to the Edition

    Statement of Responsibility Relating to a Named Revision of an Edition

    Parallel Statement of Responsibility Relating to a Named Revision of an Edition

- **Series Statement sub-elements:**

    Statement of Responsibility Relating to Series

    Parallel Statement of Responsibility Relating to Series

    Statement of Responsibility Relating to Subseries

    Parallel Statement of Responsibility Relating to Subseries

---

RDA ESSENTIALS **TIP**

Statements of responsibility may also be recorded in other elements such as descriptions used to record Related Work, Related Expression, Related Manifestation, and Related Item.

Transcribe a statement of responsibility as it appears on the source of information. Apply guidelines: *Transcription* (p. 263).

Capitalize words within statements of responsibility as applicable to the language involved (RDA A.4).

Optional omission. Abridge a statement of responsibility only if this can be done without loss of essential information. Do not use a mark of omission (...) to indicate such an omission. Always record the first name appearing in the statement.

Element	Example
Statement of Responsibility Relating to Title Proper	by Harry Smith
Source of information reads: by Dr. Harry Smith.	

When omitting names from a statement of responsibility naming more than one person, etc., apply the instruction for the optional omission for *Statement naming more than one person, etc.*

Exception. *Serials.* Record a statement of responsibility identifying an editor of a serial only if the name of the editor is considered an important means of identifying the serial (e.g., if a particular person edited the serial for all or most of its existence; if the person's name is likely to be better known than the title of the serial).

More than one statement of responsibility (RDA 2.4.1.6)

Record the statements in the order indicated by the sequence, layout, or typography of the source of information from which the corresponding title, edition, or series information is taken.

If the sequence, layout, and typography are ambiguous or insufficient to determine the order, record the statements in the order that makes the most sense.

If statements of responsibility appear in sources other than the source from which the corresponding title, edition, or series information is taken, record them in the order that makes the most sense.

Statement naming more than one person, etc. (RDA 2.4.1.5)

Record a statement of responsibility naming more than one person, family, or corporate body as a single statement whether those persons, etc., perform the same function or different functions.

Element	Example
Statement of Responsibility Relating to Title Proper	developed by Dale Kahn with Laurie Fenster

Optional omission. If a single statement of responsibility names more than three persons, families, or corporate bodies performing the same function (or with the same degree of responsibility), omit any but the first of each group of such persons, families, or bodies. Indicate the omission by summarizing what has been omitted in a language and script preferred by the agency preparing the description. Indicate that the summary was taken from a source outside the resource itself (e.g., by using square brackets).

Element	Example
Statement of Responsibility Relating to Title Proper	by Raymond Queneau, Jacques Jouet [and 4 others]
Source of information reads: by Raymond Queneau, Italo Calvino, Paul Fournel, Jacques Jouet, Claude Berge & Harry Mathews.	

If the members of a group, ensemble, company, etc., are named as well as the group, etc., omit the names of the members from the statement of responsibility. If they are considered important for identification, access, or selection, record them in a note on statement of responsibility (see *Note on Manifestation » Note on Statement of Responsibility*).

Clarification of role (RDA 2.4.1.7)

Add a word or short phrase if necessary to clarify the role of a person, family, or corporate body named in a statement of responsibility. Indicate that the information was taken from a source outside the resource itself by means of a note or some other means (e.g., by using square brackets).

Element	Example
Statement of Responsibility Relating to Title Proper	[collected by] Chet Williams

Noun phrases occurring with a statement of responsibility (RDA 2.4.1.8)

If the sequence, layout, or typography on the source of information indicates that a noun or noun phrase is intended to be part of the statement of responsibility *and* the noun phrase is indicative of the role of the person, family, or corporate body named in the statement of responsibility, *then* treat the noun or noun phrase as part of the statement of responsibility. In case of doubt, treat the noun or noun phrase as part of the statement of responsibility.

Element	Example
Statement of Responsibility Relating to Title Proper	research and text by Colin Barham

Element	Example
Title Proper	Pride and prejudice
Other Title Information	a novel
Statement of Responsibility Relating to Title Proper	by Jane Austen
On source, a novel *appears below the title proper and* by *and* Jane Austen *appear on separate lines.*	

No person, family, or corporate body named in the statement of responsibility (RDA 2.4.1.9)

Record a statement of responsibility even if no person, family, or corporate body is named in that statement.

Element	Example
Statement of Responsibility Relating to Title Proper	with a spoken commentary by the artist

19

Place of Production, Publication, Distribution, and Manufacture

(RDA 2.7.2, 2.8.2, 2.9.2, AND 2.10.2)

THESE GUIDELINES APPLY to the following elements:

- Production Statement » Place of Production
- Publication Statement » Place of Publication
- Distribution Statement » Place of Distribution
- Manufacture Statement » Place of Manufacture

Record places as they appear on the source of information. Apply guidelines: *Transcription* (p. 263). Include both the local place name (e.g., city, town) and the name of the larger jurisdiction or jurisdictions (state, province, etc., and/or country) if present on the source of information.

Element	Example
Place of Publication	Wellington, New Zealand

Element	Example
Place of Manufacture	West Hill, Ont.

Optional addition. Include the full address as part of the local place name, if considered important for identification or access.

Element	Example
Place of Production	6 Ludgate Hill, London

Optional addition. Supply the name of the larger jurisdiction (state, province, etc., and/ or country) as part of the local place name if considered important for identification or access. Indicate that the information was taken from a source outside the resource itself.

Element	Example
Place of Publication	Dublin [Ohio]

If the place name as transcribed is known to be fictitious, or requires clarification, make a note giving the actual place name, etc. (use appropriate Note on Manifestation element sub-type).

Element	Example
Place of Publication	Belfast
Note on Publication Statement	Actually published in Dublin

Place not identified in the resource—Known or probable place can be determined (RDA 2.7.2.6, 2.8.2.6, 2.9.2.6, 2.10.2.6)

If the place is not identified in the resource, supply the place or probable place if it can be determined. Apply the instructions in this order of preference: a) known place, b) probable place, c) known country, state, province, etc., d) probable country, state, province, etc., e) unknown place.

Indicate that the information was taken from a source outside the resource itself (e.g., by using square brackets).

a) Known place

If the place is known, supply the local place name (e.g., city, town). Include the name of the larger jurisdiction if necessary for identification.

Element	Example
Place of Publication	[Toronto]

b) Probable place

If the place is uncertain, supply the name of the probable local place. Include the name of the larger jurisdiction if necessary for identification.

Add a question mark after the local place name, or after the larger jurisdiction if the larger jurisdiction is also uncertain.

Element	Example
Place of Publication	[Munich?]

c) Known country, state, province, etc.

If the probable local place is unknown, supply the name of the country, state, province, etc., of production.

Element	Example
Place of Production	[Canada]

d) Probable country, state, province, etc.

If the country, state, province, etc., is uncertain, supply the name of the probable country, state, province, etc., followed by a question mark.

e) Unknown place

If neither a known nor a probable local place or country, state, province, etc., can be determined, then record the following as applicable. Indicate that the information was taken from a source outside the resource itself (e.g., by using square brackets).

Element	Example
Place of Production	[Place of production not identified]

Element	Example
Place of Publication	[Place of publication not identified]

Element	Example
Place of Distribution	[Place of distribution not identified]

Element	Example
Place of Manufacture	[Place of manufacture not identified]

20

Name of Producer, Publisher, Distributor, and Manufacturer

(RDA 2.7.4, 2.8.4, 2.9.4, AND 2.10.4)

THESE GUIDELINES APPLY to the following elements:

- **Production Statement » Producer's Name**
- **Publication Statement » Publisher's Name**
- **Distribution Statement » Distributor's Name**
- **Manufacture Statement » Manufacturer's Name**

Record names as they appear on the source of information. Apply guidelines: *Transcription* (p. 263). A name may be represented by a characterizing word or phrase.

Element	Example
Publisher's Name	Oxford University Press

Element	Example
Manufacturer's Name	CTD Printers

> **Optional omission.** Omit levels in a corporate hierarchy that are not required to identify the producer, publisher, distributor, or manufacturer. Do not use a mark of omission (...) to indicate such an omission.

If the name as transcribed is known to be fictitious, or requires clarification, make a note giving the actual name, etc. (use *Note on Manifestation* elements: *Note on Production Statement, Note on Publication Statement, Note on Distribution Statement,* and *Note on Manufacture Statement,* as applicable).

For instructions on recording the relationship to producers, publishers, distributors, and manufacturers, see *Producer of an Unpublished Resource, Publisher, Distributor, and Manufacturer.*

Statement of function (RDA 2.7.4.4, 2.8.4.4, 2.9.4.4, 2.10.4.4)

Record words or phrases indicating the function—other than solely publishing for a publisher—performed by a person, family, or corporate body as they appear on the source of information.

Element	Example
Manufacturer's Name	Manufactured and marketed by PolyGram Video, a division of PolyGram Records, Inc.

Element	Example
Publisher's Name	SAGE Publications on behalf of McGill University

Do not record phrase for publishing function. Source of information reads: Published by SAGE Publications on behalf of McGill University.

Optional addition. If the function of a person, family, or corporate body recorded is not explicit or clear, add a term indicating the function. Indicate that the information was taken from a source outside the resource itself (e.g., by using square brackets).

Element	Example
Distributor's Name	Guild Sound and Vision [distributor]

No producer, publisher, distributor, or manufacturer identified
(RDA 2.7.4.7, 2.8.4.7, 2.9.4.7, 2.10.4.7)

If the producer, publisher, distributor, or manufacturer is not named within the resource itself *and* cannot be identified from other sources, *then* record the following as appropriate. Indicate the information was taken from a source outside the resource itself (e.g., by using square brackets).

Element	Example
Producer's Name	[producer not identified]

Element	Example
Publisher's Name	[publisher not identified]

Element	Example
Distributor's Name	[distributor not identified]

Element	Example
Manufacturer's Name	[manufacturer not identified]

21

Date of Production, Publication, Distribution, and Manufacture

(RDA 2.7.6, 2.8.6, 2.9.6, AND 2.10.6)

THESE GUIDELINES APPLY to the following elements:

- Production Statement » Date of Production
- Publication Statement » Date of Publication
- Distribution Statement » Date of Distribution
- Manufacture Statement » Date of Manufacture

Record dates as they appear on the source of information. Apply guidelines: *Numbers Expressed as Numerals or as Words* (p. 267) and *Transcription* (p. 263) for words that are not numbers.

> **Optional addition.** If the date as it appears in the resource is not of the Gregorian or Julian calendar, add the corresponding date or dates of the Gregorian or Julian calendar. Indicate that the information was taken from a source outside the resource itself (e.g., by using square brackets).

If the date as it appears in the resource is known to be fictitious or incorrect, make a note giving the actual date (use *Note on Manifestation Element* sub-types, *Note on Production Statement, Note on Publication Statement, Note on Distribution Statement,* and *Note on Manufacture Statement,* as applicable).

Supplied dates (RDA 1.9)

Indicate that the date was taken from a source outside the resource itself by means of a note or some other means (e.g., by using square brackets).

Actual year known

Element	Example
Date of Manufacture	[2003]
Actual year is known; record the year.	

Either one of two consecutive years

Element	Example
Date of Publication	[1971 or 1972]
Date is known to be either one of two consecutive years; record both years separated by or.	

Probable year

Element	Example
Date of Distribution	[1969?]
Probable year is known; record the year followed by a question mark.	

Probable range of years

Element	Example
Date of Production	[between 1846 and 1853?]
Probable date falls within a range of years; record the range. Record between, *followed by the earliest probable year, then* and *and the latest probable year, followed by a question mark.*	

Earliest and/or latest possible date known

Element	Example
Date of Publication	[not before 2007]
Earliest possible data is known; record not before *followed by the date.*	

Element	Example
Date of Manufacture	[not before August 21, 1492]
Latest possible date is known; record not after *followed by the date.*	

Element	Example
Date of Distribution	[between August 12, 1899 and March 2, 1900]
Both the earliest possible and latest possible dates are known; record between *followed by the earliest possible date, then* and *and the latest possible date.*	

Date of production, publication, distribution, or manufacture not identified in a single-part resource (RDA 2.7.6.6, 2.8.6.6, 2.9.6.6, 2.10.6.6)

If the date is not identified in a single-part resource, supply the date or approximate date. If the date or an approximate date for a single-part resource cannot reasonably be determined, record the following as appropriate. Indicate the information was taken from a source outside the resource itself (e.g., by using square brackets).

Element	Example
Date of Production	[date of production not identified]

Element	Example
Date of Publication	[date of publication not identified]

Element	Example
Date of Distribution	[date of distribution not identified]

Element	Example
Date of Manufacture	[date of manufacture not identified]

Dates for multipart monographs, serials, and integrating resources (RDA 2.7.6.5, 2.8.6.5, 2.9.6.5, 2.10.6.5)

First issue, part, or iteration available, record date followed by hyphen.

Element	Example
Date of Publication	1999

Ceased or is complete, and first and last issues, parts, or iterations are available, record dates separated by a hyphen.

Element	Example
Date of Distribution	1982–2001

Ceased or is complete, and last but not first issue, part, or iteration is available, record date preceded by a hyphen.

Element	Example
Date of Production	–2002

For an integrating resource, supply the date of the last update, if considered important for identification.

Element	Example
Date of Publication	1995–1998 [updated 1999]

If the date is the same for all issues, parts, or iterations, record single date.

Element	Example
Date of Publication	1967

If first and/or last issue, part, or iteration is not available, supply an approximate date or dates (see instruction on *Supplied dates*).

Element	Example
Date of Manufacture	[1998]–

Element	Example
Date of Production	1997–[2000]

Element	Example
Date of Publication	[1998–1991]

If the date or dates cannot be approximated for a multipart monograph, serial, or integrating resource, do not record a date of production.

22

Titles of Works

(RDA 6.2.1)

THESE GUIDELINES APPLY to the following elements:

- **Title of the Work element sub-types:**

  Preferred Title for the Work

  Variant Title for the Work

Capitalization (RDA A.3)

Capitalize the title of a work as instructed for titles of manifestation. See guidelines: *Titles Associated with a Manifestation* (p. 271).

Numbers expressed as numerals or as words (RDA 6.2.1.5)

When recording a title for a work, record numbers expressed as numerals or as words in the form in which they appear on the source of information.

Element	Example
Preferred Title for the Work	3:10 to Yuma

If the title of a part of a work identified only by a generic term includes a numeric designation, record the numeric designations as a numeral (RDA 6.2.2.9).

Element	Example
Preferred Title for the Work	Season 6
Preferred title for a part of the television program Buffy, the vampire slayer.	

Diacritical marks (RDA 6.2.1.6)

Record diacritical marks such as accents appearing in a title for a work as they appear on the source of information.

> **Optional addition.** Add diacritical marks such as accents that are not present on the source of information. Follow the standard usage for the language of the data.
>
> | Element | Example |
> |---|---|
> | Preferred Title for the Work | Sur l'état du système des timars des XVIIe–XVIIIe ss. |
> | *Title appears in uppercase letters without diacritical marks.* | |

Initial articles (RDA 6.2.1.7)

When recording the title, include an initial article, if present.

Element	Example
Preferred Title for the Work	The invisible man

> **Alternative.** Omit an initial article unless the title for a work is to be accessed under that article (e.g., a title that begins with the name of a person or place) (RDA appendix C).
>
> | Element | Example |
> |---|---|
> | Preferred Title for the Work | Taming of the shrew |
> | *Not* The taming of the shrew. | |

Spacing of initials and acronyms (RDA 6.2.1.8)

When recording a title for a work:

a) Do not leave a space between a full stop and an initial following it.
b) If separate letters or initials appear on the source of information without full stops between them, record the letters without spaces between them.

Element	Example
Preferred Title for the Work	T.S. Eliot memorial lectures

Element	Example
Preferred Title for the Work	ABC of practical astronomy
Title appears as: A B C of practical astronomy.	

Abbreviations (RDA 6.2.1.9)

Use only the following abbreviations in titles of works:

a) those that are integral parts of the title

b) the abbreviation for *Number* (or its equivalent in another language) in the title for a part of a musical work when this word precedes a number used to identify that part

c) *etc.* in the title *Laws, etc.*

Names of Persons, Families, and Corporate Bodies

(RDA 8.4 AND 8.5)

THESE GUIDELINES APPLY to the following elements:

- **Name of the Person element sub-types:**

  Preferred Name for the Person

  Variant Name for the Person

- **Name of the Family element sub-types:**

  Preferred Name for the Family

  Variant Name for the Family

- **Name of the Corporate Body element sub-types:**

  Preferred Name for the Corporate Body

  Variant Name for the Corporate Body

Language and script (RDA 8.4)

Record names in the language and script in which they appear on the sources from which they are taken.

Alternative. Record a transliterated form of the name either as a substitute for, or in addition to, the form that appears on the source.

Initial articles

RDA instructs to include initial articles in names of persons and corporate bodies in cases, but offers alternative instructions to omit the initial article (see *Preferred Name for the Person* and *Preferred Name for the Corporate Body*).

Capitalization (RDA 8.5.2, A.2, A.10–A.55)

In general, capitalize the first word of each name. Capitalize other words as applicable to the language involved.

Element	Example
Preferred Name for the Person	La Roche, Mazo de
Variant Name for the Person	Roche, Mazo de la
Follow the person's use of capitalization for a prefix from a language other than English. If in doubt, capitalize it.	

For names with unusual capitalization, follow the capitalization of the commonly known form.

Element	Example
Preferred Name for the Person	lang, k. d.

Element	Example
Preferred Name for the Corporate Body	netViz Corporation

For Name of the Person element sub-types

Words or phrases characterizing persons: Capitalize a word, or the substantive words in a phrase characterizing a person and used as a name as applicable to the language involved. Capitalize proper names contained in such a phrase as applicable to the language involved (RDA A.10–A.55). Capitalize a quoted title within a personal name as instructed for titles of manifestations.

Element	Example
Preferred Name for the Person	A Physician

Element	Example
Preferred Name for the Person	Citizen of Albany

Element	Example
Preferred Name for the Person	Author of Early impressions

Other terms associated with names of persons: If a title and other term is treated as an integral part of the name of a person, then capitalize the title or term as applicable to the language involved (RDA A.10–A.55).

Numbers expressed as numerals or as words (RDA 8.5.3)

When recording a name, record numbers expressed as numerals or as words in the form in which they appear on the source of information.

Element	Example
Preferred Name for the Person	50 Cent

Element	Example
Preferred Name for the Corporate Body	Thirteenth Avenue Presbyterian Church

Accents and other diacritical marks (RDA 8.5.4)

Record accents and other diacritical marks appearing in a name as they appear in the source of information. Add them if it is certain that they are integral to a name but have been omitted in the source from which the name is taken.

Element	Example
Preferred Name for the Person	Lefèvre d'Étaples, Jacques

In some cases, the application of the instructions on capitalization in RDA appendix A can result in lower-case letters without the accents and other diacritical marks that are standard usage for the language in which the data is recorded. When this occurs, add accents and other diacritical marks according to the standard usage for the language.

Hyphens (RDA 8.5.5)

Retain a hyphen between given names if the hyphen is used by the person.

Element	Example
Preferred Name for the Person	Ahlers, R.-J.

Spacing of initials and acronyms (RDA 8.5.6)

For Name of the Person and Name of the Family

a) If an initial represents a given name or a surname, and the initial is followed by another initial or a name, leave a space after the full stop following the first initial.

Element	Example
Preferred Name for the Person	Rowling, J. K.

b) If the name consists entirely or primarily of separate letters, leave a space between the letters (regardless of whether they are followed by full stops or not).

Element	Example
Preferred Name for the Person	A. E. I. O. U.

c) If the name includes initials or abbreviations forming part of a title or term of address, leave a space between the initial or abbreviation and a subsequent initial, abbreviation, numeral, or word.

Element	Example
Preferred Name for the Person	Dr. X

For Name of the Corporate Body

a) If an initial is followed by another initial, do not leave a space after the full stop, etc., following the first initial.

Element	Example
Preferred Name for the Corporate Body	J.A. Folger and Company

b) If separate letters or initials appear on the source of information without full stops between them, record the letters without spaces between them.

Element	Example
Variant Name for the Corporate Body	IEEE

Abbreviations (RDA 8.5.7, B.2)

For Name of the Person and Name of the Family

Use only the abbreviations that are integral parts of the name (e.g., "Wm.") if the person uses the abbreviation.

Element	Example
Preferred Name for the Person	Fry, Benjamin St. James

For Name of the Corporate Body

Use only the abbreviations that are integral parts of the name if the corporate body uses the abbreviation. Use abbreviations for certain names of larger places recorded as part of the name of another place. See guidelines: *Places* (p. 305).

Element	Example
Preferred Name for the Corporate Body	Domus Lugdunensis Soc. Jesu

Element	Example
Preferred Name for the Corporate Body	Washington (D.C)

Dates Associated with Persons, Families, and Corporate Bodies

(RDA 9.3.1.3, 10.4.1.3, AND 11.4.1.3)

THESE GUIDELINES APPLY to the following elements:

- **Date Associated with the Person element sub-types:**

    Date of Birth

    Date of Death

    Period of Activity of the Person

- **Date Associated with the Family**

- **Date Associated with the Corporate Body element sub-types:**

    Date of Conference, Etc.

    Date of Establishment

    Date of Termination

    Period of Activity of the Corporate Body

Recording

Record dates in terms of the calendar preferred by the agency creating the data.

For the Christian calendar, use the abbreviation B.C. for dates in the pre-Christian era. Place the abbreviation at the end of a date or each date in a span in that era. Use the abbreviation A.D. only when the dates span both eras.

Record a date associated with a person, family, or corporate body by giving the year.

Element	Example
Date of Establishment	1965

Optional addition. *For persons and families.* Add the month or month and day in the form *[year] [month]* or *[year] [month] [day]*. Record the month in a language and script preferred by the agency creating the data.

Element	Example
Date of Birth	1936 December 17

Exception. For *corporate bodies.* If necessary to distinguish between two or more conferences, etc., with the same name held in same year, record the date in the form *[year] [month] [day]*. Record the month in a language and script preferred by the agency creating the data.

Element	Example
Date of Conference, Etc.	1978 February 13–15

For persons and families

Indicate a probable date by adding a question mark following the year.

Element	Example
Date of Birth	1816?

If the year is uncertain but known to be either one or two years, record the date in the form *[year] or [year]*.

Element	Example
Date of Death	1966 or 1667

For persons, families, and corporate bodies

If the year can only be approximated, record the date in the form *approximately [year]*.

Element	Example
Period of Activity of the Person	approximately 680

Record a period of activity expressed as a range of dates in the form *[year]-[year]*.

Element	Example
Period of Activity of the Corporate Body	1687–approximately 1735

Record a period of activity expressed as a range of centuries in the form *[century]-[century]*.

Element	Example
Date Associated with the Family	1st century B.C.–1st century A.D.

Element	Example
Period of Activity of the Corporate Body	16th century–17th century

25

Places

(RDA 16)

THESE GUIDELINES APPLY to elements that require the name of a place to be recorded. Two groups of elements differ in some guidelines for recording a place name. One group (hereafter referred to as Group 1 elements) consists of the element sub-types of Name of the Corporate Body. The second group (hereafter referred to as Group 2 elements) consists of place names recorded in other elements for works, persons, families, and corporate bodies.

Group 1 elements

Name of the Corporate Body element sub-types:

Preferred Name for the Corporate Body

Variant Name for the Corporate Body

Recording

When recording the place name used as the conventional name for a government or for a community that is not a government, do not abbreviate the place name.

If the name of a place is qualified by a larger jurisdiction, enclose the name of the larger place in parentheses and abbreviate the name of the larger place (RDA B.11).

Element	Example
Preferred Name for the Corporate Body	Oregon

Element	Example
Preferred Name for the Corporate Body	Budapest (Hungary)

Element	Example
Preferred Name for the Corporate Body	New York (N.Y.)

Element	Example
Preferred Name for the Corporate Body	Tribeca (New York, N.Y.)
Variant Name for the Corporate Body	Triangle Below Canal Street (New York, N.Y.)

The place names in Group 1 elements may be used in access points with the qualifying element Other Designation Associated with the Corporate Body » Type of Jurisdiction (RDA 11.13.1.6):

Access point	Example
Authorized Access Point Representing a Corporate Body	New York (State)

The qualifying element Other Designation Associated with the Corporate Body » Other Designation may also be used in access points with names of places from Group 1 elements (RDA 11.13.1.7):

Access point	Example
Authorized Access Point Representing a Corporate Body	Korea (South)

Group 2 elements

For a work (recorded as separate elements and/or in access points representing a work)

Place of Origin of the Work

For a person

Place of Birth

Place of Death

Country Associated with the Person

Place of Residence, Etc.

For a family (recorded as separate elements and/or in access points representing a family)

Place Associated with the Family

For a corporate body (recorded as separate elements and/or in access points representing a corporate body)

Place Associated with the Corporate Body element sub-types:

Location of Conference, Etc.

Other Place Associated with the Corporate Body

Recording

When recording the place name for group 2 elements, abbreviate the name (RDA B.11).

If the name of a place is qualified by a larger jurisdiction, precede the name of the large place by a comma and abbreviate the name of the larger place (RDA B.11).

Element	Example
Country Associated with the Person	Canada

Element	Example
Place of Birth	Or.

Element	Example
Place of Origin of the Work	Budapest, Hungary

Element	Example
Place of Death	New York, N.Y.

Element	Example
Other Place Associated with the Corporate Body	Toronto, Ont.

Element	Example
Location of Conference, Etc.	Oakdale, Stearns County, Minn.

Sources of information (RDA 16.2.2.2)

Preferred Name for the Place (for Group 1 and Group 2 elements)

Determine the preferred name for a place from (in order of preference):

a) gazetteers and other reference sources in a language preferred by the agency creating the data

b) gazetteers and other reference sources issued in the jurisdiction in which the place is located in the official language or languages of that jurisdiction

Variant Name for the Place (for Group 1 element Variant Name for the Corporate Body)

Take variant names from any source.

Choosing the Preferred Name for the Place (RDA 16.2.2.3)

Choose as the preferred name of a place (in this order):

a) the form of the name in the language preferred by the agency creating the data, if there is one in general use

b) the form of the name in the official language of the jurisdiction in which the place is located

Different language forms of the same name

Form is in a language preferred by the agency creating the data and that form is general use

Choose that form. Determine the form from gazetteers and other reference sources published in that language.

Form is found in a language preferred by the agency creating the data and that form is the name of the government that has jurisdiction over the place

Choose that form.

No form in general use in a language preferred by the agency creating the data

Choose the form in the official language of the jurisdiction in which the place is located.

No form in general use in a language preferred by the agency creating the data and the jurisdiction has more than one official language

Choose the form most commonly found in sources in a language preferred by the agency.

Change of name

Changes to the name of a place affect the Preferred Name for the Corporate Body (Group 1 element) for governments, and access points for persons, families, and corporate bodies when a place element is used in the construction of the access point (Group 2 elements).

Recording the Preferred Name for the Place
(RDA 16.2.2.4–16.2.2.5, 16.2.2.8–16.2.2.14)

Record as the preferred name of a place the form most commonly found in gazetteers or other reference sources, unless a specific instruction indicates otherwise.

When recording the preferred name of a place, include an initial article if present.

> **Alternative.** Omit an initial article unless the name is to be accessed under the article (RDA appendix C).

Place names that include a term indicating type of jurisdiction (RDA 16.2.2.8.1)

If the first part of a place name is a term indicating a type of jurisdiction *and* the place is commonly listed under another part of its name in lists published in the language of the country in which it is located, *then* omit the term indicating the type of jurisdiction.

Element	Example
Group 1 elements	Kerry (Ireland)
Group 2 elements	Kerry, Ireland
Not County Kerry.	

In all other cases, include the term indicating the type of jurisdiction.

Element	Example
Group 1 elements	Mexico City (Mexico)
Group 2 elements	Mexico City, Mexico
Term City *included.*	

State, province, territory, etc. of Australia, Canada, the United States, the former U.S.S.R., or the former Yugoslavia; England, Northern Ireland, Scotland, and Wales; overseas territories, dependencies, etc. (RDA 16.2.2.9 16.2.2.11)

Do not record the name of the larger jurisdiction as part of the preferred name.

Element	Example
Group 1 elements	Puerto Rico
Group 2 elements	Wales

Element	Example
Group 1 and 2 elements	Wales

Element	Example
Group 1 and 2 elements	French Guiana

If the place is in one of these jurisdictions, record the name of the jurisdiction as part of the preferred name.

Element	Example
Group 1 elements	Washington (D.C.)
Group 2 elements	Washington, D.C.

Element	Example
Group 1 elements	Bangor (Northern Ireland)
Group 2 elements	Bangor, Northern Ireland

Places in other jurisdictions (RDA 16.2.2.12)

Record the name of the country in which a place is located as part of the preferred name for the place if that place is in a jurisdiction not covered by the instructions for Australia, Canada, the United States, the former U.S.S.R., and the former Yugoslavia; England, Northern Ireland, Scotland, and Wales; and overseas territories, dependencies, etc.

Element	Example
Group 1 elements	Paris (France)
Group 2 elements	Paris, France

Alternative. Record the name of a state, province, or highest-level administrative division preceding the name of the country.

Element	Example
Group 1 elements	Wiesbaden (Hesse, Germany)
Group 2 elements	Wiesbaden, Hesse, Germany

Places with the same name (RDA 16.2.2.13)

If the inclusion of the name of the larger place or jurisdiction is insufficient to distinguish between two or more places with the same name, include as part of the preferred name a word or phrase commonly used to distinguish them.

Element	Example
Group 1 elements	Alhama de Granada (Spain)
Group 2 elements	Alhama de Granada, Spain
Short name Alhama *used for two places in Spain;* de Granada *added to distinguish.*	

If there is no commonly used word or phrase to distinguish between places in the same larger place or jurisdiction, record the name of an intermediate place between the name of the place being identified and the larger place or jurisdiction.

Element	Example
Group 1 elements	Farnham (Essex, England)
Group 2 elements	Farnham, Essex, England
Essex *added to distinguish from Farnham in Dorset, England.*	

Places within cities, etc. (RDA 16.2.2.14)

For the name of a place within a city, etc., record as part of the preferred name for the place a) the name of the city, etc. *and* b) the larger place within which the city, etc., is located.

Element	Example
Group 1 elements	Chelsea (London, England)
Group 2 elements	Chelsea, London, England

Recording the Variant Name for the Place (RDA 16.2.3)

The variant name for the place is used in the Variant Name for the Corporate Body element.

Variant names for places, if access is affected, include: expanded forms of abbreviations and initialisms, abbreviated form or initialism for full form, absence or presence of articles, numbers expressed as words or numerals, and forms with or without full stops.

If the name recorded as the preferred name for a place has one or more alternative linguistic forms (e.g., different language form, different script, different spelling, different transliteration) record them as variant names.

Record other variant names and variant forms of the name if considered important for identification or access.

Constructing
Access Points

26

Persons

AN AUTHORIZED ACCESS point is one of the techniques used to represent a person. The Authorized Access Point Representing a Person is constructed by using the Preferred Name for the Person element followed by other elements identifying a person as instructed. The Variant Access Point Representing a Person is an alternative access point representing a person.

If no suitable addition is available to distinguish access points representing persons with the same name, use the same access point for all persons with the same name.

Authorized Access Point Representing a Person
(RDA 9.19.1; punctuation in RDA E.1.2.2)

Preferred Name for the Person
Use Preferred Name for the Person as the basis for the authorized access point representing a person.

Access point	Example
Authorized Access Point Representing a Person	Fitzgerald, Ella

Make additions to the name using the following elements, as applicable.

Title of the Person—A title of royalty (RDA 9.19.1.2.1)

Add a title of royalty even if it is not needed to distinguish access points representing different persons with the same name. Add the title of royalty after the preferred name. Add the title before adding date of birth and/or date of death or period of activity of the person.

Access point	Example
Authorized Access Point Representing a Person	Anne, Queen of Great Britain

Access point	Example
Authorized Access Point Representing a Person	Isabella, of Parma, consort of Joseph II, Holy Roman Emperor
Isabella, of Parma *is preferred name. Title of royalty begins with* consort.	

Title of the Person—A title of nobility (RDA 9.19.1.2.2)

If the title of nobility or part of the title commonly appears with the name in resources associated with the person or in reference sources, add the title to the name. In this context, disregard reference sources dealing with the nobility. In case of doubt, add the title. Add the title of nobility even if it is not needed to distinguish access points representing different persons with the same name.

Add the title after the preferred name unless adding Fuller Form of Name. If adding Fuller Form of Name, add the title after the fuller form of name. Add the title before adding date of birth and/or date of death or period of activity of the person.

Access point	Example
Authorized Access Point Representing a Person	Puymaigre, Th. de (Théodore), comte

Title of the Person—A title of religious rank (RDA 9.19.1.2.3)

Popes

Add the title *Pope* or *Antipope* after the preferred name.

Access point	Example
Authorized Access Point Representing a Person	Pius XII, Pope

Bishops, etc., and other persons of religious vocation

If the given name is recorded as the first element in the preferred name *and* the title or part of the title commonly appears with the name in resources associated with the person or in reference sources, *then* add the title, even if it is not needed to distinguish access points representing different persons with the same name. In case of doubt, add the title.

Add the title after the preferred name unless adding Fuller Form of Name. If adding Fuller Form of Name, add the title after the fuller form of name. Add the title before adding date of birth and/or date of death or period of activity of the person.

Access point	Example
Authorized Access Point Representing a Person	M. Alicia (Mary Alicia), Sister, S.C.N.
Preferred name + Fuller Form of Name + Title including initials representing a Christian religious order.	

but

Access point	Example
Authorized Access Point Representing a Person	Augustine, of Canterbury, Saint
Title Archbishop *not commonly used in resources associated with the person or in reference sources.*	

Other Designation Associated with the Person—Saint (RDA 9.19.1.2.4)

Add the term *Saint* to the preferred name unless the access point represents a pope or an emperor, empress, king, or queen. Add the term after the fuller form of name and title of nobility or title of religious rank, as applicable. Add the designation before adding date of birth and/or date of death or period of activity of the person.

Access point	Example
Authorized Access Point Representing a Person	Manyanet, José (Manyanet I Vives), Saint

Other Designation Associated with the Person—Spirit (RDA 9.19.1.2.5)

For the spirit of a person add the term *Spirit* to the authorized access point for the person. Add the term *Spirit* as the last element.

Access point	Example
Authorized Access Point Representing a Person	Elijah (Biblical prophet) (Spirit)

Other Designation Associated with the Person—Person named in sacred scriptures or apocryphal books (RDA 9.19.1.2.6)

Add a term indicating a person named in a sacred scripture or an apocryphal book if needed to distinguish one access point from another. Add the term after the fuller form of name, title of royalty, title of nobility, title of religious rank, or the term *Saint*, as applicable.

Access point	Example
Authorized Access Point Representing a Person	Adam (Biblical figure)

> **Optional addition.** Add a term even if there is no need to distinguish one access point from another.

Other Designation Associated with the Person—Fictitious or legendary persons (RDA 9.19.1.2.6)

Add a term indicating fictitious or legendary character for a fictitious or legendary person whose name consists of a phrase or appellation not conveying the idea of a person. (RDA 9.19.1.1)

Access point	Example
Authorized Access Point Representing a Person	Wolverine (Fictitious character)

Add the term *Fictitious character, Legendary character,* or another appropriate designation if needed to distinguish one access point from another. Add the term after the fuller form of name, title of royalty, title of nobility, title of religious rank, or the term *Saint,* as applicable.

> **Optional addition.** Add a term even if there is no need to distinguish one access point from another.

Access point	Example
Authorized Access Point Representing a Person	Leibowitz, Isaac Edward, Saint (Fictitious character)

Other Designation Associated with the Person—Real nonhuman entities (RDA 9.19.1.2.6)

Add a term indicating type, species, or breed for real nonhuman entities whose name consists of a phrase or appellation not conveying the idea of a person. (RDA 9.19.1.1)

Access point	Example
Authorized Access Point Representing a Person	Splash (Dog)

Add a term indicating type, species, or breed if needed to distinguish one access point from another. Add the term after the fuller form of name, title of royalty, title of nobility, title of religious rank, or the term *Spirit,* as applicable.

> **Optional addition.** Add a term even if there is no need to distinguish one access point from another.

Date Associated with the Person element sub-types: Date of Birth, Date of Death (RDA 9.19.1.3)

Add the date of birth and/or date of death if needed to distinguish one access point from another. Record the year alone, except add the month or month and day if needed to distinguish one access point from another.

Access point	Example
Authorized Access Point Representing a Person	Blount, Harry, 1880–1913

Access point	Example
Authorized Access Point Representing a Person	Smith, John, 1936 December 17–

> **Optional addition.** Add the date of birth and/or death even if there is no need to distinguish between access points.
>
> | Access point | Example |
> |---|---|
> | Authorized Access Point Representing a Person | Hemingway, Ernest, 1899–1961 |

Fuller Form of Name (RDA 9.19.1.4)

Add a fuller form of the person's name if needed to distinguish one access point from another. Make this addition when the person's date of birth or date of death is not available.

Access point	Example
Authorized Access Point Representing a Person	Johnson, A. W. (Anthony W.)

> **Optional addition.** Add a fuller form of name even if there is no need to distinguish between access points. Add the fuller form of name before the date of birth and/or death.
>
> | Access point | Example |
> |---|---|
> | Authorized Access Point Representing a Person | Eliot, T. S. (Thomas Stearns), 1888–1965 |

Date Associated with the Person » Period of Activity of the Person (RDA 9.19.1.5)

Add the period of activity of the person if needed to distinguish one access point from another. Make this addition when the person's date of birth or date of death is not available.

Access point	Example
Authorized Access Point Representing a Person	Smith, John, active 1719–1758

Access point	Example
Authorized Access Point Representing a Person	Allen, Charles, 18th century–19th century

Optional addition. Add the period of activity of the person even if there is no need to distinguish between access points.

Profession or Occupation (RDA 9.19.1.6)

Add a term indicating profession or occupation for human entities whose name consists of a phrase or appellation not conveying the idea of a person. (RDA 9.19.1.1).

Add the profession or occupation if needed to distinguish one access point from another. Make this addition when the person's date of birth or date of death is not available.

Access point	Example
Authorized Access Point Representing a Person	Stone Mountain (Writer)

Add profession or occupation if needed to distinguish one access point from another.

Access point	Example
Authorized Access Point Representing a Person	Watt, James (Gardener)

Optional addition. Add the profession or occupation even if there is no need to distinguish between access points.

Title of the Person—Other term of rank, honor, or office (RDA 9.19.1.7)

Add a term indicative of rank, honor, or office if the term appears with the name if needed to distinguish one access point from another. Make this addition when the person's date of birth or date of death is not available.

Access point	Example
Authorized Access Point Representing a Person	Wood, John, Captain

Access point	Example
Authorized Access Point Representing a Person	Shah, Seema, Ph. D.

> **Optional addition.** Add a term indicative of rank, honor, or office even if there is no need to distinguish between access points.

Other Designation Associated with the Person—Other designation (RDA 9.19.1.8)

Add an appropriate other designation if needed to distinguish one access point from another. Make this addition when the person's date of birth or date of death is not available, and another designation associated with the person is not available (e.g., title of royalty, nobility, religious rank).

Access point	Example
Authorized Access Point Representing a Person	Nichols, Chris (of the North Oxford Association)

Access Point	Example
Authorized Access Point Representing a Person	Budd, Henry (Cree Indian)

> **Optional addition.** Add a designation even if there is no need to distinguish between access points.

Variant Access Point Representing a Person (RDA 9.19.2)

Variant Name for the Person

Use Variant Name for the Person to construct a variant access point representing a person.

Make additions to the name, if considered important for identification. Apply the instructions for the additional elements for the authorized access point representing the person, as applicable.

27
Families

AN **AUTHORIZED ACCESS** point is one of the techniques used to represent a family. The Authorized Access Point Representing a Family is constructed by using the Preferred Name for the Family element followed by other elements identifying a family as instructed. The Variant Access Point Representing a Family is an alternative access point representing a family.

Access Point	Example
Authorized Access Point Representing a Family	Nayak (Dynasty : 1529–1739 : Madurai, India)

Authorized Access Point Representing a Family (RDA 10.11.1; punctuation in RDA E.1.2.3)

Preferred Name for the Family
Use Preferred Name for the Family as the basis for the authorized access point representing a family.

Make additions to the name using the elements in the following order, as applicable.

Type of Family (RDA 10.11.1.2)
Add even if not needed to distinguish access points representing different families with the same name.

Access Point	Example
Authorized Access Point Representing a Family	Donald (Clan)

Date Associated with the Family (RDA 10.11.1.3)

Add even if not needed to distinguish access points representing different families with the same name.

Access Point	Example
Authorized Access Point Representing a Family	Pahlavi (Dynasty : 1925–1979)

Place Associated with the Family (RDA 10.11.1.4)

Add if needed to distinguish one access point from another.

Access Point	Example
Authorized Access Point Representing a Family	James (Family : Jamestown, Wash.)

Access Point	Example
Authorized Access Point Representing a Family	James (Family : Summerton, S.C.)

> **Optional addition.** Add if the addition assists in the identification of the family.

Prominent Member of the Family (RDA 10.11.1.5)

Add if needed to distinguish one access point from another. Make this addition when a place associated with the family is not available.

> **Optional addition.** Add if the addition assists in the identification of the family.
>
> | Access Point | Example |
> |---|---|
> | Authorized Access Point Representing a Family | Medici (Royal house : Medici, Lorenzo de', 1449–1492) |

Variant Access Point Representing a Family (RDA 10.11.2)

Variant Name for the Family

Use Variant Name for the Family to construct a variant access point representing a family. Hereditary Title can be used as a variant name for the family.

Add Type of Family.

Make other additions to the name, if considered important for identification. Apply the instructions for the additional elements for the authorized access point representing the family, as applicable.

28

Corporate Bodies

AN **AUTHORIZED ACCESS** point is one of the techniques used to represent a corporate body. The Authorized Access Point Representing a Corporate Body is constructed by using the Preferred Name for the Corporate Body element followed by other elements identifying a corporate body as instructed. The Variant Access Point Representing a Corporate Body is an alternative access point representing a corporate body.

Authorized Access Point Representing a Corporate Body (RDA 11.13.1; punctuation in RDA E.1.2.4)

Preferred Name for the Corporate Body

Use Preferred Name for the Corporate Body as the basis for the authorized access point representing a corporate body.

Access Point	Example
Authorized Access Point Representing a Corporate Body	Royal Aeronautical Society

Make additions to the name using the elements in the following order, as applicable. Separate instructions for additions to the preferred name of a conference, etc. follow.

Other Designation Associated with the Corporate Body »
Type of Corporate Body (RDA 11.13.1.2)

Add if needed to distinguish one access point from another (i.e., when two or more bodies have the same name or names so similar that they may be confused).

Add Type of Corporate Body or Other Designation if the preferred name for the body does not convey the idea of a corporate body even if not needed to distinguish access points representing different corporate bodies with the same name. (RDA 11.13.1.1)

Access Point	Example
Authorized Access Point Representing a Corporate Body	Niagara (Passenger ship)

Place Associated with the Corporate Body » Other Place Associated
with the Corporate Body (RDA 11.13.1.3)

Add if needed to distinguish one access point from another (i.e., when two or more bodies have the same name or names so similar that they may be confused). Add the name of the country, state, province, etc., or the name of a local place with which the body is associated.

Access Point	Example
Authorized Access Point Representing a Corporate Body	Newport High School (Newport, R.I.)

Optional addition. Add the name of the place associated with the body if the addition assists in the identification of the body.

Access Point	Example
Authorized Access Point Representing a Corporate Body	Bushcare (Program : Australia)
Name of place added to Type of Corporate Body (enclosed in parentheses, separated by space, colon, space).	

If a chapter, branch, etc., is recorded as a subdivision of a higher body *and* it carries out the activities of the higher body in a particular locality *and* the name of the locality is not already part of the name of the chapter, branch, etc., *then* add the name of the locality.

Access Point	Example
Authorized Access Point Representing a Corporate Body	Knights Templar (Masonic order). Grand Commandery (Ohio)

Add the name of the local place or jurisdiction if it is not clearly indicated in the name of a local church, temple, mosque, etc., or radio or television station.

Access Point	Example
Authorized Access Point Representing a Corporate Body	St. Mary (Church : Abberley, England)

If the name of the place associated with the body changes during the lifetime of the body, record the latest name in use during the lifetime of the body.

If the following elements provide better identification than the name of the local place, use one of these elements instead of the name of the local place: Associated Institution, Date Associated with the Corporate Body, Other Designation Associated with the Corporate Body » Other Designation.

Associated Institution (RDA 11.13.1.4)

Add if needed to distinguish one access point from another (i.e., when two or more bodies have the same name or names so similar that they may be confused).

Add the name of an associated institution if the institution's name is commonly associated with the name of the corporate body. Prefer this addition instead of the local place name.

Access Point	Example
Authorized Access Point Representing a Corporate Body	B'nai B'rith Hillel Federation Jewish Student Center (University of Cincinnati)
Associated Institution preferred over local place name, Cincinnati, Ohio.	

Optional addition. Add the name of an institution associated with the body if the addition assists in the identification of the body.

Access Point	Example
Authorized Access Point Representing a Corporate Body	Delta Tau Delta Fraternity. Beta Omicron Chapter (Cornell University)

Date Associated with the Corporate Body element sub-types: Date of Establishment, Date of Termination, Period of Activity of the Corporate Body (RDA 11.13.1.5)

Add if needed to distinguish one access point from another when the following elements are not available: Place Associated with the Corporate Body » Other Place Associated with the Corporate Body and Associated Institution.

Access Point	Example
Authorized Access Point Representing a Corporate Body	Double Image (Musical group : 1989–)
Date of Establishment added to distinguish the access point. Type of Corporate Body precedes date.	

> **Optional addition.** Add a date or dates associated with the body if the addition assists in the identification of the body.

Other Designation Associated with the Corporate Body » Type of Jurisdiction (RDA 11.13.1.6)

Add if needed to distinguish one access point from another (i.e., when two or more bodies have the same name or names so similar that they may be confused). Add the term to the name of a government other than a city or a town.

Access Point	Example
Authorized Access Point Representing a Corporate Body	New York (State)
Type of Jurisdiction added to distinguish from New York (N.Y.). The term for type of jurisdiction, (State), added to the name of a state (a "state" being a government other than a city or town).	

Other Designation Associated with the Corporate Body » Other Designation (RDA 11.13.1.7)

If none of the other additions is sufficient or appropriate for distinguishing between the access points for two or more bodies, add a suitable designation.

Access Point	Example
Authorized Access Point Representing a Corporate Body	Korea (South)

Add Type of Corporate Body or Other Designation if the preferred name for the body does not convey the idea of a corporate body even if not needed to distinguish access points representing different corporate bodies with the same name. (RDA 11.13.1.1)

Access Point	Example
Authorized Access Point Representing a Corporate Body	CD (Center for Democracy)

> **Optional addition.** Add such a designation if the addition assists in the understanding of the nature or purpose of the body.

Access Point	Example
Authorized Access Point Representing a Corporate Body	Oxford University International (Chess tournament)

If a designation is required to distinguish between the access points for two or more bodies with the same name and associated with the same place, add the designation following the place name.

Access Point	Example
Authorized Access Point Representing a Corporate Body	All Hallows (Church : London, England : Bread Street)

If two or more governments claim jurisdiction over the same area (e.g., occupying powers and insurgent governments), add a designation to the access point to distinguish between the two. Add the designation before the date or dates associated with the government.

Access Point	Example
Authorized Access Point Representing a Corporate Body	Germany (Territory under Allied occupation, 1945–1955)

Additions for Access Points Representing Conferences, Etc. (RDA 11.13.1.8)

Use Preferred Name for the Corporate Body as the basis for the authorized access point representing a conference, etc.

Access point for a single instance of a conference, etc. (RDA 11.13.1.8.1.)

Apply this instruction to a one-time conference, etc., or a single instance of a series of conferences. Apply this instruction also to a conference recorded subordinately.

Add the following elements to the name of a conference, etc., if applicable and readily ascertainable. Add them in this order: Number of the Conference, etc.; Date of Conference, etc.; Location of Conference, etc.

Access Point	Example
Authorized Access Point Representing a Corporate Body	Governor's Conference on Aging (Fla.) (3rd : 1992 : Tallahassee, Fla.)

Exception. Add the name of the associated institution instead of the local place name if the name of an associated institution provides better identification than the local place name or the local place name is not known or cannot be readily determined.

Access Point	Example
Authorized Access Point Representing a Corporate Body	International Conference on Georgian Psalmody (2nd : 1997 : Colchester Institute)

Exception. If the conference, etc., was held online, record *Online* as the location.

Access Point	Example
Authorized Access Point Representing a Corporate Body	Electronic Conference on Land Use and Land Cover Change in Europe (1997 : Online)

If the sessions of a conference, etc., were held in two or more locations, add each of the place names.

Access Point	Example
Authorized Access Point Representing a Corporate Body	Danish-Swedish Analysis Seminar (1995 : Copenhagen, Denmark; Lund, Sweden; Paris, France)

Access point for a series of conferences, etc. (RDA 11.13.1.8.2)

If the access point represents a series of conferences, etc., do not add the number, date, or location of the conferences, etc.

Access Point	Example
Authorized Access Point Representing a Corporate Body	Blue Ridge Folklife Festival

If additions are required to distinguish two or more series of conferences, etc., with the same name or a name so similar that they may be confused, apply the instructions for the additional elements for authorized access points representing corporate bodies, as applicable.

Variant Access Point Representing a Corporate Body
(RDA 11.13.2)

Variant Name for the Corporate Body

Use Variant Name for the Corporate Body to construct a variant access point representing a corporate body.

Make additions to the name, if considered important for identification. Apply the instructions for the additional elements for the authorized access point representing a corporate body, as applicable.

29
Works

AN AUTHORIZED ACCESS point is one of the techniques used to represent a work. The Authorized Access Point Representing a Work is constructed by using the Preferred Title for the Work element followed by other elements identifying works as instructed. In many cases the Preferred Title for the Work is preceded by an authorized access point representing a person, family, or corporate body responsible for the work. The Variant Access Point Representing a Work is an alternative access point representing a work.

An authorized access point representing a work can be for an original work or a new work based on a previously existing work.

RDA Essentials does not include instructions for constructing access points for these types of works: musical works (RDA 6.28), legal works (RDA 6.29), religious works (RDA 6.30), and official communications (RDA 6.31).

Authorized Access Point Representing a Work (RDA 6.27.1–6.27.2; punctuation in RDA E.1.2.5)

Works created by one person, family, or corporate body (RDA 6.27.1.2)

Construct access point by combining in this order:

> Authorized access point representing the person, family, or corporate body responsible for creating a work (see *Scope of Creator*)
>
> **+** Preferred Title for the Work

Access Point	Example
Authorized Access Point Representing a Work	Cassatt, Mary, 1844–1926. Children playing on the beach

Access Point	Example
Authorized Access Point Representing a Work	Coldplay (Musical group). Parachutes

Access Point	Example
Authorized Access Point Representing a Work	O'Connor, Flannery. Short stories
Preferred title for the compilation of complete works in the form of short stories is the conventional collective title Short stories.	

For works of uncertain attribution, see instruction for *Works of uncertain or unknown origin.*

Collaborative works (RDA 6.27.1.3)

Collaborative work which two or more persons, families, or corporate bodies are responsible for creating (*see* Scope of Creator*)*

Construct access point by combining in this order:

Authorized access point representing the person, family, or corporate body with principal responsibility
+ Preferred Title for the Work

Access Point	Example
Authorized Access Point Representing a Work	Porter, Douglas R. Making smart growth work
Resource described: Making smart growth work / principal author, Douglas R. Porter ; contributing authors, Robert T. Dunphy, David Salvesen.	

See RDA 6.27.1.3 for alternative to include all creators in access point.

Exception. Collaborative work which one or more corporate bodies and one or more persons or families are responsible for creating that falls into one or more of the categories for which corporate bodies are considered to be creators (see *Scope of Creato*r).

Construct access point by combining in this order:

Authorized access point representing the corporate body with principal responsibility
+ Preferred Title for the Work

Access Point	Example
Authorized Access Point Representing a Work	California Academy of Sciences. Catalog of the asteroid type-specimens and Fisher voucher specimens at the California Academy of Sciences

Exception. *Collaborative moving image work (e.g., motion pictures, videos, video games).*

Construct access point by using:

Preferred Title for the Work

Access Point	Example
Authorized Access Point Representing a Work	Gunner palace

Collaborative work for which two or more persons, families, or corporate bodies are represented as having principal responsibility

Construct access point by combining in this order:

Authorized access point representing the first-named person, family, or corporate body
+ Preferred Title for the Work

Access Point	Example
Authorized Access Point Representing a Work	Cordell, H. Ken. Footprints on the land
Resource described: Footprints on the land : an assessment of demographic trends and the future of natural lands in the United States / H. Ken Cordell, Christine Overdevest, principal authors.	

Collaborative work for which principal responsibility is not indicated

Construct access point by combining in this order:

Authorized access point representing the first-named person, family, or corporate body

+ Preferred Title for the Work

Access Point	Example
Authorized Access Point Representing a Work	Tracey, John Paul. Managing bird damage to fruit and other horticultural crops
Resource described: Managing bird damage to fruit and other horticultural crops / John Tracey, Mary Bomford, Quentin Hart, Ron Sinclair.	

Collaborative work for which there is no consistency in the order in which the persons, families, or corporate bodies responsible are named either in resources embodying the work or in reference sources

Construct access point by combining in this order:

Authorized access point representing the first-named person, family, or corporate body in the first resource received

+ Preferred Title for the Work

Compilations of works by different persons, families, or corporate bodies (RDA 6.27.1.4)

Construct access point by using:

Preferred Title for the Work representing the compilation

Access Point	Example
Authorized Access Point Representing a Work	The best of Broadway

If the compilation lacks a collective title, construct separate access points for each of the works in the compilation.

> **Alternative.** Construct an authorized access point representing the compilation by using a devised title as the preferred title for the work. Construct this access point instead of, or in addition to, access points for each of the works in the compilation.

Adaptations and revisions (RDA 6.27.1.5)

Work that is an adaptation or revision of a previously existing work that substantially changes the nature and content of that work and the adaptation or revision is presented as the work of one person, family, or corporate body

Construct access point by combining in this order:

Authorized access point representing the person, family, or corporate body responsible for the adaptation or revision, as applicable

+ Preferred Title for the Work representing the adaptation or revision

Access Point	Example
Authorized Access Point Representing a Work	Gray, Patsey. J.R.R. Tolkien's The hobbit

Exception. *Work that is an adaptation or revision of a compilation of works by different persons, families, or corporate bodies.*

Apply the instructions for *Compilations of works by different persons, families, or corporate bodies.*

Access Point	Example
Authorized Access Point Representing a Work	North American mammals

Exception. Work that is an adaptation or revision of a work of uncertain origin.

Apply the instructions for *Works of uncertain or unknown origin.*

Work that is an adaptation or revision for which more than one person, family, or corporate body is responsible

Apply the instructions for *Collaborative works.*

Access Point	Example
Authorized Access Point Representing a Work	Abrams, Anthony. Dead man on campus
Resource described: Dead man on campus / a novelization by Tony Abrams and Adam Broder.	

Work that is not an adaptation or revision but is presented simply as an edition of the previously existing work

Treat it as an expression of that work. Use the authorized access point representing the previously existing work.

Access Point	Example
Authorized Access Point Representing a Work	Carroll, Bradley W. Introduction to modern astrophysics
Authorized access point representing the first and second edition of a work by Bradley W. Carroll and Dale A. Ostlie. Each edition in this case is an expression of the same work, and the same authorized access point representing the work is used in each case.	

Commentary, annotations, illustrative content, etc., added to a previously existing work (RDA 6.27.1.6)

Work that consists of a previously existing work with added commentary, annotations, illustrative content, etc. and is presented as the work of the person, family, or corporate body responsible for the commentary, etc.

Construct access point by combining in this order:

> Authorized access point representing the person, family, or corporate body responsible for the commentary, etc., as applicable
>
> **+** Preferred Title for the Work representing the commentary, etc.

Access Point	Example
Authorized Access Point Representing a Work	Akram, Malik M. Comprehensive and exhaustive commentary on the Transfer of Property Act, 1882
A commentary by Akram that includes the text of the law and its amendments.	

Work that consists of a previously existing work with added commentary, annotations, illustrative content, etc. and *more than one person is responsible for the added commentary, etc.*

Apply the instructions for *Collaborative works* for the commentary, etc.

Work that consists of a previously existing work with added commentary, annotations, illustrative content, etc. but is presented simply as an edition of a previously existing work

Treat it as an expression of that work. Use the authorized access point representing the previously existing work. If it is considered important to identify the particular expression, construct an authorized access point representing the expression.

Access Point	Example
Authorized Access Point Representing a Work	Joyce, James, 1882–1941. Dubliners
Resource described: James Joyce's Dubliners : an illustrated edition with annotations / [edited by] John Wyse Jackson & Bernard McGinley.	

Different identities for an individual responsible for a work (RDA 6.27.1.7)

Work for which the individual responsible has more than one identity and there is no consistency in how that individual is identified on resources embodying the work

Construct access point by combining in this order:

> Authorized access point representing the identity most frequently used on resources embodying the work
>
> **+** Preferred Title for the Work

Access Point	Example
Authorized Access Point Representing a Work	Cunningham, E. V., 1914–2003. Sylvia

Not Fast, Howard, 1914-2003. Sylvia. *The author's novel* Sylvia *was originally published under the pseudonym E.V. Cunningham. On some resources embodying the work the author is identified by his real name, Howard Fast; the identity most frequently used on resources embodying the work is E.V. Cunningham.*

Work for which the individual responsible has more than one identity and the identity used most frequently cannot be readily determined

Construct access point by combining in this order:

Authorized access point representing the identity appearing in the most recent resource embodying the work

+ Preferred Title for the Work

Works of uncertain or unknown origin (RDA 6.27.1.8)

Work that has been attributed to one or more persons, families, or corporate bodies, but there is uncertainty as to the probable person, family, or corporate body responsible

Construct access point by using:

Preferred Title for the Work

Access Point	Example
Authorized Access Point Representing a Work	The law scrutiny

Resource described: The law scrutiny, or, Attornies' guide. *Variously attributed to Andrew Carmichael, William Norcott, and others.*

Work which reference sources indicate one person, family, or corporate body is probably responsible for creating

Construct access point by combining in this order:

Authorized access point representing the person, family, or corporate body

+ Preferred Title for the Work

Work for which the person, family, or corporate body responsible is unknown or work that originated from an unnamed group

Construct access point by using:

Preferred Title for the Work

Access Point	Example
Authorized Access Point Representing a Work	The log-cabin lady
Resource described: The log-cabin lady : an anonymous autobiography. *Person responsible unknown.*	

Access Point	Example
Authorized Access Point Representing a Work	A memorial to Congress, against the tariff law of 1828
Resource described: A memorial to Congress, against the tariff law of 1828 / by citizens of Boston.	

Additions to Access Points Representing Works (RDA 6.27.1.9)

Make additions to access points if needed to distinguish the access point for a work from one that is the same or similar but represents a different work *or* from one that represents a person, family, corporate body, or place.

Add one or more of the following elements as appropriate:

Form of Work

Access Point	Example
Authorized Access Point Representing a Work	Charlemagne (Play)

Access Point	Example
Authorized Access Point Representing a Work	Charlemagne (Tapestry)

Date of Work

Access Point	Example
Authorized Access Point Representing a Work	Connecticut Commission on Children. Annual report (2005)
Title changed from Annual report *to* Year's summary *in 2004; title* Annual report *resumed in 2005.*	

Place of Origin of the Work

Access Point	Example
Authorized Access Point Representing a Work	Advocate (Boise, Idaho)

Access Point	Example
Authorized Access Point Representing a Work	Advocate (Nairobi, Kenya)

Other Distinguishing Characteristic of the Work

Access Point	Example
Authorized Access Point Representing a Work	Othello (Television program : 1963 : Canadian Broadcasting Corporation)

Access Point	Example
Authorized Access Point Representing a Work	Othello (Television program : 1963 : WOR–TV (Television station : New York, N.Y.))

Examples use Form of Work, Date of Work, and Other Distinguishing Characteristic of the Work.

Authorized Access Points Representing a Part or Parts of a Work

Construct the authorized access point representing a part or parts of a work by applying the instructions for *One part* or *Two or more parts,* as applicable.

One part (RDA 6.27.2.2)

Construct the authorized access point representing a part of a work by combining in this order:

> Authorized access point representing the person, family, or corporate body responsible for the part, as applicable
>
> **+** Preferred Title for the Work representing the part

Access Point	Example
Authorized Access Point Representing a Work	Tolkien, J. R. R. (John Ronald Reuel), 1892–1973. The two towers

Exception. *Nondistinctive titles.*

If the part is identified only by a general term (with or without a number), construct the authorized access point representing the part by combining in this order:

Authorized access point representing the work as a whole

+ Preferred Title for the Work representing the part

Access Point	Example
Authorized Access Point Representing a Work	Homer. Iliad. Book 1

Exception. *Serials and integrating resources.*

If the part is a section of, or supplement to, a serial or an integrating resource, whether the title of the section or supplement is distinctive or not, construct the authorized access point representing the part by combining in this order:

Authorized access point representing the work as a whole

+ Preferred Title for the Work representing the section or supplement

Access Point	Example
Authorized Access Point Representing a Work	Colorado. Judicial Branch. Annual report. Statistics and charts

Exception. *Television programs, radio programs, etc.*

If the part is a season, episode, excerpt, etc., of a television program, radio program, etc., whether the title of the part is distinctive or not, construct the authorized access point representing the part by combining in this order:

Authorized access point representing the work as a whole

+ Preferred Title for the Work representing the part

Access Point	Example
Authorized Access Point Representing a Work	Buffy, the vampire slayer (Television program). Season 6

If the preferred title for the work as a whole is used as the authorized access point representing the work, use the preferred title for the part as the authorized access point representing the part. Apply the exceptions for *One part*, if applicable, such as for nondistinctive titles of parts.

Access Point	Example
Authorized Access Point Representing a Work	Sindbad the sailor
This authorized access point for a part follows the same instruction as the authorized access part for the work as a whole, The Arabian nights.	

CHAPTER 29: WORKS | 341

Access Point	Example
Authorized Access Point Representing a Work	Encyclopedia of philosophy. Supplement
This authorized access point for a part with a nondistinctive title for the part includes the authorized access point for the work as a whole, Encyclopedia of philosophy.	

Two or more parts (RDA 6.27.2.3)

If two or more parts of a work are consecutively numbered *and* each is identified only by a general term and a number, *then* construct the authorized access point by combining in this order:

> Authorized access point representing the work as a whole
>
> **+** Preferred Title for the Work representing the sequence of parts

Access Point	Example
Authorized Access Point Representing a Work	Homer. Iliad. Book 1–6

When identifying two or more parts that are unnumbered or nonconsecutively numbered, construct authorized access points for each of the parts. Apply the instructions for *One part.*

Access Point	Example
Authorized Access Point Representing a Work	Dante Alighieri, 1265–1321. Purgatorio
Authorized Access Point Representing a Work	Dante Alighieri, 1265–1321. Paradiso

Alternative. When identifying two or more parts of a work that are unnumbered or nonconsecutively numbered, identify the parts collectively. Construct the authorized access point representing the parts by combining in this order:

> Authorized access point representing the work as a whole
>
> **+** Preferred Title for the Work consisting of the conventional collective title *Selections*

Access Point	Example
Authorized Access Point Representing a Work	The Simpsons (Television program). Selections
A compilation of four party-themed episodes.	

Variant Access Point Representing a Work (RDA 6.27.4)

Apply this instruction to individual works and compilations of works by different persons, families, or corporate bodies.

Construct variant access points representing a work by combining in this order:

Authorized access point representing the person, family, or corporate body responsible for the work, as applicable

+ Variant Title for the Work (or in some cases Preferred Title for the Work)

+ Form of Work; Date of Work; Place of Origin of the Work; and/or Other Distinguishing Characteristic of the Work as instructed if appropriate

Access Point	Example
Authorized Access Point Representing a Work	Dickens, Charles, 1812–1870. The Pickwick papers
Variant Access Point Representing a Work	Dickens, Charles, 1812–1870. The posthumous papers of the Pickwick Club

Variant Title for the Work: The posthumous papers of the Pickwick Club. *Option to omit the initial articles for Title of the Work not applied in these cases.*

In some cases the Preferred Title for the Work is used in a Variant Access Point Representing a Work if the authorized access point for a person, family, or corporate body is different from the one used in the Authorized Access Point Representing a Work. For example, a work may have two creators. The second creator is used with the Title of the Work to form a Variant Access Point Representing a Work:

Access Point	Example
Authorized Access Point Representing a Work	Christo, 1935– . Wrapped Reichstag
Variant Access Point Representing a Work	Jeanne-Claude, 1935– . Wrapped Reichstag

A work of art created jointly by Christo and Jeanne-Claude.

Make additions to the variant access point, if considered important for identification, by using Form of Work, Date of Work, Place of Origin of the Work, and/or Other Distinguishing Characteristic of the Work:

Access Point	Example
Authorized Access Point Representing a Work	Schwartz, David M. Science series
Variant Access Point Representing a Work	Science series (Cypress, Calif.)

Preferred title is identical to preferred and variant titles of other works, and so a qualifying element is added to variant access point which begins with the preferred title for the work.

Variant access points representing a part of a work (RDA 6.27.4.3)

A variant access point representing a part of a work can be constructed in several ways based upon how the authorized access point for the part is constructed.

Authorized access point has title of work as a whole and a distinctive title of part

Construct variant access point by using:

Preferred Title for the Work representing the part if the title is distinctive and used in an authorized access point for a work

Access Point	Example
Authorized Access Point Representing a Work	Acta Universitatis Upsaliensis. Studia musicologica Upsaliensia
Variant Access Point Representing a Work	Studia musicologica Upsaliensia
Title of part, Studia musicologica Upsaliensia, *is distinctive and used in the authorized access point.*	

Authorized access point has title of work as a whole, distinctive title of part, and access point for person, family, or corporate body

Construct variant access point by combining in this order:

Authorized access point representing the person, family, or corporate body **+** Preferred Title for the Work representing the part if the title is distinctive

Access Point	Example
Authorized Access Point Representing a Work	Williams, Kim, 1966– . Young explorer series. Penguins
Variant Access Point Representing a Work	Williams, Kim, 1966– . Penguins
Authorized Access Point Representing a Work has same authorized access point for the person, the preferred title for the work as a whole, followed by the preferred title for the part.	

Authorized access point does not have title of work as a whole

Construct variant access point by combining in this order:

Preferred Title for the Work representing the work as a whole **+** Preferred Title for the Work representing the part used in an authorized access point for a work on its own

Access Point	Example
Authorized Access Point Representing a Work	Sinbad the sailor
Variant Access Point Representing a Work	Arabian nights. Sinbad the sailor

Authorized access point does not have title of work as a whole and has access point for person, family, or corporate body

Construct variant access point by combining in this order:

> Authorized access point representing the person, family, or corporate body
>
> **+** Preferred Title for the Work representing the work as a whole
>
> **+** Preferred Title for the Work representing the part

Access Point	Example
Authorized Access Point Representing a Work	Raven, Simon, 1927–2001. Come like shadows
Variant Access Point Representing a Work	Raven, Simon, 1927–2001. Alms for oblivion. Come like shadows

Authorized Access Point Representing a Work has same authorized access point for the person, followed only by the preferred title for the part.

Additions to the variant access point

Make additions to the variant access point, if considered important for identification.

Access Point	Example
Authorized Access Point Representing a Work	Cheers (Television program). King of the hill
Variant Access Point Representing a Work	King of the hill (Television program : Episode of Cheers)

Additional variant access points

Construct additional variant access points if considered important for access.

Access Point	Example
Authorized Access Point Representing a Work	Occasional papers of the California Academy of Sciences
Variant Access Point Representing a Work	California Academy of Sciences. Occasional papers of the California Academy of Sciences

Corporate body does not fall into the scope of a Creator, and is used here in a variant access point representing a work.

Access Point	Example
Authorized Access Point Representing a Work	Cunningham, E. V., 1914–2003. Sylvia
Variant Access Point Representing a Work	Fast, Howard, 1914–2003. Sylvia

Novel originally published under the pseudonym E.V. Cunningham. Author's real name, Howard Fast, appears on some resources embodying the work, but the identity most frequently used is Cunningham.

30

Expressions

AN **AUTHORIZED ACCESS** point is one of the techniques used to represent an expression. The Authorized Access Point Representing an Expression is constructed by using the Authorized Access Point Representing a Work followed by other elements identifying expressions as instructed. The Variant Access Point Representing an Expression is an alternative access point representing an expression.

See RDA for additional instructions that apply to expressions of these types of works: musical works (RDA 6.28), legal works (RDA 6.29), religious works (RDA 6.30), and official communications (RDA 6.31).

Authorized Access Point Representing an Expression
(RDA 6.27.3; punctuation in RDA E.1.2.5)

Construct an authorized access point to represent a particular expression of a work (or of a part or parts of a work) by using the authorized access point representing the work and adding one or more elements identifying the expression.

Combine in this order:

Authorized access point representing the work (or the part or parts of a work)
+ One or more of the following elements: Content Type, Date of Expression, Language of Expression, Other Distinguishing Characteristic of the Expression

Content Type

Access Point	Example
Authorized Access Point Representing an Expression	Brunhoff, Jean de, 1899–1937. Babar en famille. English. Spoken word
Added Language of Expression and Content Type Spoken word.	

Date of Expression

Access Point	Example
Authorized Access Point Representing an Expression	Wilde, Oscar, 1854–1900. Works. Selections. 2000
Added Date of Expression.	

Language of Expression

Access Point	Example
Authorized Access Point Representing an Expression	Piave, Francesco Maria, 1810–1876. Ernani. Spanish
Added Language of Expression.	

Other Distinguishing Characteristic of the Expression

Access Point	Example
Authorized Access Point Representing an Expression	Blade runner (Motion picture : Final cut)
Added Other Distinguishing Characteristic of the Expression Final cut. *Form of Work* Motion picture *is part of authorized access point representing the work.*	

Access Point	Example
Authorized Access Point Representing an Expression	Pushkin, Aleksandr Sergeevich, 1799–1837. Evgeniĭ Onegin. English (Beck)
Added Language of Expression English *and Other Distinguishing Characteristic of the Expression* Beck *(for translator Tom Beck).*	

Variant Access Point Representing an Expression (RDA 6.27.4.5)

Construct variant access points representing an expression, if appropriate, by combining in this order:

> Authorized access point representing the work
>
> **+** A variant of an addition used in constructing an authorized access point representing the expression (i.e., Content Type, Date of Expression, Language of Expression, Other Distinguishing Characteristic of the Expression)

Access Point	Example
Authorized Access Point Representing an Expression	Theodore bar Konai, 8th century–9th century. Liber scholiorum (Urmiah version)
Variant Access Point Representing an Expression	Theodore bar Konal, 8th century–9th century. Liber scholiorum (Ourmia version)

Access Point	Example
Authorized Access Point Representing an Expression	Blade runner (Motion picture : Final cut)
Variant Access Point Representing an Expression	Blade runner (Motion picture : 2007 version)
Variant Access Point Representing an Expression	Blade runner (Motion picture : 25th anniversary edition)
Variant Access Point Representing an Expression	Blade runner (Motion picture : Definitive version)
Authorized access point representing the work is Blade runner (Motion picture).	

If the authorized access point representing the expression has been constructed with:

- the authorized access point representing a person, family, or corporate body
- the preferred title for the work
- one or more additions identifying the expression

and a variant title for a work is associated with a particular expression,
then construct a variant access point representing the expression by combining in this order:

> Authorized access point representing the person, family, or corporate body
>
> **+** Variant Title for the Work associated with the particular expression

Access Point	Example
Authorized Access Point Representing an Expression	Munro, Alice, 1931– . Lives of girls and women. Danish
Variant Access Point Representing an Expression	Munro, Alice, 1931– . Pigeliv & kvindeliv

Authorized access point representing the Danish expression uses the English Preferred Title for the Work. The Danish title is a Variant Title for the Work and is used in constructing the variant access point representing the expression.

Make additions to a variant access point representing an expression, if considered important for identification.

Construct additional variant access points representing an expression if considered important for access.

Other Additional Instructions

31

Cases Involving Multiple Elements

Facsimiles and Reproductions (RDA 1.11)

When describing a facsimile or reproduction, record the data relating to the facsimile or reproduction in the appropriate element. Record any data relating to the original manifestation in Related Work or Related Manifestation, as applicable.

Resources Consisting of More Than One Carrier Type
(RDA 3.1.4)

Apply the method that is appropriate to the nature of the resource and the purpose of the description. See RDA 3.1.4 for additional instructions (e.g., containers and accompanying material).

Method 1

If a detailed description of the characteristics of the carriers is not considered necessary, record only the applicable carrier type or types *and* extent of each type of carrier.

Method 2

If a detailed description of the characteristics of each carrier is considered important for identification or selection, record the applicable carrier type *and* the extent of each carrier *and* other characteristics of each carrier.

Method 3

For a resource consisting of many different types of carriers, record the predominant carrier type *and* the extent of the resource as a whole, describing the units as *various pieces* (e.g., *27 various pieces*). Record details of the pieces in a note if considered important for identification or selection (see *Note on Carrier » Note on Extent of Manifestation*).

> **Optional omission.** If the number of units cannot be readily ascertained or approximated, omit the number (e.g., various pieces).

Example of Method 2 (recording Carrier Type, Extent, and other characteristics of each carrier)

Resource consisting of slides and an audiocassette.

Element	Example
Carrier Type	slide
Extent	46 slides
Dimensions	5 × 5 cm
Carrier Type	audiocassette
Extent	1 audiocassette
Dimensions	10 × 7 cm, 4 mm tape
Type of Recording	analog
Configuration of Playback Channels	mono

Dimensions for resources consisting of more than one carrier
(RDA 3.5.1.6)

If the resource consists of more than one carrier, and the carriers are all of the same type and size, record the dimensions of a single carrier.

If the carriers are of the same type but differ in size, record the dimensions of the smallest or smaller and the largest or larger size.

Element	Example
Dimensions	24–28 cm

Alternative. If the carriers are all of two sizes, record both. If they are of more than two sizes, record the dimensions of the largest followed by *or smaller.*

Element	Example
Dimensions	8 × 13 cm and 10 × 15 cm

Element	Example
Dimensions	26 × 21 cm or smaller

For a resource consisting of more than one type of carrier, record the dimensions of the carriers if recording a detailed description of the characteristics of the carriers (RDA 3.1.4, Method 2).

Online Resources (RDA 3.1.5)

Record *online resource* as the carrier type for all online resources.

For an online resource that is complete (or if the total extent is known), record the extent as *1 online resource.* Add subunits as appropriate (see *Extent*).

Record other characteristics of the carrier, as applicable (e.g., Digital File Characteristic elements such as Encoding Format), if considered important for identification or selection.

If the online resource consists of more than one file *and* a description of the characteristics of each file is considered important for identification or selection, *then* record the characteristics of each file.

Element	Example
Carrier Type	online resource
Extent	1 online resource
File Type	text file
Encoding Format	RTF
File Size	73 KB
File Type	audio file
Encoding Format	WAV
File Size	18 MB

32

Changes That Result in the Creation of a New Description

For multipart monographs

Mode of Issuance (RDA 1.6.1.1, 2.13)

Create a new description if a multipart monograph changes to a serial or an integrating resource. Create a new description if a serial or integrating resource changes to a multipart monograph.

Media Type (RDA 1.6.1.2, 3.2)

Create a new description if there is a change in the media type of a multipart monograph.

For serials

Mode of Issuance (RDA 1.6.2.1, 2.13)

Create a new description if a serial changes to a multipart monograph or an integrating resource. Create a new description if a multipart monograph or integrating resource changes to a serial.

Media Type (RDA 1.6.2.2, 3.2)

Create a new description if there is a change in the media type of a serial.

Carrier Type = Online resource (RDA 1.6.2.2, 3.3)

If the carrier type of a serial changes to *online resource* from another computer carrier *or* changes from *online resource* to another computer carrier, *then* create a new description.

Edition Statement (RDA 1.6.2.5)

Create a new description when there is a change in an edition statement indicating a significant change to the scope or coverage of a serial.

Major change in the Title Proper of a serial affecting identification of the work (RDA 1.6.2.3, 2.3.2.12.2)

If there is a major change in the title proper on a subsequent issue or part of a serial, make a new description for the issues or parts appearing under the new title. Treat the two descriptions as descriptions for related works (see *Related Work*).

Construct the authorized access point representing the work to reflect the title as represented in the issue or part of the serial used as the basis for the new description (see *Authorized Access Point Representing a Work* and *Preferred Title for the Work*).

Title proper—Major changes (RDA 2.3.2.13.1)

In general, consider the following to be major changes in a title proper written in a language and script that divides text into words:

a) the addition, deletion, change, or reordering of any of the first five words (the first six words if the title begins with an article) unless the change belongs to one or more of the categories listed as minor changes

b) the addition, deletion, or change of any word after the first five words (the first six words if the title begins with an article) that changes the meaning of the title or indicates a different subject matter

c) a change of name for a corporate body included anywhere in the title if the changed name is for a different corporate body

See RDA 2.3.2.13.1.2 for titles in a language and script that does not divide text into words.

Title proper—Minor changes

In general, consider the following to be minor changes in a title proper of a serial and do not make a new description:

a) a difference in the representation of a word, words, or other component (i.e., a character or group of characters) anywhere in the title such as

> change in the form of the character
> one spelling versus another
> abbreviated word or sign or symbol versus spelled-out form
> arabic numeral versus roman numeral
> number or date versus spelled-out form
> hyphenated word versus unhyphenated word

one-word compound versus two-word compound, whether hyphenated or not

acronym or initialism versus full form

or

change in grammatical form (e.g., singular versus plural)

b) the addition, deletion, or change of articles, prepositions, or conjunctions (or, in languages which do not use those, analogous parts of speech that have little lexical meaning but express grammatical relationships) anywhere in the title

c) a difference involving the name of the same corporate body and elements of its hierarchy or their grammatical connection anywhere in the title (e.g., the addition, deletion, or rearrangement of the name of the same corporate body, the substitution of a variant form)

d) the addition, deletion, or change of punctuation, including initialisms and letters with separating punctuation versus those without separating punctuation, anywhere in the title

e) a different order of titles when the title is given in more than one language on the source of information, provided that the title chosen as title proper still appears as a parallel title proper

f) the addition, deletion, or change of a word, words or other component (i.e., a character or group of characters) anywhere in the title that link the title to the numbering

g) two or more titles proper used on different issues of a serial according to a regular pattern

h) the addition to, deletion from, or change in the order of a word, words, or other component (i.e., a character or group of characters) in a list anywhere in the title, provided that there is no significant change in the subject matter

i) the addition, deletion, or rearrangement anywhere in the title of a word, words, or other component (i.e., a character or group of characters) that indicate the type of resource, such as "magazine," "journal," or "newsletter" or their equivalent in other languages

In case of doubt, consider the change to be a minor change.

Change in responsibility for a serial affecting identification of the work
(RDA 1.6.2.4, 6.1.3.2)

Create a new description if there is a change in responsibility that requires a change in the authorized access point representing the serial as a work.

Construct the new Authorized Access Point Representing a Work to reflect responsibility for the work as represented in the issue or part of the serial used as the basis for the new description.

Consider changes in responsibility requiring the construction of a new authorized access point representing the work to include the following.

a) a change affecting the authorized access point representing a person, family, or corporate body that is used in constructing the authorized access point representing the work (see *Authorized Access Point Representing a Work*).

Access Point	Example
Authorized Access Point Representing a Work	Western Cape Housing Development Fund. Annual report
Authorized Access Point Representing a Work	Western Cape Housing Development Board. Annual report
Name change in corporate body results in a new authorized access point representing the work and therefore a new description is made.	

    b) a change affecting the name of a person, family, or corporate body used as an addition to the authorized access point representing the work (see *Authorized Access Point Representing a Work* and *Other Distinguishing Characteristic of the Work*).

Access Point	Example
Authorized Access Point Representing a Work	Bulletin (Council for Geoscience (South Africa))
Authorized Access Point Representing a Work	Bulletin (Geological Survey (South Africa))
Name change in corporate body used in qualifier element Other Distinguishing Characteristic of the Work results in a new authorized access point representing the work, and therefore a new description is made.	

For integrating resources

Mode of Issuance (RDA 1.6.3.1, 2.13)

Create a new description if an integrating resource changes to a multipart monograph or serial. Create a new description if a multipart monograph or serial changes to an integrating resource.

Media Type (RDA 1.6.3.2, 3.2)

Create a new description if there is a change in the media type of an integrating resource.

Re-basing of an integrating resource (RDA 1.6.3.3)

Create a new description for an integrating resource if a new set of base volumes is issued for an updating loose-leaf.

Edition Statement (RDA 1.6.3.4, 2.5)

Create a new description when there is a change in an edition statement indicating a significant change to the scope or coverage of an integrating resource.